COMMERCE IN COLOR

Commerce in Color

Race, Consumer Culture,

and American Literature,

1893–1933

JAMES C. DAVIS

The University of Michigan Press ANN ARBOR

2010   2009   2008   2007   4   3   2   1

A CIP catalog record for this book is available from the British Library.

Library of Congress Cataloging-in-Publication Data

Davis, James C.
    Commerce in color : race, consumer culture, and American
literature, 1893-1933 / James C. Davis.
        p.   cm. — (Class : culture)
    Includes bibliographical references (p.   ) and index.
    ISBN-13: 978-0-472-09987-0 (acid-free paper)
    ISBN-10: 0-472-09987-6 (acid-free paper)
    ISBN-13: 978-0-472-06987-3 (pbk. : acid-free paper)
    ISBN-10: 0-472-06987-X (pbk. : acid-free paper)   1. American
literature—20th century—History and criticism.   2. Consumption
(Economics) in literature.   3. Material culture—United States—
History—20th century.   4. Popular culture—United States—History—
20th century.   5. Racism in popular culture.   6. African American
consumers—Social conditions.   I. Title.

PS228.C65D38   2007
810.9'3553—dc22   2006036411

for Jody

Acknowledgments

THOUGH WRITING A BOOK is often solitary, hard work, I'm mindful of just how much others have done for me to make that work possible, even enjoyable. Much of this book derives from my doctoral dissertation, and from that early stage onward Robyn Wiegman has been the most wonderful of mentors, supporting and challenging me in ways that not only benefited this book but also taught me a great deal about teaching and learning. Her generosity and intellectual courage are an inspiration, and she deserves credit for whatever strengths this book may possess; its weaknesses are of course mine alone.

Tom Foster and Patrick Brantlinger were dedicated and insightful readers of this project in its early stages, marshalling it through several revisions. I'm grateful for the brilliance of their observations and for their commitment to improving upon its humble beginnings. Eva Cherniaysky provided terrific feedback on my work at an early stage, for which she has my warmest thanks.

I've been fortunate to have many colleagues who went above and beyond the call of duty or friendship to support the work that went into this book. Many thanks to Janet Cutler, Art Simon, and Amy Srebnick for providing the institutional and intellectual climate in which I could conduct my research and writing. Hilary Englert helped see me and this project through some harrowing times; her impact on it is legible nowhere but felt everywhere by its author. My current colleagues at Brooklyn College have been a consistent source of inspiration and a veritable chorus of wisdom. The number who deserve my thanks is too great to list. But I would especially like to thank Ellen Tremper, who offered timely and useful feedback on my writing and is a pillar of support; Roni Natov, whose generosity, forthrightness, and intellectual curiosity are a continual source of strength for me; Joseph Entin, without whom this book may never have made it into print and from whom I'm continually learning; and Martha Nadell, Geoffrey Minter, and Nicola Masciandaro, whose wonderfully inquisitive imaginations have invigorated my commitment to research, writing, and teaching. I'm grateful to the Mrs. Giles Whiting Foundation for a fellowship that made it possible for me to complete this book, and to the PSCCUNY Research Foundation for two generous grants. I would also like to thank my students at Brooklyn College, who amaze and rejuvenate me.

My editor, LeAnn Fields, has been a tireless advocate for this book through circumstances that would tire weaker souls, and for that, as much as for the thoughtfulness of her editorial advice, she has my eternal gratitude. I have benefited from the suggestions of three outside readers who challenged me to revise both my thinking and my writing in productive ways. In addition, I'd like to thank the series editors, Bill Mullen and Amy Schrager Lang, for their abiding interest in this book, and Anna Szymanski, Rebecca Mostov, and Marcia LaBrenz of the University of Michigan Press for the many things they have done to see it into print.

My debt to friends and family is enormous. Special thanks go to Casey Smith, Aaron Jaffe, Lisa Cowan, Jonathan Spear, Jill Bloomberg, Adam Lessuck, Sumati Devadutt, Anthony Bradfield, Pete Bartkowski, Tryon Woods, and Tanya Friedman. Their interest and encouragement have meant more than they know. My immediate and extended family has supported me unwaveringly throughout what must often have seemed like an endless process. I'm particularly grateful to Jane and Rob Madell for their boundless generosity, and to my parents, Jim and Jody Davis, for their faith in me and their enthusiasm for my work. The inspiration that I draw from my daughters, Eva and Rose, defies expression; may their eagerness and passion remain undimmed. Finally, the person to whom I'm most grateful is Jody Madell. Her kindness has allowed me to pursue this work to the extent that I wished, and the steadfast commitment and care she shows in her own work has served as a model for how to do so.

Contents

Introduction

Emergence is thus the entry of forces; it is their eruption, the leap from the wings to center stage, each in its youthful strength.
—Michel Foucault, "Nietzsche, Genealogy, History" (1971)

By THE TIME the stock market crashed and the Great Depression provoked a widespread reappraisal of U.S.-style capitalism, Americans were already well on the way to defining themselves as a nation of consumers. We tend to think of consumerism as a recent or even "postmodern" phenomenon, but as historians Richard Wightman Fox and T. J. Jackson Lears note, "the American culture of consumption did not emerge full-blown at mid-century" (ix). In the late nineteenth century, many Americans felt uneasy about the economic transformation they were witnessing, from the facelessness of corporations owned by stockholders dispersed around the country to the blandishments of advertisers who challenged the prevailing Protestant ethic of thrift and industry. But by the early 1930s, they and their children had grown accustomed to the signature experiences of the new consumer society, such as buying on credit, shopping in department stores, seeing national brands advertised in local newspapers, watching the "talkies" made in Hollywood, and being the subjects of market research and public relations campaigns. What had happened? An "economy of abundance" had come to rival and supplant an "economy of scarcity," as sociologist Simon Patten put it in 1907. But why had this occurred?

The industrial revolution had enabled the manufacture of more and better goods than there were markets for those goods, so the long-term stability of the economy required that demand be manufactured as well. "Mass production has made mass distribution necessary," the department store magnate Edward Filene told the American Economic Associ-

ation in 1927. He continued, "Certain types of retailing are in effect
dams in the stream of distribution—a stream which should be broad,
deep, and swift flowing" (1). For the first time ever, the 1933 edition of
the federal study *Recent Social Trends in the United States* included a chapter entitled "The People as Consumers." As this title suggests, the democratization of the marketplace of goods had effected a dramatic change in
the way many Americans—affluent and working-class, urban and rural—
imagined their identities and conducted their lives, a transformation
that became in turn the ideological and material basis for the flourishing
of consumer society later in the twentieth century. In part, this book is
about that transformation, about the emerging consumer society's consolidation and contestation, about its institutions, and above all about
the written discourses—literary, imaginative, and critical—to which it
gave rise.

Though this story is somewhat familiar by now, I want to make a case
here for revising it by considering its relationship to the concurrent history of race. Reading the influential scholarly accounts of America's consumer revolution, we encounter provocative references to racial thinking and racism, but they are mainly confined to footnotes and
digressions. For example, we note that in the late nineteenth century,
rumors that Sears and Roebuck were "a Jew" and "a Negro" were widely
circulated by rural merchants who were anxious about the displacement
of locally owned stores by mail-order entrepreneurs.[1] We learn that
world's fairs and other popular turn-of-the-century exhibitions not only
identified commodity consumption with American citizenship and historical progress but sometimes barred African Americans from participation in exhibitions and employment and placed pseudocommunities
of live, exotic "savages" on display. In material culture, we are confronted with commercial iconography that relied routinely on racial
stereotypes and subtexts, even when the advertised products bore no
self-evident relationship to anyone's race, as, for instance, in the ubiquitous images of "pickaninnies" pursued by alligators. In "high" culture, we
read in the work of many modernist writers and intellectuals a critique of
modernity's "commercial values" and "overcivilization," casting whites as
the special victims of modern society and nonwhites as the repositories
of pastoral virtue.

However, with few exceptions, most of them recent, race has been rel-

egated to the margins of analyses of consumer culture during this
period. This neglect is all the more striking considering that the period
in which our consumer society took shape was one in which race in the
United States was transformed decisively by Jim Crow segregation; the
"new immigration"; imperial forays into Cuba, the Philippines, and
Panama; and the Great Migration, through which two million African
Americans moved to northern industrial centers. Further attention to
the relationship between these developments and emerging consumerism will allow us to raise new questions, cross disciplinary boundaries, and produce a "reconfigured genealogy" of the culture of segregation and the culture of consumption.[2] As the preceding examples
indicate, the development of racial identities and communities did not
occur in isolation from the consumer revolution. To the contrary, this
book suggests, they were bound up intimately with one another, not by
mere accident of simultaneity or the machinations of powerful individuals but by an articulation of discourses—a process in which the struggle
for hegemonic power requires the performance of ideological work on
multiple fronts at once and thus generates reciprocity and tension
among them.[3] The emergence of consumer society relied on the concept of race and the persistence of white-supremacist thinking. Likewise,
the ways in which people thought and wrote about consumer society
helped to maintain the concept of race and reproduce assumptions
about white supremacy.

   This is not to say that the articulation of race with consumer culture
during this period was monolithic or unambivalent. It occasioned transgressions of social roles and expectations; it was subject to regional variations and informed by issues of class and gender; and in certain ways
and in certain areas, it unsettled and even subverted prevailing social
relations.[4] But I argue in this study that it primarily served to maintain
the viability of racial thinking and the normativity of whiteness. Though
I here make no attempt to chart a teleological narrative of historical
progress (if "progress" is the appropriate word here), I cannot help but
think that the legacy of this articulation is our inheritance today. In the
contemporary United States, consumption and the private interest of
corporations shape our identities, our desires, our public sphere, and
our horizons of political possibility in ways that are certainly unprecedented but not, given the period under discussion, entirely unpre-

dictable. Race continues to differentially determine our access to resources and life chances and to conceal its status as a social construction behind a false screen of nature and common sense. That this is the case despite the efforts of the civil rights struggle and the discrediting of biological accounts of race testifies to its resilience and utility in the U.S. social imaginary. "Race is as healthy today as it was during the Enlightenment," wrote novelist Toni Morrison in 1992, because it has "become metaphorical."

> [It is] a way of referring to and disguising forces, events, classes, and expressions of social decay and economic division far more threatening to the body politic than biological "race" ever was . . . It seems that it has a utility far beyond economy, beyond the sequestering of classes from one another, and has assumed a metaphorical life so completely embedded in daily discourse that is perhaps more necessary and on display than ever before. (63)

In what ways might thinking across the disciplines that have constituted race and consumer culture as objects of historical study help to demystify their antidemocratic force and contest their authority to frame our contemporary common sense? What critical perspective emerges when we "read together . . . the putative 'objects and subjects' of disciplines which are thought to be distinct and mutually exclusive" (Brody 6)?

Pursuing these questions has required me to leave the comfort of my training in literary studies for long stretches in order to acquaint myself with relevant work in history, sociology, anthropology, ethnic studies, and critical race studies. My limitations in this effort are reflected in this book, but so, I think, are the strengths of work that is not indigenous to the fields from which scholars typically approach these questions. Disciplinary conventions have shaped the significance of the period between the 1890s and 1930s very differently for different groups of observers: "the culture of consumption" and "the culture of segregation" are spoken of in ways that do not fully acknowledge their concurrence, much less their conjunctions. It was in the same year, 1890, that two of the most critical pieces of legislation that spurred the consumer revolution and the Jim Crow era were both passed. One, the Sherman Antitrust Act, was a formal recognition of the dangers of concentrated power in the hands of corporations, while the other, crafted by lawmakers in

Louisiana, enforced racial segregation on train cars. Both laws soon acquired tremendous symbolic and material significance, the Louisiana law for its effectiveness and the Sherman Act for its ineffectiveness. Affirming the Louisiana law in the landmark case *Plessy v. Ferguson* six years later, the U.S. Supreme Court put the official stamp of the federal government on "Jim Crow." The concentration of corporate power at which the Sherman Act was aimed quickly accelerated beyond the reach of this and other similarly toothless antitrust legislation. Corporations, possessed now of the legal status of persons and unprecedented wealth and influence, began the arduous but ultimately successful task of selling consumption as a way of life. Just as segregation was intended to resolve a crisis that emancipation and Reconstruction had precipitated in a white-supremacist society structured by relations of dominance, so the reorientation of the economy toward consumption aimed to resolve a crisis in American capitalism, which was terribly embattled at the time by overproduction, labor uprisings, and severe depressions. Both of these attempts at crisis management, historians have argued, served to exacerbate existing social and political inequities, and both had a dramatic impact on the realm of culture. It is now commonplace to speak of a culture of consumption and a culture of segregation, however contentiously the exact nature of these cultures is debated.

So familiar have these rubrics become in U.S. cultural studies that they seem to suggest discrete entities, their distinguishing features and dominant figures falling neatly into parallel columns. But in fact their historical coincidence bound the culture of segregation inextricably with the culture of consumption; indeed, the phrase "historical coincidence" is misleading insofar as it suggests an arbitrary simultaneity and implies the autonomy of the developments said to coincide. For one, the regime of visibility on which race depends found a hospitable climate in the visual orientation and technological innovation of consumer culture, from the two-dimensional spaces of print advertising and increasingly inexpensive reproductions of images to the semipublic spaces of chain stores, Pullman cars, restaurants, expositions, shop windows, and leisure and amusement sites that constituted this emerging culture of spectacle and display.

In addition, the consumer revolution occurred at a time in which the authority to define racial categories was vigorously contested, the con-

ventional discourses for framing race—legal, scientific, and popular—
having fallen out of sync. If it was clear that the Manichaean opposition
between white and black would continue to determine people's legal status and shape their social identities, and if who was black and who was
white was also clear to many people, it was far less clear what these categories would continue to mean or whether they could be reconciled with
a citizenry whose national origins, somatic features, languages, and religious and ethnic affiliations increasingly troubled the neat legal fiction
of black versus white. Historian Matthew Guterl expresses the turn-of-
the-century conundrum well.

> In this moment of widespread social, economic, and cultural tumult,
> a vast tide of racial categories washed over American culture, its ambi-
> guities and confusions hidden by multiple political motives. Several
> fundamental questions plagued discussions about "race problems"
> throughout the United States. What, exactly, was a race? Where, pre-
> cisely, should the boundary lines of racial difference be drawn? What,
> specifically, marked race physically upon or within the body? Race, it
> was argued, could be marked by language, nation, skin color, rela-
> tions between the sexes, arts and technology, social standing, govern-
> ment and laws, or religion. One popular encyclopedia, capturing the
> depth of the problem perfectly, listed several conflicting definitions
> of race without explaining or exploring the contradictions. Scientists,
> journalists, politicians, and cultural figures wavered between alle-
> giance to one set of physical traits and to another, leaving a remark-
> able looseness of fit in the language of race. And as "the science of
> races" grew more sophisticated, "race charts" and "purely somatical
> classifications" became ever more confused and complicated. (16)

For that matter, the stability of the supposedly self-evident distinction
between black and white was not entirely secure. Despite Jim Crow legislation (and arguably because of it), this distinction came under attack,
and indeed the integrity of the very concept of race was subjected to
intense skepticism in the late nineteenth century and again beginning in
late 1920s. Having formerly been associated with nation or geographic
origin, race had been "biologized" by eighteenth-century comparative
anatomists and by nineteenth-century eugenicists and physiognomists.
But this biologist paradigm, despite enjoying a renaissance in the years

around World War I, was undermined by postwar anthropologists, among others, who took an ethnicity-oriented approach to the question of race. Navigating these competing discourses was, as this book demonstrates, a regular endeavor for many U.S. writers, some of whom did so deliberately and with an intent to imaginatively intervene, others of whom wound up writing about race more or less unwittingly.

Thus, the historical moment of consumer culture's emergence was one in which neither science nor the law fully shouldered the ignominious burden of stabilizing and reproducing race, as they often competed with each other and with conventional wisdom for cultural authority. The crucial part that emerging commercialism and the cultural conversation to which it gave rise played in deepening or managing this crisis has yet to be fully examined. Though a significant body of work exists on "commodity racism"—the racially coded material artifacts of consumer culture—what occupies me here are the ways in which race was inscribed within the imaginative and critical discourses that consumer culture provoked, working itself into what W. E. B. DuBois called "the warp and woof of our daily thought with a thoroughness that few realize," into the fabric of novels and short stories, nonfiction prose and travel writing, white-authored and nonwhite-authored texts alike.[5]

A first step toward "reading together" the disciplines that have focused on the history of consumption and the history of race is to acknowledge the whiteness of the scholarly tradition on consumer culture. By this I mean its tendency to universalize white experiences, to proceed as though whiteness signifies the absence of race, and to subordinate race to class and gender as its primary categories of analysis. Recall, for example, that the urbanization of America in the late nineteenth and early twentieth centuries that historians identify as a chief catalyst in consumer society's emergence—that cityward drift chronicled in much of the classic fiction from the turn of the twentieth century—was accompanied and fueled by the demographic shift of African Americans from the rural south to northern cities. According to the 1935 U.S. Census, the decade between 1910 and 1920 saw the "Negro" populations of New York, Chicago, Cleveland, and Detroit grow 66 percent, 148 percent, 308 percent, and 611 percent, respectively—figures that would each increase again by over 100 percent during the following decade (C. Hall 55). A migration of this scale could not possibly change the

racial makeup of urban America neutrally and without fallout. If it facilitated for many African Americans access to the wages and material
goods that whites enjoyed, it also engendered the anxiety and resentment that led to widespread racial violence and rioting in 1919. Our
scholarly tradition has in effect magnified the significance of white experiences without actually treating them as white, obscuring both the experiences of nonwhites and the role of whiteness in whites' experiences. As
recently as 2000, Blackwell Publishers brought out an anthology entitled
The Consumer Society Reader—one of many such collections of foundational essays and subsequent interventions in the field, but an especially
ambitious one—and among its thirty-nine chapters there are exactly two
references to race.[6]

Far more interest has also been shown in consumerism's relationship
to ethnicity than in its relationship to race. This is a fairly recent distinction; it did not really obtain during the period I discuss here (when many
differences we would now call ethnic were considered racial), but it is
meaningful for our current scholarship. Its significance is clearly demonstrated in *Making a New Deal,* Lizabeth Cohen's analysis of Chicago's
industrial workers between the wars. Against the notion that consumer
culture homogenized society and flattened social differences, Cohen
contends that the second generation of European immigrants—the Italians, Jews, and Poles who enthusiastically embraced mainstream mass
culture—did not perforce "abandon ethnic and class affiliations" but
rather integrated these disparate concerns in ways "that preserved the
boundaries between themselves and others." However, African Americans, she adds, "developed a different and complex relationship to mass
culture."

> Black more than ethnic workers satisfied those who hoped a mass
> market would emerge during the twenties. Unlike ethnic workers,
> blacks did not reject commercial insurance, chain stores, and stan-
> dard brands. But blacks disappointed those who assumed an inte-
> grated American culture would accompany uniformity in tastes. For
> ironically, by participating in mainstream commercial life, which
> black Chicagoans did more than their ethnic co-workers, blacks came
> to feel more independent and influential as a race, not more inte-
> grated into white middle-class society. Mass culture—chain stores,

brand goods, popular music—offered blacks the ingredients from which to construct a new, urban black culture. (147–48)

The excellent existing scholarship on ethnicity's relationship to emergent consumer culture has brought welcome attention to social differences other than those of class and gender, but as Cohen's account indicates, this work cannot simply be extended by analogy or implication to African Americans. Rather, additional attention to race as distinct from ethnicity is required.[7]

Indeed, the storied refashioning of "the people as consumers" was not confined to those whites and "not-yet-white ethnics" whom the scholarly tradition typically treats as "the people."[8] When the National Negro Business League announced in 1931 its "determined fight for the Negro to gain for him some more secure economic place in American life," it tellingly cast that struggle in terms of the strength of collective consuming practices: "[T]he strongest argument we have is the power represented in the dollars we spend through stores of various kinds" (Weems 19). That same year, DuBois wrote in an editorial in *The Crisis* that "advertisement and installment buying have made the nation blind and crazy." He explained: "We think we must buy whatever is offered. The orgy must be stopped, and no group is strategically better placed than the American Negro" (*Emerging Thought* 393). In the following year, 1932, African American economist Paul K. Edwards published a groundbreaking study, *The Southern Urban Negro as a Consumer*. Of course, the highly segmented marketing practices we see today—the hyperrationalized mapping of potential purchasers along axes of race, gender, class, ethnicity, age, and sexuality—had not evolved yet. But as these three examples illustrate, the period leading to the 1930s had already constructed "the Negro as a consumer" (albeit differentially), and "the Negro" had come to participate in and experience consumer culture in ways that overlap with but are not reducible to the participation and experiences of other groups.

Attending to the complexity of this process does not require us to neglect the importance of class and gender on which the critical tradition was established. In fact, one recognizes immediately how thoroughly the relationship between consumer culture and race is shot through with gender and class ideologies. A few examples will illustrate this point. Women's experiences and issues of gender have an unusually and understandably important place in the scholarship on consumer culture. Because of women's traditional role as the point-of-purchase agent for the family, and because of prevalent assumptions about their innate predisposition toward irrationality, emotion, and appearances, women figured in many ways as the paradigmatic consumers. It is therefore significant that no less an authority than the eminent sociologist Robert Park, founder of the Chicago school of urban sociology, relied on an explicitly gendered construction of materialistic desire in distinguishing "the Negro" from other races. In a claim that rehearses long-standing stereotypes about the inferiority of "the Negro," Park wrote in 1924 that "the Negro" expresses "an interest and attachment to external, physical things rather than to subjective states and objects of introspection," exhibits a "disposition for expression rather than enterprise and action," and is therefore, "so to speak, the lady among races" (quoted in D. Baldwin 127). Thus, questions of gender are never far from the analysis of race and consumer culture, as several of the chapters in this book demonstrate.

Nor is it possible to delimit race from those issues of class that have traditionally concerned scholars of consumer culture. The most economistic critiques of consumer culture treat race as a second-order phenomenon, merely one among many instruments through which the ruling class has exploited and contained the poor and working classes. But race is not reducible to class, even as it is also unthinkable apart from class. Recent work in labor history, for example, has shown that the vastly widened and internally differentiated version of whiteness that emerged after the 1920s was the result of a hegemonic struggle over the self-affiliation of the millions of immigrant workers who might otherwise have cast their lot, so to speak, with the African Americans *with* whom they worked rather than the white bosses *for* whom they worked. Moreover, the question of the relationship of African Americans to consumer culture is always already a question of class. This is so not only because the majority of African Americans in this period were left impoverished by the failures of Reconstruction and by de facto and de jure racism, effectively barring their entry into the "able-to-buy" class that advertisers targeted, but also because the African American population in the

United States was itself highly stratified by class and thus differentially affected by the socioeconomic changes in the arena of consumption.

For example, anthropologist Paul Mullins has explored the ambivalent relationship between African Americans and the ideal of the "genteel consumer." On one hand, Mullins notes, it was primarily in the arena of consumption (rather than politics, work, or social life) that African Americans of means could demonstrate their equality with whites and express, through their "modern" appearance and lifestyle, a fitness for modernity. This was of no small value at a time when many whites still thought that African Americans constituted a premodern race or indeed represented the very antithesis of civilization itself. Replacing folk consumer practices of barter and domestic production with genteel practices within the cash economy (e.g., brand-name, store-bought products and services) served symbolic as well as material purposes. On the other hand, African Americans who approximated this genteel consumer ideal were routinely subjected to the ridicule of both whites and lower-class African Americans, to whom they appeared to be "acting white," pretending to be something they were not. Buying the markers of social prestige set African Americans up for the accusation— always close to hand among the legions of "observers of Negro behavior"—that they could not improve their actual economic standing because of their inherent weakness to spend their earnings on the outward pretense of that standing. One white essayist put it thus in 1928:

> The Negro must learn the secret of the application of wealth; he acquires it, but he does not know how to apply it to advantage. The Negro is a spendthrift; he is reckless and also a hypocrite. He tries to make people believe what he is not, by the imitation of the shadow and not the real substance. (Quoted in Mullins 102)

In short, there is an extensive, politically charged history of the class inflections of African American consumerism and of the meanings that white observers have made of African American consumption, a history to which I return in chapter 1.

Even if our scholarship were to continue to privilege white experiences of consumer culture, it could no longer, in the current critical moment, be imagined to transcend race. As a great deal of recent work has shown, race is something everyone has in a racialized society, such as the United States—albeit not in equivalent ways. Further, race is produced relationally and differentially, at least in the binary U.S. racial imaginary—the categories white and black existing in a mutually constitutive, dynamic tension. Consumer culture's institutions, artifacts, and imaginative and critical discourses elaborated blackness and whiteness relationally, deploying them in multiple and conflicting ways. Examples abound in the chapters of this book. The 1893 World's Columbian Exposition, whose role as a "cultural pedagogy" for consumerism has been widely remarked, forged an unspoken but unmistakable equation between whiteness and consumer citizenship. However, in the following decade, Henry James's *The American Scene* relied on the inverse equation, keying a nostalgic ideal of American culture to a whiteness that was being tarnished by consumer culture's "black" vulgarity and impudence. Later, as literary modernism elaborated its critique of consumer capitalism, "the Negro" became an atavistic, antimodern hero, his romanticized blackness the repository of a supposed authenticity and proximity to nature (and human nature) from which whites had been alienated. Yet in the popular fiction and drama of that same period, blackness was also deployed as a figure for consumer desire itself.[9]

Thus fraught with contradictions, the articulation of consumer culture and race in this period resists neat, totalizing analytical claims. This book proposes that the discourses of consumer culture served to reproduce racial thinking and the normativity of whiteness, but it does not attempt a comprehensive survey of the period's cultural history or literature. Having sketched in chapter 1 the theoretical terrain from which my own approach emerged, I offer readings of the articulation of race and consumer culture in several literary texts and cultural institutions. Three of the chapters (chapters 3, 4, and 6) attend closely to a particular literary text or set of texts, while the other two (chapters 2 and 5) focus principally on institutional conditions of circulation and reception. Close reading does not require a narrow formalism, however, and what I have done is to trace—through a sustained treatment of figures, rhetorical gestures, and formal devices—the connection between a text and its social context. I have tried to avoid reductively interpreting works of imaginative writing as mere mirrors that reflect dominant ideologies, and I have sought to ask, as Dominick Lacapra puts it, how "a text relate[s] in symptomatic, critical, and possibly transformative ways to its pertinent contexts" (4).

I do not take the critical and imaginative literature at the emergence of consumer society to be derivative of a more authentic object of study, of the institutions and commodities "in and of themselves." Such representations matter vitally because there is no such thing as an unmediated experience of these institutions and commodities, no extradiscursive experience of them "in and of themselves." Far from standing as second-order evidence, the work of the fiction writers on which I focus—Henry James, James Weldon Johnson, Nathanael West, and George Schuyler— was integral to the social changes they lived through and observed. Whether deliberately or unwittingly, they offer forceful reimaginings of the dynamic relationship between race and consumer culture. Although these writers are canonical (with the possible exception of Schuyler), reconceptualizing their work from this perspective produces unconventional readings. I have purposely avoided discussing writers—such as Theodore Dreiser, John Dos Passos, Sinclair Lewis, F. Scott Fitzgerald, and Nella Larsen—whose concern with consumer society is already thoroughly established, if still debated.

In chapter 2, "'Stage Business' as Citizenship," I examine a performance at the 1893 World's Columbian Exposition of what we might (following Lauren Berlant) call "diva citizenship,"[10] were it not for the decidedly stoic disposition of the performer. To publicize and compensate for the fair's policies of racial exclusion, the African American journalist Ida B. Wells solicited contributions from three other black public intellectuals for what would become an eighty-one-page polemic that she distributed in person on the fairgrounds. *The Reason Why the Colored American is Not in the World's Columbian Exposition* exposed the systemic racism behind the fair's refusals of African American contributions and, highlighting black culture and accomplishment since emancipation, served as an unofficial exhibit itself. I argue that Wells's decision to produce not just a pamphlet but also her body on the fairgrounds was particularly responsive to the racialized, commercialized public sphere that the fair represented. In contrast with other black women who managed to break through the fair's color line, the body Wells produced was neither depoliticized for ready consumption nor assimilable to a white political agenda.

In chapter 3, "Thrown into Relief," I examine Henry James's *The American Scene* (1907). James's ostensible account of his two-year return tour of the East Coast of the United States after twenty years in Europe stages a series of reflections on and revulsions from commercialism and nonwhites. He calls both "presumptuous" challenges to the continuity of American national character and consequently to the observer's capacity to represent that character in writing. Recent scholarship has addressed this and other late James texts in relation to either issues of race or issues of consumer culture, but I argue that these issues are inseparable. I situate this text at the juncture of two strands of racial thinking at the turn of the twentieth century—one scientific, the other popular. Rejecting the "100 percent Americanism" ascendant at this time, yet pulling up short of the cultural pluralism that emerged after World War I, *The American Scene* is exceptional in the anxious determination with which it raises the contradictions of racial and national discourse, contradictions that James himself concedes to harboring and ultimately needing to resubmerge. He casts himself in competition with mass culture, immigrants, and nonwhites for the authority to represent the American national character. Framed as an exercise in the rigors of observation and distinction making, *The American Scene* both advances a critique of mass cultural forms and is itself a performance of opposition against them. Chief among the distinctions James wishes to make are those he casts as racial. I argue that the process of excavating and papering over the problematic of race and national identity leads James to produce a consoling version of whiteness, one that does not reduce to color or blood. He recovers whiteness for American national identity through the idea of "consanguinity," which holds in tension its literal meaning of shared blood and its figurative meaning of fraternity and fellow feeling.

Chapter 4, "Race-changes as Exchanges," focuses on James Weldon Johnson's 1912 novel *The Autobiography of an Ex-Coloured Man,* whose narrator decides on several occasions to trade his racial identity for a better one. The neoclassical economic model of the rational consumer, *homo economicus,* who is imagined to choose freely within the marketplace of goods, has tacitly informed most readings of the narrator's changes. Perhaps most significant among these readings is Henry Louis Gates's introduction to the Vintage edition, in which he writes that the narrator changes race "at his whim and by his will" (xviii). While I endorse the

trend in recent criticisms of this novel—Gates's included—toward reading it as a constructivist account of race that challenges the dominant
biological essentialism of its time, the notion that "passing" involves free
choice among equivalent categories of identity obscures the economic
context and social structures determining race. By emphasizing instead
the novel's attention to the commodification of blackness after the turn
of the twentieth century and to the performative dimension of racial
identities, I argue that consumer capitalism is a crucial determining context for the narrator's repeated movements across the color line. Moreover, Johnson's novel represents a color line that is not only productive
of consumer culture (as race makes possible certain commodities, spectacles, and lucrative performances of the transgression of racial identity)
but also one of consumer culture's important products.

Chapter 5, "A Black Culture Industry," takes the concurrence of a
rapid commercialization in book publishing and a burst of African
American literary production between World War I and the Great
Depression as an occasion to examine their reciprocal impact. The firm
of Boni and Liveright (1917–33) focuses this inquiry for two reasons.
Although it cultivated high-culture ambitions and a stable of "difficult"
modernists, it also embodied the pronounced shift toward the aggressive
promotion and marketing practices that (to use book historian John
Tebbel's term) "revolutionized" the industry. This was a shift that
Edward Bernays, the father of twentieth-century public relations, actively
encouraged as B&L's chief public relations officer. Also, B&L was among
the first and most prominent venues for "New Negro" writers, publishing
books by Jean Toomer, Jessie Fauset, and Eric Walrond, as well as playing
a vital role in the Boni brothers' publication of *The New Negro*. Although
Horace Liveright and Charles Boni enjoy considerable prominence in
histories of the Harlem Renaissance, the African American writers and
editors who raised B&L's stature earn hardly a mention in accounts of its
history or in its officers' biographies, a symptomatic omission that invites
a critical reassessment. Likewise, the established critical accounts of the
Harlem Renaissance tend to overlook the role consumer capitalism
played in reproducing racial thinking, because they highlight individual
patronage relations rather than the history of institutions and the
broader economic transitions in which these individuals were participating.[11] By examining the advertising and public relations campaigns for

Toomer's *Cane* (1923) and Fauset's *There Is Confusion* (1924), chapter 5 argues that the reception of the "New Negro" had to contend with the persistence of the "Old Negro" in advertising discourse, which included the book-jacket blurbs, print ads, promotional materials for bookstores, ready-to-print reviews for newspapers, and staged publicity events that proliferated as advertising and public relations professionalized themselves in the 1920s. Though B&L is the immediate concern of chapter 5, the chapter raises questions about the translation of race between the "literary-art world," as Toomer called it, and the world of literary commodities and celebrity with which these writers had to make their peace to extend their audience beyond the readers of *Opportunity*, *The Crisis*, and the "little magazines."

In chapter 6, "Confessions of the Flesh," I discuss two arch satirists of the 1930s, Nathanael West and George Schuyler. Although the Depression provoked widespread challenges to capitalism and realigned the class affiliations of many Americans (in the process of impoverishing them), it only outwardly and temporarily changed the consumer society consolidated in the post–World War I years.[12] By the early thirties, the diffusion of advertising into new arenas of everyday life, the commodification of experience and discourse, and the rhetorical fashioning of the public as consumers became sites of frequent literary reflection. At the same time, among African Americans, the limitations of social advancement programs based on culture rather than economics had become more evident. Chapter 6 argues that while West is concerned with mass culture and commodification and Schuyler is concerned with white-supremacist thinking and racialized embodiment, the overt themes of one writer turn out to be the implicit concerns of the other. In the process, I discuss *U.S. v. Ozawa* (1922) and *Thind v. U.S.* (1923), the only two petitions for citizenship naturalization ever to reach the Supreme Court, both of which turned on a highly contested legal definition of a "white person," meeting which was a prerequisite for naturalization.[13]

West wrote what many consider the first "Hollywood novel," *The Day of the Locust* (1937), but his effort to skewer the burgeoning culture industries began in the late twenties, when he embarked on *Miss Lonelyhearts* (1933), a short novel about a spiritually enervated advice columnist for a New York newspaper. Schuyler is best known for his essay "The Negro-

Art Hokum"—which provoked Langston Hughes's famous rebuttal, "The Negro Artist and the Racial Mountain"—and perhaps also for the conservative positions he went on to adopt as a columnist for the *Pittsburgh Courier*. Early in his career, however, his picaresque novel *Black No More* (1931) performed a reductio ad absurdum on white-supremacist thinking, imagining that the so-called Negro problem could be solved by a machine that turns dark skin light at the touch of a button, effectively "eliminating Negroes." As it follows the paradoxical ascendance of the first "whitened Negro" from the Harlem offices of Black-No-More, Incorporated, to a high office in a white-supremacist organization, Schuyler's critique of American racial hierarchy also confronts consumer capitalism, the cynical manufacturing of desire that it requires, and the possessive individualism that it fosters. West's critique of consumer society ends up smuggling in issues of race because it invokes skin color as an index of fitness for citizenship in the commercial public sphere. I trace the peculiar kinds of attention paid to skin color in West and Schuyler to the Supreme Court's effort to bury the contradictions in racial discourse by freighting skin with an almost textual kind of legibility and referentiality.

While this book confines its attention to the significance of a roughly forty-year period, its conclusion, "Leaving Muncie," suggests our inheritance of the negotiations of racism, race thinking, and consumer capitalism in the present. I take Robert Lynd's decision to base the research for his seminal work on consumer culture, *Middletown* (1933), in Muncie, Indiana, as emblematic of the methodological problem this book invites us to redress. Confronted with what he took to be the unnecessary complication of a racially mixed citizenry in South Bend, Indiana, Lynd wished to restrict his inquiry "to the white American stock" and ultimately relocated to Muncie, 92 percent of whose citizens were native-born whites. The critical tradition that *Middletown* helped launch has impoverished itself by following suit and relegating questions of race to the margins. Further, the conclusion challenges the willful optimism of current popular reflections on the relationship between race and consumer culture as exemplified in Leon Wynter's recent book *American Skin: Pop Culture, Big Business, and the End of White America* (2002), which takes the racial "diversity" of mass culture images as the death knell for the normative whiteness of American national identity.

Bringing race out of the footnotes of our scholarship on consumer culture and according it an analytical priority should not be a strictly academic exercise, an esoteric corrective. The assumptions about race that have shaped American social and political practices and that continue to enjoy pernicious currency despite our supposed multicultural moment have reproduced themselves in part through social relations that do not announce themselves as racial. But race lives and breathes through these social relations; it does not exist outside of them. It is their effect, as well as their antecedent. How has our neglect of the reciprocity between the hegemonic development of race and consumer culture made them more resilient? How might we better recognize the ways in which they have worked—and have been worked—to mystify their mutual investments? I hope this study, rooted in the past, can begin to address these critical issues of the present and future.

This book represents but one of many possible ways into the question of the relationship between race and consumer culture. Of necessity, it makes but a modest contribution to the kind of far-reaching genealogy we need. Because of the complexity and even obscurity of this relationship in U.S. history, because of the contingencies involved in its articulation, what is needed is precisely not a traditional history that seeks determinate moments of origin or that "pretend[s] to go back in time to restore an unbroken continuity" with the present "beyond the dispersion of forgotten things" but one that "disturbs what was previously considered immobile; fragments what was thought unified; [and] shows the heterogeneity of what was imagined consistent with itself."[14] Therefore, before turning to the particular sites of my own research, I begin by tracing a history of the scholarship on consumption in the United States, but one that does not, I trust, function blandly as a "review of the literature." It focuses not only on this critical history's moments of influence, revision, and repudiation but also on its aporias, its nonconversations across disciplines, and on recent efforts to make these conversations happen. In so doing, my hope is to inspire others to pursue related projects, even and especially those with little concern for the literary studies questions that tend to preoccupy me in this book.

1 *No Place of Race*

CONSUMER CULTURE'S
CRITICAL TRADITION

For students of African American history and of race in the
United States, the years between *Plessy v. Ferguson* and the Great Depression were pivotal in the renewal of racial thinking—the retrenchment of
racism, the disenfranchisement of African Americans, and the consolidation of a whiteness that would include the massive "second wave" of
European immigrants but few others. For scholars in contiguous fields of
cultural history, however, the primary significance of this period is that it
marked the birth of a full-blown consumer society. To borrow the titles
of several influential works on this transformation, the "incorporation of
America" turned the United States into a "land of desire," as the commercial "captains of consciousness" set about "advertising the American
dream" and other "fables of abundance" in order to carve enduring
"channels of desire." Given the critical importance that the period from
the 1890s to the 1930s held for both of these defining transformations
of U.S. culture, why has each one mattered so little in the scholarship
about the other? Sustained attention to the articulations of race and consumer culture is more often found in scholarship on contemporary culture than in work addressing those earlier eras in which the patterns of
their articulations were established. Historically, how have ideas about
consumption and national citizenship been shaped by race thinking? In
what ways has consumer culture animated race? As I stated in the introduction, understanding these articulations requires a kind of
"reconfigured genealogy" that has only recently begun to emerge.

The title of this chapter alludes to the magisterial study *No Place of
Grace* (1981), whose author, T. J. Jackson Lears, has arguably done more

than any other individual scholar to define and advance the recent study
of U.S. consumer culture, not only through *No Place of Grace* and his
more recent *Fables of Abundance* (1994), but also through coediting, with
Richard Wightman Fox, two pivotal volumes of essays, *The Culture of Consumption* (1983) and *The Power of Culture* (1993). The scholarship in
these books is representative of a broader tendency, a culturalist shift in
the study of U.S. capitalism in recent years. Within this scholarship, culture has come to mean not just the superstructural expressions of an economic base, as more mechanistic accounts suggested, but a field of contestation in a hegemonic struggle to naturalize modern capitalism.
Likewise, recent years have also witnessed a corresponding culturalist
shift in the study of race in the United States—an interest in culture as a
mediator of racial formation. Culture is here understood as a form of
agency that is distinct from but works in concert with the law, science,
and the state in maintaining and redefining our ideas about race. These
two notable developments have taken place concurrently but almost
independently over the past twenty-five years.

As varied and extensive as the cultural history of consumer society has
become, one is still hard-pressed to find scholarship in which race is central to the inquiry. If questions of race are posed at all, they are usually
secondary to the questions of class or gender that have traditionally
interested scholars of U.S. consumer culture. To begin to account for
this tendency, we can look to the major strands of theoretical and historical scholarship that have informed the critical discourse. As importantly, we can in turn recognize the possibilities that are available for a
sustained consideration of race. The examination of the critical tradition that I offer in this chapter begins with the influential analytical
frameworks of Marx, Veblen, and the Frankfurt and Birmingham
schools. I turn to the "native" tradition in U.S. scholarship, which has
over the years adopted and adapted elements from each of the aforementioned frameworks. I then take up the less-known but robust critical
conversation in African American scholarship that has coexisted alongside this "native" U.S. tradition, bearing its imprint in certain respects
and departing in others, without having been much noted in turn by the
mainstream. I end with several recent, promising interventions generated by critical race studies and the vigorous conversation on the concept of the "public sphere." Though it is not an exhaustive survey of the

relevant scholarship, this discussion suggests that a reconsideration of the place of race in consumer culture scholarship is urgently required and potentially transformative.

Consumer Culture's Critical Tradition:
Marx, Veblen, Frankfurt, and Birmingham

Critical analyses of American capitalism that emphasize the period between the Gilded Age and the Great Depression rely, of course, on intellectual traditions not only that precede this period but for which this period has no peculiar significance. Karl Marx's critique of private property and political economy conditioned the possibility for a theory of capitalist societies that remains viable despite his inaccuracy at predicting the course of history. In the 1844 *Economic and Philosophical Manuscripts,* Marx defined "the world of objects" created by workers as estranged labor, the concretization of relations of production that alienate workers from the processes and the products of their work (Fromm 122). In the first volume of *Capital,* Marx advanced a critique of the "fetishization" of commodities under capitalism. Although "a commodity appears at first sight a very trivial thing, and easily understood," he suggests, "its analysis shows that it is, in reality, a very queer thing, abounding in metaphysical subtleties and theological niceties" (319). To illustrate the source of "the mystical character of commodities," he proceeded to distinguish use value from exchange value (320). Moreover, he argued in *Capital* that social relations are obscured in capitalism as economic relations and that people and goods are "reified" and falsely rendered equivalent by their abstraction as money. Thus, what Marx bequeathed the critical study of consumer culture was a theoretical framework and a fundamental premise: that capitalism replaces actual human needs with false desires. The notion that capitalism systematically produces desires it cannot satisfy, channeling natural human needs for individual fulfillment and social relationships through commodities that spectacularly fail to fulfill them, has informed an entire critical tradition.

Marxist historiography put consumer culture on the U.S. scholarly map in the mid-twentieth century, as historians sought to explain the failures of workers' political movements in the United States and to refute the prevailing liberal orthodoxy that capitalism's triumph was expressed through an American "democracy of goods." Their rebuttal contended, rather, that the working class had in effect been "bought off" by the promise of more and better commodities, that class-based grievances against an exploitative economic system were mollified by the appearance of equality, and that the oversupply of consumer goods and diversions offered a palliative distraction from the actual conditions of economic exploitation. The elite class had effectively tricked the working class, many of whom considered themselves middle-class, into acting against their own interests. These scholars subscribed to a notion of ideology as "false consciousness."

In its adherence to the classical Marxist ideas of the commodity as alienated labor, of consumption as the impossible satisfaction of false desires, and of exchange value as a perversion of a commodity's natural, inherent use value, the false consciousness approach differs dramatically from another foundational analysis: Thorstein Veblen's. By troubling the neat distinction between use value and exchange value, Veblen's *Theory of the Leisure Class* (1899) left an indelible mark on consumer culture scholarship. Veblen contended that there were in fact vital social functions served by the "conspicuous" consumption and display of expensive consumer goods among the genteel class. His argument that commodities have an invidious social utility that is not reducible to its use value in Marxist terms compelled a reconsideration of objects, spectacles, dress, and display as status markers. Although Veblen confined his claims too narrowly to the upper class and mistakenly forecast a return to "feudalism," he nevertheless anticipated, in some respects, arguments advanced many decades later in such pivotal work as Jean Baudrillard's *The Mirror of Production* (1975), Mary Douglas and Baron Isherwood's *World of Goods* (1979), and Pierre Bourdieu's *Distinction* (1984).

If late twentieth-century consumer culture scholarship was therefore shaped decisively by Marx and Veblen, certain interventions have nevertheless been acts of apostasy within these traditions. Two such projects of particular significance received support from the Frankfurt Institute for Social Research in Germany and the Centre for Contemporary Cultural Studies in Birmingham, England. While the work of the scholars affiliated with these institutions is far from uniform, some consistent lines of analysis illustrate their formative influence on the field.

In response to the rise of fascism in Europe in the early twentieth century, the German social theorists Georg Lukacs, Max Horkheimer, Theodor Adorno, Hannah Arendt, Leo Lowenthal, and Walter Benjamin developed a method of dialectical analysis that Marx had himself adapted from Hegel for his own historical-materialist purposes. "Negative dialectics," as they called their revision, rejected historical positivism—the notion that civilization was advancing progressively toward greater emancipation and "enlightenment." By calling attention to the ways in which culture was instrumentalized for ideological purposes, their work dramatically expanded the definitions of politics and power, beyond their conventional associations with the state, parliamentary procedures, and the law, into the quotidian corners of daily life and the circulation and consumption of popular, "mass" culture. Because these theorists were above all concerned with the Enlightenment-era promise of the public's capacity to dissent, to forge community, and thereby to serve as a check on both state power and private power wielded by corporations, their work attended as thoroughly to the tyranny of a highly managed sphere of cultural production as to the specter of official state fascism. In the surfeit of commodities that Western civilization furnished to the ruling class and the working class alike, the Frankfurt theorists identified insidious instruments of social control. "The ruthless unity in the culture industry is evidence of what will happen in politics," Adorno and Horkheimer wrote in *The Dialectic of Enlightenment,* "Something is provided for all so that none may escape; the distinctions are emphasized and extended. The public is catered for with a hierarchical range of mass-produced products of varying quality, thus advancing the rule of complete quantification" (123).

Unlike Marx, the Frankfurt theorists saw culture as the contested terrain on which ideological battles were fought rather than as simply the superstructural expression of the dominant ideology. Unlike Veblen, they suggested that the most important of these battles took place not in the practices of "leisure-class" consumption but rather through "mass" culture—the commodities, amusements, and spectacles systematically manufactured, they argued, by the distraction factory of the commercial "culture industries." Not only did the Frankfurt theorists write a great deal about American mass culture (e.g., jazz, Hollywood, and the language of advertisements), but several emigrated to the United States to escape the Third Reich, trained American students, and left an indelible mark on subsequent scholarship. Their cultural pessimism resonated provocatively with concurrent work on consumer society from such American critics as Walter Lippmann, Robert and Helen Lynd, and Dwight MacDonald.

With few exceptions (most notably Benjamin), the Frankfurt theorists tended to identify "mass" culture forms with false consciousness and passivity and "high" culture forms with reason, rigor, and dissent. Therefore, their critique of the culture industry tacitly reinforced some unflattering assumptions about precisely those ordinary, working people on whose behalf they ostensibly sought to salvage the political and philosophical ideals of the Enlightenment. In stark contrast to this elitism, an alternate analytical model emerged in the second half of the century from the Birmingham Centre, a model that has been tremendously influential in shaping the critical conversation. Drawing on the work of Italian Marxist Antonio Gramsci, French sociologist Claude Levi-Strauss, French philosopher Michel Foucault, and Britain's own rich tradition of working-class history, Birmingham scholars recast politics, redefined ideology, and, in so doing, asserted the political agency of the mass public of consumers. While classical Marxism saw class interests as static and definable in advance of the conflict between labor and capital (an assumption the Frankfurt theorists tended to share), Gramsci defined social conflict as hegemonic, a dynamic process by which an always-precarious consent of the governed is only ever won provisionally. He argued that class interests were not simply the cause but also the effect of class conflict; because this conflict was continuous, class interests were always provisional. Ideology could therefore be understood not as "false consciousness," since this model presupposes a working class that is duped into adopting the interests of the ruling class, but as "spontaneous philosophy," or the "common sense" produced as political power is maintained through the negotiation of competing interests.[1] Similarly, Foucault reimagined power as social and diffuse rather than formally political and exercised from the top down. Because power is wielded at particular institutional sites and dependent on the availability of particular, socially privileged discourses, Foucault argued, the real work of social control is difficult to locate and therefore to resist but is nevertheless impossible to shore up completely. As the Birmingham theorists read them, Gramsci and Foucault suggested a social field that was suffused with relations of domination, but a domination that could not be secured without also conditioning possibilities for its own resistance and reversal, opportunities for subordinated subjects to exercise agency at the interstices.

Chief among these sites of resistance, the Birmingham school contended, is the consumption of mass culture. They took seriously a set of questions for which the Frankfurt school had little use: what do consumers actually do with the products they buy, at the spectacles they observe, to the texts they read? While the Frankfurt theorists saw the reflection of ruling-class interests in mass culture, such Birmingham theorists as Raymond Williams, Richard Hoggart, Stuart Hall, John Fiske, and Dick Hebdige pursued highly nuanced analyses of reception and recast consumption as activity rather than passive absorption. To express this activity, they drew on Levi-Strauss's notion of bricolage, a figure for the consumer's practices of decoding and reassembling fragments of consumer culture for the consumer's own purposes. Mary Douglas and Baron Isherwood (an anthropologist and an economist, respectively) captured this intervention succinctly in their decidedly anti-Frankfurt assertion that "commodities are good for thinking" and that scholars should therefore "treat them as a nonverbal medium for the human creative faculty." Similarly, Fiske contended, "All the culture industries can do is produce a repertoire of texts or cultural resources for the various formations of the people to use or reject in an ongoing process of producing their popular culture."[2] Thus, to recent U.S. consumer culture scholarship, the Birmingham school contributed models in which consumption, spectatorship, and other modes of participation in mass culture are understood as politically ambivalent, if not emancipatory, practices. Their political significance is, at any rate, not decidable in advance or immanent in the mass cultural forms themselves.

Moreover, due in large part to Birmingham's influence, it became virtually impossible, by the 1990s, to overstate the importance of the study of consumer culture, as the following excerpt from a major 1982 study illustrates.

Just as the Industrial Revolution of the eighteenth century marks one of the great discontinuities in history, one of the great turning points in the history of human experience, so, in my view, does the matching

revolution in consumption. For the consumer revolution was the necessary analogue to the Industrial Revolution, the necessary convulsion
on the demand side of the equation to match the convulsion on the
supply side. We are only just beginning to realize how pervasive were
the social and economic effects of this change, and how considerable
were the pressures needed to bring it about. For the results were such
as to bring about as great a change in the lifestyle of the population as
was brought about by the neolithic revolution in agriculture which
began some eight thousand years before the birth of Christ. (Mc-
Kendrick, Brewer, and Plumb 9)

According to this somewhat breathless claim, the great epochs of civilization have been defined by the agricultural revolution, the industrial
revolution, and now the consumer revolution. The place and time of
"the birth of consumer society" to which McKendrick, Brewer, and
Plumb refer in their book's title are identified in its subtitle, *The Commercialization of Eighteenth-Century England*. Clearly, another set of intellectual
traditions and political and economic conditions must be considered in
order to understand the U.S-based scholarship that locates this "birth"
much more recently and on the other side of the Atlantic.

The "Native" Critical Tradition in the United States

Although contemporary U.S. scholarship on consumer culture is
indebted to European critical traditions—a familiar example, Frederic
Jameson's essay "Reification and Utopia in Mass Culture," appeared in
the inaugural issue of *Social Text* in the same year (1979) that Douglass
and Isherwood published *World of Goods*—the main tributary to U.S.
scholarship was the revisionist impulse in American studies that had its
roots in the liberation movements of the civil rights era. In the 1960s and
1970s, challenges arose to the foundational narratives that underwrote
American studies in the post–World War II years, narratives in which the
myth of American exceptionalism was pressed into service as a Cold War
defense of liberal capitalism.[3] American democracy expressed itself best
in a "democracy of goods," this story went, in the power of liberal capitalism to offer an ever-broadening spectrum of consumer-citizens access
to ever-cheaper and better goods and services. In the challenges to this

narrative, it was the subtle but decisive redefinition of "the people as consumers," as the title of Robert Lynd's 1933 essay had put it, that scholars sought to highlight and revisit. To be sure, these challenges had ample precedent in American letters. A powerful Puritan suspicion of luxury and a Protestant ethic of delayed gratification had long informed American critiques of materialism and incipient consumer society, from colonial-era jeremiads to Franklin's "Poor Richard" to Thoreau's early nineteenth-century romantic humanism. More than the European traditions, it was this "native" tradition, formalized by academic sociology, that informed such twentieth-century analyses as *The Phantom Public* (1925) by Walter Lippmann, *Middletown* (1933) by Robert and Helen Lynd, *People of Plenty* (1954) by David Potter, *The Hidden Persuaders* by Vance Packard (1957), *The Affluent Society* by John Kenneth Galbraith (1958), *Against the American Grain* (1962) by Dwight Macdonald, *The Image; or, What Happened to the American Dream* (1962) by Daniel Boorstin, and *Abundance for What?* (1964) by David Riesman.

Over the past two decades, two strands of scholarship have made the critical study of consumer capitalism central to social and cultural history and have made the period between the Gilded Age and the Great Depression central to that study. One is a social history that challenges the consensus, grand-narrative approach by focusing on previously marginalized historical subjects—workers, women, and ethnic, racial, and sexual minorities—and on the popular and material culture that was previously thought unworthy of scholarly consideration.[4] A second, related strand of influential scholarship has come from historians of advertising and theorists of its social and cultural impact. Warren Susman's essays collected in *Culture as History* (1984) argue that the development of U.S. consumer capitalism provoked a corresponding shift at the level of individual consciousness and social identity, supplanting a nineteenth-century, Protestant-based belief in "character" with a twentieth-century, consumption-oriented belief in "personality." As they constituted consumer culture as a major field of scholarly inquiry within American studies, Stuart Ewen's *Captain's of Consciousness* (1976), Alan Trachtenberg's *The Incorporation of America* (1982), and the essays collected by Richard Wightman Fox and T. J. Jackson Lears in *The Culture of Consumption* (1983), staged an implicit exchange about "hegemony" as a privileged category for the study of consumer culture.[5]

While there is little agreement among these scholars regarding the persuasiveness of the hegemony thesis, there is near consensus that the period of the 1880s through the 1930s were the definitive years of transformation in American capitalism and the culture of consumption it engendered.[6] But why did this transformation occur? Traditionally, historians stressed the technological conditions of possibility for consumer capitalism's emergence, such as the establishment by the late 1890s of railroads, telephone systems, and electricity in urban transportation. Though this infrastructure was necessary, it was not sufficient, and as the later set of scholars point out, a purely mechanistic treatment is doubly obscuring: it posits an immanent, progressive logic to capitalist development, thereby concealing the role of a deliberate incorporation and merger movement; and it fails to recognize how much ideological work was performed to overcome the tremendous discrepancy in the late nineteenth century between the unprecedented supply of manufactured goods resulting from industrialization and the relatively tepid demand for them.

Trachtenberg notes that incorporation had already been occurring on "a modest scale," but by the 1870s, "it had become commonplace, changing the face and character of American capitalism."

The merger movement at the turn of the century was a dramatic outcome of the process inaugurated in the Gilded Age, underlining the change in the entrepreneurial history of the previous decades. That movement resulted in a major realignment of economic power. By 1904, for example, about three hundred industrial corporations had won control over more than two-fifths of all manufacturing in the country, affecting the operations of about four-fifths of the nation's industries. And the trend has continued, as any student of twentieth-century history well knows. By 1929, the two hundred largest corporations held 48 percent of all corporate assets (excluding banks and insurance companies) and 58 percent of net capital assets such as land, buildings, and machinery. By 1962, that ratio of ownership and control had narrowed even further, to the hundred largest corporations. In the era of multinationals, certain corporations exceed many countries in wealth. Of the hundred largest economic units in the

world in 1974, forty-nine were nations and fifty-one multinational corporations. (*Incorporation* 4–5)

Richard Ohmann points out that by the late 1890s, the U.S. economy
had effectively industrialized at twice the rate as had England's during its
industrial revolution. The value of manufactured goods grew at roughly
two and one-half times the rate of the population over the last four
decades of the century, he goes on to note, and the gross national product climbed precipitously, suggesting a greater ability to buy than ever
before (49). However, wealth, income, and the means of production
were concentrated in the hands of a few, and those who could buy were
not inclined to do so; Americans were saving their money at a higher rate
than at any other time in U.S. history. Thus, concludes Ohmann, at the
very moment when the accumulation of capital was at its highest
(1881–96), the "flow of goods to consumers was the lowest" (51). This
crisis of overproduction was succinctly expressed by the president of the
stovemaker's association who said in 1888, "It is a chronic case of too
many stoves and not enough people to buy them" (Ohmann 54). Or as
sociologist Simon Patten put it in *The New Basis of Civilization* (1907), an
"economy of scarcity" had given way to an "economy of abundance," but
Americans' values and social practices had not yet caught up to accommodate and take advantage of the shift. The effects on culture, society,
and ideology of the ensuing efforts to encourage consumption as a way
of life—"the remaking of cultural perceptions this process entailed"
(Trachtenberg, *Incorporation* 3)—gave rise to a rich and variegated field
of "native" U.S. scholarship.

   If the "crucial formative" period for the culture of consumption was
1880 to 1930, this was an equally formative period for race in the United
States (Leach xiii). They were not only the pivotal Jim Crow years that
would have long-term social and economic reverberations. They were
also the gestational years for the full-blown racial nativism that emerged
out of late nineteenth-century antiforeign radical sentiments and that
was authorized by racialist natural science (Higham 131–57). They were
the years in which the basis of race in biology, which had been the dominant account since slavery, was contested on several fronts—by social
scientists, by African American writers, and by petitioners for naturaliza-

tion to U.S. citizenship, among others. Racial biologism began to yield in the 1930s to the challenge of an ethnicity paradigm espoused by such "cultural pluralists" as Horace Kallen and Robert Park (Omi and Winant 14–16). Although it got two intellectual shots in the arm with the 1911 translation of Houston Stewart Chamberlain's *Foundations of the Nineteenth Century* (originally published in Germany in 1899) and the 1912 translation of Arthur de Gobineau's *Essay on the Inequality of Human Races* (originally published in France between 1853 and 1855), and although popular white-supremacist thinking was elevated to quasi-scientific status by such American authors as Madison Grant and Lothrop Stoddard, the authority of racial science was further undermined in the 1930s by the response to the Nazis' belief in Aryan supremacy and to the violence perpetrated in its name.

Despite what we may therefore recognize as a concurrence in convulsive periods of development, race figures only peripherally in the aforementioned scholarship, whose primary categories of analysis have been class, gender, and, more recently, ethnicity.[7] Traditional class-oriented scholarship has revealed the ways in which consumer culture has at once exacerbated economic inequalities and acted as their smoke screen. Because consumption is the one arena of economic activity in which women historically played a more active role than men, gender analysis also has a long-standing priority. Moreover, the subordination of questions of race in the critical tradition may be attributed in part to the fact that until fairly recently, advertisers did not consider nonwhites among the "able-to-buy" class that would constitute the mass market. Of course, African Americans have long constituted a niche market, but it was not until the 1930s that it was thought to "pay" to market to the working class and other nonnormative consumers (Marchand 64). Robert Weems writes that as late as 1910, "before African Americans began to proliferate noticeably in U.S. urban areas, 76.4 percent of gainfully employed African Americans worked in either agriculture or domestic service." Weems continues, "The vast majority of these workers were at the absolute bottom of the U.S. wage hierarchy, alongside self-employed black farm owners" (14).

Thus, one way to account for the neglect of race in the scholarly tradition is to see it as simply a faithful reflection of the normativity of whiteness in consumer culture itself. However, I think there are two additional and related issues that are much more decisive. One is the great extent to which the critical tradition failed to enter into dialogue with the concurrent, extensive body of writing about consumer culture by African Americans. The other is the privilege that whiteness has enjoyed to not signify as any race at all, to stand tacitly for universal personhood, to remain invisible as whiteness in the critical discourse.

Black Countertraditions

As professional writers and researchers, black authors represent an intellectual, rather than a vernacular, tradition. Theirs ought not to be taken as the definitive statements by African Americans about the relationship between race and consumer culture, which has been the subject of vigorous exchanges in beauty parlors, living rooms, and nightclubs longer than in the pages of books and journals. However, they do represent the effort of trained professionals to assess and intervene in this relationship, and I do not wish to enter into a discussion of the relative "authenticity" of intellectual and vernacular expression. In many cases, the work of these authors calls into question the very distinction between intellectual and vernacular, either because it relies heavily on the vernacular accounts the authors obtained through ethnographic fieldwork or because they situate themselves as both practitioners of intellectual work and participants in the vernacular folkways of their black communities.[8]

Understandably, turn-of-the century commentators trained their critical eyes more fixedly on the place of African Americans in production than in consumption, for until the Great Migration, jobs outside the economy of agricultural indentured servitude were neither abundant nor remunerative. Nevertheless, the question of consumption arose consistently in their work on racial equality and integration into the mainstream life of the nation. The three authors I wish to discuss—Booker T. Washington, Frances E. W. Harper, and W. E. B. DuBois—wrote in the spirit of Progressivism that infused the arena of letters and politics at the time. They tended to cast conspicuous consumption and materialism in general as antithetical to racial "uplift." However, interesting contradictions arise within and among their arguments. Moreover, in the work of DuBois in particular, whose career spanned seven tumultuous decades, we see the extent to which this early Progressivism had to be either reconciled with or sacrificed to the material and ideological pressures that followed.

Washington, as is well known, stressed the importance of work, both as a builder of "character" and as a means to saving money, acquiring real estate, establishing a financial stake in a community, and helping the race to generate its own stable middle class. This philosophy adamantly opposed conspicuous consumption, the lavish expenditure of one's hard-earned wages. But it tacitly endorsed another, more genteel version of consumerism: one's lifestyle and object choices served, as Washington well knew, as outward evidence of that solidly middle-class status that he saw as the path to parity, if not full integration, with the white mainstream. His work drew heavily on the moralist and individualist discourses of the nineteenth century, and his impact was far-reaching. Washington founded the National Negro Business League, an organization that would, under the later direction of Robert Moton, mobilize African Americans explicitly to compete against the vast resources of a white retail establishment of department stores and chain stores.

Like Washington, Frances E. W. Harper, a poet, novelist, and activist in the women's suffrage and temperance movements, represented the desire for material possessions as antithetical to the cause of racial equality. She also shared with Washington an almost hyperbolically producerist faith in the value of work, even and especially for respectable women—a rare position in her time. The protagonist of her novel *Iola Leroy* (1892) says: "I have a theory that every woman ought to know how to make her own living. I believe that a great amount of sin and misery springs from the weakness and inefficiency of women" (205). Materialism figures prominently in *Iola Leroy,* as a kind of false consciousness in Harper's African American characters, a surrender to the values of the dominant white society, and a form of treason to the race. "To be the leader of a race to higher planes of thought and action, to teach men clearer views of life and duty, and to inspire their souls with loftier aims, is a far greater privilege than it is to open the gates of material prosperity and fill every home with sensuous enjoyment," says Iola. Her ideal is "not simply a nation building up a great material prosperity, founding magnificent cities, grasping the commerce of the world, or excelling in literature, art, and science, but a nation wearing sobriety as a crown and righteousness as the girdle of her loins" (219). The cause of the race in this novel requires an unswerving commitment to temperance, church-going, and teaching in the "colored" schools of the South. The question *Iola Leroy* continually poses—has the nation's "moral life" kept pace with its "mental development" and "material progress"?—limns a familiar set of conflicts, but with the additional implication that the nation's "material progress" threatens the racial justice that Harper makes synonymous with the nation's "moral life."

Early in his career, W. E. B. DuBois sounded a similar note. In response to the mutual ignorance between the races that he felt was the sinister root of America's racial hierarchy, DuBois proposed a concerted exchange between what was "best" in the white and Negro races. To such an exchange, he wrote, "we the darker ones come even now not altogether empty handed." He explained, "in all, we black men seem the sole oasis of simple faith and reverence in a dusty desert of dollars and smartness" (*Souls of Black Folk* 8). The figure is provocative: it is a caustic indictment of what he saw as the spiritual and moral poverty of the ascendant culture of "getting and spending"; it is a valorization of a critical perspective borne of oppression and marginalization; and it is an identification of blackness with a kind of cultural innocence. This was an ambivalent identification, however, because it could be deployed not only for purposes like DuBois's own but for reactionary ones as well. Over the course of a long career, DuBois continued to write about issues of race and consumer culture in ways that are too varied and extensive to fully summarize here. But an examination of a few excerpts will illuminate the trajectory of his thinking on these issues and raise some important historiographic questions.

The DuBois of *The Souls of Black Folk* could imagine a good-faith cultural exchange between mutually respectful races, but he nevertheless recognized the priority of an intensive and extensive project of disabusing whites of pervasive, resilient, and insidious stereotypes of African Americans. In the following passage, which echoes the earlier figure of the black oasis in the desert of modern industrialization and rationalization, DuBois revalues the "shiftlessness" widely attributed to "young Negroes" by framing it as a reasoned response to structural conditions.

To the car-window sociologist, to the man who seeks to understand and know the South by devoting the few leisure hours of a holiday trip to unravelling the snarl of centuries,—to such men very often the whole trouble with the black fieldhand may be summed up by Aunt Ophelia's word, "Shiftless!" . . . Shiftless? Yes, the personification of shiftlessness. And yet follow those boys: they are not lazy; to-morrow morning they will be up with the sun; they work hard when they do work, and they work willingly. They have no sordid, selfish, money-getting ways, but rather a fine disdain for mere cash. They'll loaf before your face and work behind your back with good-natured honesty. They'll steal a watermelon, and hand you back your lost purse intact. Their great defect as laborers lies in their lack of incentive beyond the mere pleasure of physical exertion. They are careless because they have not found that it pays to be careful; they are improvident because the improvident ones of their acquaintance get on about as well as the provident. Above all, they cannot see why they should take unusual pains to make the white man's land better, or to fatten his mule, or save his corn. (107)

In the process of refuting the "car-window sociologist," DuBois suggests that the young Negro's real virtue is that he is materialistic, in the strictest sense of the term. Yes, he wants things, but he wants the things themselves, in order to use them, not the cash that merely signifies an ability to spend—the watermelon, not the lost purse. DuBois is arguably as patronizing here toward young, working-class African Americans as he is critical of the "sordid, selfish, money-getting ways" of their employers. But the passage extends the dual implication of his earlier remarks: it offsets the white presumption of cultural superiority with a representation of mainstream society as ruthlessly (and witlessly) profiteering, and it recontextualizes stigmatized behavior among African Americans as a testament to their pragmatic "good nature."

Later in his career, DuBois lost faith in the more Progressive-oriented aspects of the "uplift" project—the incremental reeducation of white America and the agency of a black "talented tenth." Among other factors, the race riots of 1919 and the failure of the cultural "renaissance" of the twenties to translate into the political and economic gains it was said to augur prompted him to question the capacity of the American melting pot ever to assimilate African Americans as it did the "ethnic" Americans. Additionally, the imperialist dimensions of World War I, the

execution of Sacco and Vanzetti in 1927, and the collapse of the economy into the Great Depression pushed DuBois politically to the radical
Left, new ground for the formerly centrist leader of the NAACP. Once a
fairly unapologetic bourgeois, DuBois's identification with the intelligentsia and cultural elite gave way to a working-class consciousness and
even, by the mid-1930s, an explicit internationalism and Communism.
His muted and somewhat vague 1903 criticism of the dominant values of
capitalist society became sharper and shriller. In 1931, in a passage
quoted in my introduction, DuBois took special aim in a *Crisis* editorial
at the new consumer orientation of the economy. "[A]dvertisement and
installment buying have made the nation blind and crazy," he wrote,
adding: "We think we must buy whatever is being offered. The orgy must
be stopped, and no group is strategically better placed than the Negro"
(*Emerging Thought* 393).

Four years later, DuBois published *Black Reconstruction*, at once a magisterial scholarly reappraisal of the Reconstruction era and a forceful critique of nineteenth-century American laissez-faire capitalism. Among
the dearest costs of the decimation of the Reconstruction program,
DuBois argues, was the sacrifice of the identification among workers of
all races with the nobility of their work and with others in their class.

> "[F]olks who were American and for whom America was, became
> ashamed of their destiny. Sons of ditch-diggers aspired to be spawn of
> bastard kings and thieving aristocrats rather than of rough-handed
> children of dirt and toil. The immense profit from this new exploita-
> tion and world-wide commerce enabled a guild of millionaires to
> engage the greatest engineers, the wisest men of science, as well as pay
> high wage to the more intelligent labor and at the same time to have
> left enough surplus to make more thorough the dictatorship of capi-
> tal over the state and over the popular vote, not only in Europe and
> America but in Asia and Africa. (634)

From his vantage in the aftermath of World War I and in the midst of
what he calls "World Depression," DuBois's prescription for "rebuilding"
synthesizes (or, less generously, conflates) revolutionary Communism
with the ideals of the earliest days of Reconstruction. He maintains that
this "rebuilding, whether it comes now or a century later, will and must
go back to the basic principles of Reconstruction in the United States

during 1867–1876—Light, Land and Leading for slaves black, brown, yellow, and white, under a dictatorship of the proletariat" (635). DuBois's political philosophy would continue to evolve, of course, and his analysis of American capitalism (and global capitalism) was as dynamic as one would expect over such a long and prolific career. However, as the passages I have excerpted here indicate, DuBois's work represents as responsive an engagement with emerging consumerism in the United States as one finds in the concurrent mainstream scholarship—indeed, an engagement that is all the more fascinating because it pits the evils of the dominant white culture's acquisitive individualism against the benefits to African Americans of integration into that very culture.

Up to this point, I have been examining interventions that largely antedated the rigidity of academic discipline and genre that began to set in after the turn of the twentieth century. Particularly in African American letters, distinctions among novelistic, journalistic, philosophical, and sociological writing were, if not immaterial, at least flexible and widely flouted, as the work of each of the foregoing authors demonstrates. However, along with the increasing specialization of academic disciplines and a modestly increasing appearance of African American practitioners in those disciplines came new sorts of approaches to the intersection of race and consumption.

The critical stance we find DuBois adopting in the 1930s found perhaps its starkest counterpoint in the work of Paul K. Edwards in *The Southern Urban Negro as Consumer* (1932). Edwards, a Fisk University economist, was the first to undertake a systematic sociological study of the role of African American consumers in the economy: how much they spent, where and what they bought, how they were addressed by the commercial media. Edwards's sanguine thesis was that the "purchasing power" of southern urban Negroes was being grossly underestimated, that they represented a vast, untapped market, and that a more sustained and savvy reconsideration of the empirical data on Negro consumers would lead not only to the greater satisfaction of the Negroes' needs but also to the financial gain of businesses willing to market to them. A firm adherent to the promise of the "democracy of goods," Edwards framed his work as a scientific approach to redressing inefficiencies in the market that the history of racial discrimination had produced. In this sense, he was committed less to a political ideology than to a faith—certainly characteristic of his time—in the technocratic solutions of specialized experts.

Far from decrying the role of advertising as productive of false needs, *The Southern Urban Negro* counsels manufacturers and distributors in how best to reach the Negro market.

> Of importance are the answers to such pertinent questions as the following: Can the Negro character be utilized advantageously in advertising copy toward securing the attention of the Negro? Does the use of racial elements that might be distasteful to the Negro serve to gain his ill will and build up sales resistance? On the other hand, do pleasing racial elements tend to gain his good will and build up his acceptance of the product concerned? (214)

Edwards's responses are based on what was surely the first marketing research involving an African American focus group. He documents the responses of sixty housewives and heads of families from Richmond and Nashville to print advertisements for such products as P&G laundry soap, Rinso soap powder, Squibb's pharmaceutical products, and Aunt Jemima pancake flour, controlling for "occupation classification" (i.e., economic class) (215).

In thus framing his research for the technicians of the emerging consumer culture, Edwards's study represents an early form of racially segmented marketing, a field that would flourish in the second half of the century. An excellent example of this development away from the moralistic, Progressive critique of commodity consumption and the Depression era's economistic critique toward an embrace of consumption as a means to self-actualization and racial equality is Norman Govoni and George Joyce's edited volume *The Black Consumer: Dimensions of Behavior and Strategy* (1971). "This book serves a two-fold purpose," reads the preface: "[I]t identifies those areas that are critical to successful stimulation of positive buying action in the black-consumer market, and it contributes to the marketing-planning effort by providing a framework within which subculture marketing might be better understood and evaluated by the marketing decision maker" (vii). Its contents include such chapters as "Racial Factors in Shopping Behavior," "Racial Brand Usage and Media Exposure Differentials," and "Ghetto Marketing: What Now?"

Thus, Edwards's 1932 study left a paradoxical legacy: it helped initiate a "subculture marketing" industry by rationalizing African Americans' consumption practices to make them legible for an audience with the institutional investment in "better serving" them by relieving them of their wages; yet it has also served a potentially more counterhegemonic function as the first sustained African American work at the intersection of race and consumption. Though Edwards's objectives are clearly at odds with those of later critics of advertising, his fieldwork and analyses of the rhetorical elements of particular advertisements anticipate, in interesting ways, the pioneering critical work on advertising by, for example, semiotician Roland Barthes and cultural studies scholar Judith Williamson. Moreover, Edwards's attention to the significance of national brands in the consumption practices of African Americans has been consistently revisited ever since.[9]

Two of the most provocative and witheringly critical texts in the sociological tradition appeared in the years following World War II: Horace Cayton and St. Clair Drake's *Black Metropolis* (1945) and E. Franklin Frazier's *Black Bourgeoisie* (1955, 1957). Both were rooted in, yet departed significantly from, the Chicago school of urban sociology, which had virtually invented the field in the 1910s and long dominated it thereafter. Both left indelible marks on urban sociology in general and on the study of race and consumption in particular.

A breathtaking analysis of ethnographic evidence and empirical data about 1930s Chicago, *Black Metropolis* was, as William Julius Wilson writes, "a fundamental revision in the Chicago framework," because it flew in the face of the ethnicity model for the study of African Americans that Chicago professors Robert Park and Ernest Burgess had established. "Their analysis clearly revealed the existence of a color line that effectively blocked black occupational, residential, and social mobility," writes Wilson, who maintains, "Thus, any assumption about urban blacks duplicating the immigrant experience has to confront the issue of race." Wilson goes on to quote historian Alice O'Connor, who claimed that "Drake and Cayton recognized that the racial configuration of Chicago was not the expression of an organic process of city growth," as the Park-Burgess approach would have it, "but the product of human behavior, institutional practices, and political decisions" (xlviii). If the previous year's publication of Gunnar Myrdal's *An American Dilemma* "marked the ascent of the ethnicity paradigm to a position of theoretical dominance," as Michael Omi and Howard Winant have observed, *Black Metropolis* cast severe doubts on that paradigm's adequacy to account for the persistence of urban African Americans' social and economic challenges. Myrdal had argued optimistically that the contradiction between the "American creed" of democracy, equality, and justice and the facts of racial segregation and prejudice would inevitably "give way to racial equality and the eventual integration of blacks into the mainstream of American life" (Omi and Winant 17). But the evidence in *Black Metropolis* belied this narrative of ineluctable assimilation, revealing instead the ways in which the "blackness" of African Americans of all classes, shades, ethnic backgrounds, and geographic origins invoked a very different dynamic of national (non)belonging than did the immigrants on whom the Chicago approach was modeled. The residential segregation that confined the vast majority of Chicago's African Americans to Bronzeville, the community in which Cayton and Drake conducted their research, exemplified this difference from the more porous ethnic communities, for even when the class mobility on which mainstream assimilation relied was achieved, the result was usually just a change of address within Bronzeville.

In Cayton and Drake's study, the issue of African Americans' relationship to consumer culture figures prominently and is perhaps best illustrated in the authors' discussion of the tensions between members of the genteel upper class and their nearest rivals, the "upper shadies." Distinct practices of conspicuous consumption served to differentiate the two classes yet also reflected a prevalent desire among "upper shadies" to displace members of the genteel upper class from their position of social privilege. Whereas the upper class took "respectability" for granted and was "concerned with 'refinement,' 'culture,' and graceful living as a class-ideal," the "upper shadies" had made their money—often amounting to vast sums—through administering the underground lottery, also known as "policy" (Cayton and Drake 531). Many of these "policy kings" were wealthier than members of the genteel upper class, but because their wealth was recent and disreputable in origin, they were excluded from upper-class society. In their discussion of the mechanisms by which the upper class differentiated itself from and excluded the "upper

shadies," Cayton and Drake pursue an argument similar to Thorstein
Veblen's in *Theory of the Leisure Class:* that conspicuous consumption was
used as "invidious display."

> Interview-observation studies of these persons' families revealed
> extreme emphasis on maintaining a "good home," with fine furni-
> ture, linen, glassware, china, and silver much in evidence. Before the
> Second World War the majority kept at least a part-time maid, and a
> few had more than one servant, even during the Depression. The men
> dressed expensively, but conservatively; the women smartly, but in
> good taste. All of the families carried accounts with exclusive down-
> town shops. The majority owned automobiles, and one family had
> three cars and a chauffeur. (Cayton and Drake 530–31)

By contrast, the "upper shadies," whom Cayton and Drake also call the
"Gentlemen Racketeers," were more ostentatious, not to say vulgar,
about their displays of wealth. They were not "home-centered" "good livers," as the upper-class people identified themselves, but, rather, "high
livers": their identities sprang from their social lives, which were comprised of frequent, lavish entertainment, horseback riding, cabaret parties, and high-stakes poker games.

> The women's lives, like the men's, are centered on conspicuous con-
> sumption—display of the most lavish kind. This set is organized
> around a cult of clothes. Nothing but the right labels at the right
> prices will do. Both the men and the women know how to buy and
> wear clothes—and with taste rather than garishness. Clothes are both
> an end in themselves and an adjunct to the social ritual of this *café au
> lait* society. (Cayton and Drake 547)

Thus, both the upper class and the "Gentlemen Racketeers" are said to
engage in highly stylized rituals of conspicuous consumption, but with
significant differences. The former relied far more than the latter on
symbols of refinement rather than mere wealth and put into heavy circulation "performances of vicarious leisure"—the maids, servants, and
chauffeurs (and even the conspicuously idle housewives) whose primary
purpose, Veblen argued, was to exhibit their employer's "abstention
from productive labor" (36–37). The "Gentlemen Racketeers" pursued
a dual strategy of emulating the consumption practices of the upper class

insofar as was possible while also seeking to undermine the prestige of the upper class by becoming, themselves, the class to which others aspired.

Indeed, Cayton and Drake note that the Depression jeopardized the preeminence of the upper class because most of its members relied in their professional lives as doctors and lawyers on the now diminishing patronage of clients who had been impoverished by the economic crisis. Suddenly, not only was their community standing rivaled by people on fixed incomes, such as civil servants, but the "fast set" of "'Gentlemen Racketeers' and their coterie emerged as the most widely publicized group in Bronzeville" (Cayton and Drake 544–46). Nevertheless, the latter still revealed a great deal of anxiety, Cayton and Drake maintain, about what the "true" upper class thought of them. They recognized that ostentatious display and conspicuous consumption could only go so far toward generating the respectability attached to the upper class, all of whom were considered "Race Men." To acquire this standing, they had begun conspicuously displaying wealth in the service of civic- and race-oriented activities.

> [T]he policy kings all have legitimate businesses as well as their shady enterprises. They give regularly and generously to all fund-raising drives for Bronzeville charities. With the outbreak of the war they began to play a prominent part in bond rallies and in the sponsoring of a service men's center. Their motives appear to be highly mixed, but undoubtedly one motive is their hope that such activities will wipe away the stain of policy. (Cayton and Drake 548)

Black Metropolis thus addresses the aspirations and struggles of the several classes comprising Bronzeville (other chapters examine the middle class and the poor), with unprecedented sensitivity and a tone of studied neutrality that departs from the explicitly moralistic and the ideological critiques that preceded them. Cayton and Drake reject and offer an alternative to conventional explanations for the practices of consumption they discuss. It is not that African Americans simply want a more comfortable material existence (though of course they do), for this explanation privileges use value far and above symbolic value, which they saw as vitally important. Nor is it that African Americans simply mimic white Americans' patterns of consumption and thus reveal their desire to be white, a notion that Cayton and Drake show to be reductive because it collapses a whole complex of class-oriented desires into a monolithic white-supremacist imaginary.

E. Franklin Frazier's *Black Bourgeoisie,* though similarly versed in the conceptual lexicon of Veblen and indebted to the Chicago school in which Frazier trained, is far less neutral in tone than *Black Metropolis* and is in fact avowedly polemical. Whereas *Black Metropolis* seems aimed chiefly at reformers and policy makers who have thus far neither recognized nor confronted specifically antiblack forms of institutional discrimination, *Black Bourgeoisie* performs such an exuberant and derisive critique of the "new middle class" that it seems calculated to delight both the abstemious African American reader with whom Frazier implicitly aligns himself and the white cynic, for whom Frazier's dramatic rendering of the foibles and "false pretenses" of upwardly mobile African Americans provide great pleasure and affirmation. It must have gratified many a white reader in the 1950s, for example, to hear a Negro sociologist declare: "The black bourgeoisie, especially the section which forms Negro 'society,' scarcely ever read books for recreation. Consequently, their conversation is trivial and exhibits a childish view of the world" (Frazier 172). Cayton and Drake's measured perspective on such "strivers" becomes, in *Black Bourgoisie,* a searing indictment of their expensive "world of make-believe."

Cayton and Drake had conceded that prestige-driven conspicuous consumption among African Americans was "in actuality . . . a substitute for complete integration into the general American society," suggesting that African Americans' authentic desire for social equality had been rerouted into a more readily fulfilled but artificial desire for material possessions. Cayton and Drake quickly added, however, that such consumption "has compensations of its own which allow individuals to gain stability and inner satisfaction, despite conditions in the Black Ghetto and their rejection by white America" (557). This dialectical approach to the multiple meanings of consumption is absent from Frazier's study, which casts conspicuous consumption as a symptom of the unfortunate desperation with which affluent African Americans pursue a white middle-class ideal. Cayton and Drake addressed this notion of affluent Negroes "pining to be white, or to associate with whites socially," by citing survey responses indicating instead that "[t]hey are almost com-

pletely absorbed in the social ritual and in the struggle to 'get ahead,'"
both goals "inextricably bound up with 'advancing the Race' and with
civic leadership" (557). Ten years later (*Black Bourgeoisie* was first published in Paris in 1955), Frazier either remained unconvinced of this
argument or had observed a decline in the civic- and race-minded
engagement observed by Cayton and Drake. He casts conspicuous consumption strictly as false consciousness, devoid of any of the redemptive
functions they identified.

> Having become less isolated and thus more exposed to the contempt
> of the white world, but at the same time cherishing the values of the
> white world, the new black bourgeoisie, with more money at their dis-
> posal, have sought compensations in the things that money can buy.
> Moreover, their larger incomes have enabled them to propagate false
> notions about their place in American life and to create a world of
> make-believe. (126)

Frazier's analysis hews closely in this respect to Marx's critique of the
fetishization of the commodity, with the added complication now that
the subject is not the universal worker but the African American possessed of DuBois's "double consciousness," a member of the economic
middle class for whom race functions to endlessly defer the social and
political entitlements of that class's national belonging. Some find ways
of shielding themselves from "the harsh social and economic realities of
American life," Frazier writes, but many more "seek an escape in delu-
sions."

> They seek an escape in delusions involving wealth. This is facilitated by
> the fact that they have had little experience with the real meaning of
> wealth and that they lack a tradition of saving and accumulation.
> Wealth to them means spending money without any reference to its
> source. Hence, their behavior generally reflects the worst qualities of
> the gentleman and the peasant from whom their only vital traditions
> spring. Therefore, their small accumulations of capital and the income
> which they receive from professional services within the Negro com-
> munity make them appear wealthy in comparison with the low eco-
> nomic status of the majority of Negroes . . . Moreover, the attraction of
> the delusion of wealth is enhanced by the belief that wealth will gain

them acceptance in American life. In seeking an escape in the delu-
sion of wealth, middle-class Negroes make a fetish of material things
or physical possessions. They are constantly buying things—houses,
automobiles, furniture and all sorts of gadgets, not to mention
clothes. Many of the furnishings and gadgets which they acquire are
never used; nevertheless they continue to accumulate things. (189)

All of this waste and self-delusion may be chalked up, in Frazier's view,
to the middle-class Negro's self-hatred, arising "not only from the fact
that he does not want to be a Negro but also because of his sorry role in
American society" (188). The principal response to American racism
among middle-class Negroes, claims Frazier, is to invidiously distinguish themselves from their less-affluent brothers and sisters, an illu-
sory effort to repudiate the "nigger" that they otherwise perpetually
threaten to signify. In *Black Bourgeoisie,* then, Frazier puts a finer point
on Cayton and Drake's critique of consumption as invidious display:
not only could commodity consumption and displays of leisure serve as
class delineators, but their only function was to make such invidious
distinctions.

For all its vitriol, *Black Bourgeoisie* signaled an important break with the
scholarly tradition, which still retained certain Progressive assumptions
that had gone more or less unchallenged. For example, Frazier took on
the sacred cows of the "uplift" project, from the importance placed on
"respectability" to faith placed in Negro business as an agent of race
progress. He challenged both as shibboleths propagated by the elite to
assuage an "inferiority complex." He attacked "respectability" as a vesti-
gial attachment to the one-upmanship of the "house Negro" over the
"field Negro," initiated under slavery and maintained thereafter by sanc-
timonious status seekers. He excoriated the champions of Negro business for overstating its importance to the operation of the U.S. economy
as a whole: "The myth that Negroes were spending 15 billion dollars in
1951 was widely circulated by whites as well as Negroes since it served to
exaggerate the economic well-being of Negroes in the United States and
to whet the appetites of the black bourgeoisie, both Negro businessmen
and Negroes employed by American corporations, in their efforts to
reap benefits from the increased earnings of Negroes" (145). Nevertheless, to read Frazier's study as simply a critique of the "black bourgeoisie"

themselves is to miss his identification of the sources of their desire to retreat into myth and "make-believe." Arriving as it did in the mid-1950s, amid a nascent civil rights movement and on the heels of *Brown v. Board of Education, Black Bourgeoisie* insisted that the legacies of slavery and Reconstruction were alive and well despite certain undeniable advances. This was an inconvenient reminder for those whose mounting optimism about the prospects of Negro assimilation blinded them to the persistence of far-reaching structural inequalities. As Frazier himself wrote in the preface to the 1962 edition, his book demonstrated not only "that Negroes were . . . at the bottom of the economic ladder" but "that all the pretended economic gains which Negroes were supposed to have made had not changed fundamentally their relative economic position in American life" (11). Thus, despite the special scorn that Frazier reserves for the "strivers," his broader objective was one that Cayton and Drake had shared in *Black Metropolis*—to offer a historical and materialist account of struggles that were otherwise likely to be pathologized through specious arguments about innate racial qualities or ignored in favor of a more palatable narrative of national progress.

The dialectic mapped in my discussion of *Black Metropolis* and *Black Bourgeoisie* has in many respects continued to inform more recent work on the intersection of race and consumer culture by African Americans—and, it must be added, by black Britons. I cannot do justice to so extensive a body of scholarship here. Yet some representative and influential texts highlight the persistence—indeed, the florescence—of a black countertradition that runs concurrent with, but is not much reflected in, the "native" Anglo-American tradition I have already sketched.

The side of the dialectic emphasized by Frazier—commodity consumption as racialized false consciousness—is pursued in a great deal of work that focuses on social structure, such as Manning Marable's *How Capitalism Underdeveloped Black America* (1983) and Robert E. Weems's *Desegregating the Dollar* (1998), as well as in more culturalist projects, such as Susan Willis's *A Primer for Daily Life* (1991). Marable and Willis each take explicitly Marxist approaches: Marable works in a socialist vein that has an antecedent in the 1920s work of A. Philip Randolph and Chandler Owen in *The Messenger,* while Willis is a neo-Marxist whose approach conjoins historical materialism and postmodern theory in ways that will be clarified shortly. By contrast, Weems's orientation is far more liberal-humanist, even as he also argues that consumerism has always worked unevenly to disenfranchise African Americans despite gains in other areas. "[O]ne would be hard-pressed to see where increased African American spending has improved the infrastructure and ambiance of [urban black] neighborhoods," Weems laments, but his deeply critical account of consumerism's history does not lead him to call for fundamental change so much as technocratic reform: "[T]he major challenge facing contemporary African American consumers is to develop spending strategies that will stimulate more constructive economic activity within the black community" (6). As Frazier's "world of make-believe" grew increasingly pervasive under what Frederic Jameson, Jean Baudrillard, and other postmodernist theorists call "late capitalism," many black writers have understood commodity consumption as more than ever a source of racialized alienation and the marketplace as a site of racialized exploitation. In fact, this thread in the scholarship sees the overt oppression of racism and segregation having given way in contemporary America, not to a race-blind or equitable society as some would have it, but to a hegemonic white supremacy whose effectiveness derives precisely from its insidious propagation in the arena of mass culture (hooks 24).

However, many have also urged a closer examination of the other side of the dialectic—the "compensations" of commodity consumption, as Cayton and Drake put it, "which allow individuals to gain stability and inner satisfaction" despite the strenuous trials of difficult material conditions and social marginalization. In part, this shift was the result of the pressure that the social justice movements of the 1960s and 1970s put on the academic construction of historical subjectivity among marginalized people. In addition, the study of consumption in particular was transformed by the constructivist turn of the aforementioned Birmingham Centre for Contemporary Cultural Studies. Both of these developments encouraged cultural historians to attribute less determinative agency to the intentions of the producers and distributors of commodities and to recognize instead the multiplicity of ways in which consumers experienced consumption—how they used and made meaning of commodities. These scholars reconceived mass culture as the contested terrain on which hegemonic power was not simply supported but subverted as well. In their work, the palliative, transgressive, and even liberatory possibilities of consumption are, if not celebrated uncritically, upheld as an index of ordinary people's self-determination and, further, as the one arena available to many marginalized people for constructing affirmative identities and communities.

One of the chief reasons race has been integral to much of the work affiliated with or inspired by the Birmingham school is because of its principle of studying mass culture in relation to social structures of domination, including but not reducible to "the class struggle." An additional and related reason for race's importance in this tradition is its commitment to interrogating imperialism abroad and its ramifications at home.[10] Among the finest and most representative examples of such work is that of Stuart Hall, Paul Gilroy, and Kobena Mercer. Armed with post-structuralism's critique of metaphysics, black Britons brought a new theoretical sophistication to bear on their analyses of the relationship between nation, identity, race, and mass culture. The field of "cultural studies" that has achieved such currency (and notoriety) in U.S. humanities departments since the early 1990s has been understandably criticized for taking an approach to mass culture that is apolitical or even conservative in the tacit peace it makes with the postmodern reign of the commodity. But as the work of Gilroy, Mercer, and Hall demonstrates, Birmingham's practitioners of cultural studies pursued a highly politicized engagement with mass culture as the site for generating the provisional identities and alliances from which counterhegemonic politics could emerge. Hall was quite candid about this in his closing to "Notes on Deconstructing the Popular."

Sometimes we can be constituted as a force against the power-bloc: that is the historical opening in which it is possible to construct a culture which is genuinely popular. But, in our society, if we are not constituted like that, we will be constituted into its opposite: an effective populist force, saying "Yes" to power. Popular culture is one of the sites where this struggle for and against a culture of the powerful is engaged: it is also the stake to be won or lost *in* that struggle. It is the arena of consent and resistance. It is partly where hegemony arises, and where it is secured. It is not a sphere where socialism, a socialist culture—already fully formed—might be simply "expressed." But it is one of those places where socialism might be constituted. That is why "popular culture" matters. Otherwise, to tell you the truth, I don't give a damn about it. (239)

Similarly, although Mercer and Gilroy privilege "style," "pleasure," "play," and "performance" as politically transgressive (even emancipatory), they do so finally in the service of an elucidation of the relationship between commodity consumption and the existing structures of political domination. This is clear, for example, in Mercer's deconstruction of the nature/artifice binary in black hair fashions and in Gilroy's analysis of the "dialogic rituals of active and celebratory consumption" enacted by black dance-hall DJs and MCs.[11]

Their work has both inspired and provoked criticism from African American practitioners of cultural studies, including Susan Willis, bell hooks, Sylvia Wynter, Michele Wallace, and Ann duCille, each of whom has extensively mined the intersections of race, gender, and consumer culture, especially but not exclusively in the contemporary moment of postmodernism and "late capitalism." Willis's implicit dialogue with Mercer in her essay "I Want the Black One" illustrates a productive tension between what we might call the two Birminghams that impinge on the work of these writers—one in the South of the civil rights era, the other in the United Kingdom. A commitment to historical materialism, on one hand, is expressed in these writers' attention to the history of racialized violence and oppression punctuated by such events as the 1963 bombing in Birmingham, Alabama, of the Sixteenth Street Baptist Church, which killed four African American girls. On the other hand, they take seriously the commitment in Birmingham, UK, to recognizing resistance to repressive discourses and social structures in the uses to which people put mass culture.

Although Willis treats the "utopian or transcendent" and the "ideological" functions of mass culture as inseparable (as Frederic Jameson has argued), she objects to an exaggeration of the former at the expense of the latter in such work as Mercer's.

Mercer's point is finally that black culture has at its disposal and can manipulate all the signs and artifacts produced by the larger culture. The fact that these are already inscribed with meanings inherited through centuries of domination does not inhibit the production of viable cultural statements, even though it influences the way such statements are read. (118)

Any analysis that "sees commodities giving new forms of access to black people's self-expression," Willis contends, has also to reckon with the role commodities play in performing apparent resolutions to social contradictions that they actually reproduce (117). Willis is primarily concerned with contemporary mass culture, but her analyses are historically grounded. For example, having examined characters in Toni Morrison's novels, Barbie dolls, Michael Jordan, and Michael Jackson, she closes "I Want the Black One" by tracing the sources of Mickey Mouse in nineteenth-century minstrel performances and early twentieth-century pickaninny cartoons (130–31). She first claims, "[T]he scandalous point I want to make is that Mickey Mouse is black; indeed, a minstrel performer," but she adds that he is also, "as a commodity, laundered of all possible social and historical associations." Ultimately, Willis is interested not with making a clever case for Mickey's blackness but with recognizing what Jameson and Baudrillard characterize as the collapse of all historical referents under the sign of the commodity.

> As a cultural commodity, Mickey Mouse is finally not black. He is precisely the cancellation of the black cultural subtext, and quite possibly the "retroactive" eradication of the original minstrel performer who jumped Jim Crow to the tune of "Turkey in the Straw." This first-time event, now apprehended from the cultural moment defined by Mickey Mouse, is, then, redefined as a simulacrum of the Disney tradition. (132)

The question that I think Willis's brilliant analysis leaves unanswered is whether any qualitative differences exist between consumer culture's articulation with race in our current "postmodern" era and in earlier historical periods. Based on her discussion of the characters of Pecola and Claudia in *The Bluest Eye*, it would seem not. Whether it is Shirley Temple iconography in 1935 or a Michael Jackson video in 1995, in Willis's final analysis, "commodity consumption mutilates black personhood" (114).

This is not a claim I necessarily wish to refute, but because Willis

makes a Jameson-Baudrillard regime of simulations and commodity seri-
ality stand for consumer capitalism tout court, her work may beg the
question of periodization and risk reifying the phenomenon she inter-
rogates. These are precisely the theoretical questions that have engaged
such writers as Wallace, Ducille, Wynter, and hooks. For instance, one
index of Wynter's distance from Willis and her proximity to the Birmingham school is her argument that in its earliest forms, African American self-commodification, such as blackface minstrelsy, initiated a
process of "subversion of the normative bourgeois American reality"
(155).

The partial inventory I have attempted here of African American and
black British intellectual work on the historical articulation of consumption and race omits a great deal of significant scholarship. But it indicates the breadth of the extant body of work and the responsiveness of
these black commentators to institutional and social changes, and it illu-
minates the ways in which they adopted, adapted, and intervened in the
"native" American and European critical conversations. One is compelled to wonder, for example, whether W. E. B. DuBois's 1903 essays
would have introduced a note of chastened qualification in Simon Patten's ebullient 1907 pronouncement that the "economy of scarcity" had
been supplanted by an "economy of abundance"; how E. Franklin Frazier's 1955 account of the middle-class Negro's "world of make-believe"
would have sounded to Raymond Williams as he composed his seminal
1960 essay on advertising as "the magic system"; or if Cayton and Drake's
discussion in 1945 of "The Stroll," black Chicago's shopping district,
would have prompted Adorno and Horkheimer to reflect on their cate-
gorical denunciation of the commodity form in *Dialectic of Enlightenment*
the previous year.

In or about the winter of 1979, the disciplinary segregation between
African American studies and cultural history had arguably begun to
subside: readers of the new journal *Social Text* found Jameson's
"Reification and Utopia in Mass Culture" sharing space with Wynter's
"Sambos and Minstrels," and visitors to the Birmingham Centre found
Stuart Hall ensconced in the director's chair, a position he held for ten
years. But as the foregoing discussion indicates, a great many opportunities for transdisciplinary work had been missed. I now turn to explore
some of the recent provocative efforts to do just that.

Recent Interventions

At a conference in 1991 in which several of the aforementioned scholars participated, Hazel Carby, a black feminist cultural theorist who trained at the Birmingham Centre, warned of the danger that multiculturalism's "politics of difference" posed to a clearheaded appraisal of the specific role of race in the United States.

> We need to recognize that we live in a society in which systems of domination and subordination are structured through processes of racialization that continually interact with all other forces of socialization. Theoretically, we should be arguing that everyone in this social order has been constructed in our political imagination as a racialized subject. In this sense, it is important to think about the invention of the category of whiteness as well as that of blackness and, consequently, to make visible what is rendered invisible when viewed as the normative state of existence: the (white) point in space from which we tend to identify difference. ("Multicultural Wars" 93)

One of the salutary effects of African American studies and critical race studies on the humanities since the early 1990s has been to flush whiteness out of hiding—that is, to interrogate the privilege that whiteness has enjoyed to not signify as any race at all, to stand in tacitly for universal personhood, to remain invisible as whiteness in the critical discourse. It is not that "there is no discussion of white people," as Richard Dyer puts it.

> In fact most of the time white people speak about nothing but white people, its just that we couch it in terms of "people" in general. Whites are everywhere in representation. Yet precisely because of this and their placing as norm they seem not to be represented to themselves *as* whites but as people who are variously gendered, classed, sexualised and abled. At the level of racial representation, in other words, whites are not of a certain race, they're just the human race. (*White* 3)

The critical tradition has ably treated the representation of African Americans in mass-marketed artifacts, but a fuller examination of the articulation of race and consumer culture depends on a broader construal of both of these terms.[12] Just as studies of print advertising do not exhaust the possibilities of examining consumer culture's emergence, neither do commercial images of African Americans exhaust our approaches to race.

Noteworthy advances have reached out from several fields. Eric Lott's *Love and Theft* (1995) links the development of a specifically national popular culture, blackface minstrelsy, with the consolidation of white, working-class masculinity and the "burgeoning leisure industry" of the antebellum United States (41). In Richard Ohmann's *Selling Culture* (1996), race figures prominently in the argument that mass-circulation magazines, such as *Munsey's* and the *Ladies' Home Journal,* helped create and naturalize a new, consumption-oriented professional-managerial class at the turn of the twentieth century. Richard Dyer's *White* (1997), which traces the chief source of white privilege to its discursive invisibility, examines representations of whiteness in Western visual culture from painting to photography to commercial film. In *Making Whiteness* (1998), Grace Hale argues that consumer culture between 1880 and 1940 served to reproduce racial identities through the national circulation of commercial images of blackness but also conditioned the possibility for contesting these identities through the creation of new kinds of public spaces. Paul Gilmore contends in *The Genuine Article* (2001) that the representations of "blacks and Indians" in mass cultural forms in the antebellum United States played a multifaceted role in concurrent white literary expressions of middle-class manhood.

Perhaps most consequentially for the chapters that follow, however, such studies as Ann McClintock's *Imperial Leather* (1995) and Robert Rydell's *All the World's a Fair* (1984) demonstrate the utility of racialized commodities and spectacles in justifying imperial expansion abroad and the extension of consumerism at home. McClintock's compelling account of the marketing of Pear's Soap, for example, reveals not only that images of England's imperial subjects and conquests were effective selling agents but also, more important, that the rhetoric of race in these advertisements sanitized the imperialist project by equating the purchase of such commodities with national belonging in white civilization.

From the outset, Victorian advertising took explicit shape around the reinvention of racial difference. Commodity kitsch made possible, as never before, the mass marketing of empire as an organized system of images and attitudes. Soap flourished not only because it created and filled a spectacular gap in the domestic market but also because, as a cheap and portable commodity, it could persuasively mediate between the Victorian poetics of racial hygiene and imperial progress. (209)

Indeed, McClintock goes on to argue that mass culture effectively took over for racial science in the late nineteenth-century popularization of white-supremacist thinking.

Scientific racism saturated anthropological, scientific, and medical journals, travel writing, and novels [after the 1850s, but] these cultural forms were still relatively class-bound and inaccessible to most Victorians, who had neither the means nor the education to read such material. Imperial kitsch as consumer spectacle, by contrast, could package, market and distribute evolutionary racism on a hitherto unimagined scale. No preexisting form of organized racism had ever before been able to read so large and so differentiated a mass of the populace. (209)

McClintock is concerned with the palatable "domestication" of imperialism through the consumption of racialized commodities in England, so her analysis cannot simply be generalized to the context of the United States, where imperialism was also afoot but racial thinking was still shaped chiefly by intranational social relations. Nevertheless, many parallels are discernible in the U.S. archive.

In the British context, as in the American one, massive public exhibitions and fairs were convened to supplement the work of advertising in making consumer capitalism—and its imperative to expand labor and distribution markets overseas—synonymous with national progress. British historian Thomas Richards echoes the work of many U.S. historians when he writes of the Crystal Palace Exhibition (1851), "What [it] heralded so intimately was the complete transformation of collective and private life into a space for the spectacular exhibition of commodities" (72). Like his U.S. colleagues, Richards claims such exhibitions were instrumental in fashioning "a new kind of being, the consumer, and a new kind of ideology, consumerism" (5). An additional—and, as McClintock demonstrates, related—objective of these fairs was to ritually consolidate an identification between the material abundance on display and a national community with the whiteness of advanced (and ever-advancing) civilization as its somatic sign. A number of striking illustrations of this identification arise in the research of Robert Rydell into world's fairs, perhaps none more striking than his discussion of the 1893 World's Columbian Exposition, about which he writes:

> The Chicago world's fair, generally recognized for its contributions to urban planning, beaux-arts architecture, and institutions of the arts and sciences, just as importantly introduced millions of fairgoers to evolutionary ideas about race—ideas that were presented in a utopian context and often conveyed in exhibits that were ostensibly amusing. On the Midway at the World's Columbian Exposition, evolution, ethnology, and popular amusements interlocked as active agents and bulwarks of hegemonic assertion of ruling-class authority. (*All the World's a Fair* 40–41)

Because of this fair's popularity (it had over twenty-seven million visitors) and its effort to normalize both a culture of consumption and a culture of segregation, it is the focus of my analysis in chapter 2.

Public Spheres, Critical and Contaminated

Further reformulating the premises of consumer culture scholarship, a series of vital critical conversations followed the 1989 translation into English of Jurgen Habermas's *The Structural Transformation of the Public Sphere* (originally published in Germany in 1962). The narrative of decline structuring Habermas's analysis has been criticized as falsely universalist and has been revised by those more concerned than Habermas with the particularity of historical subject positions determined by race, class, gender, sexuality, and nationality.[13] Habermas's central concept of a vital, democratic, and institutionally supported public life based on ordinary citizens' exercise of reason, though disparaged by his detractors as a utopian ideal rather than a historical reality, has served nonetheless to invigorate exchanges across the disciplines of social theory, history, and literary studies. When, if ever, did a "bourgeois public sphere" exist? Does it deserve the idealized treatment it receives in Habermas's account? How persuasive is the evidence of a shift from a

culture-debating to a culture-consuming public, and what have its consequences been? Does the concept of a public sphere reinscribe the
invidious distinction between public and private that feminist scholars
have alternately rejected and revalued? For that matter, since the conventions and boundaries of the official public sphere are never static,
can one speak intelligibly of a unified public sphere (or of multiple,
competing public spheres) in the context of the late nineteenth-century
and early twentieth-century United States, marked as it was by tremendous demographic shifts, by women's movements and labor struggles,
and by revolutions in the communication and media technology that
produced the bourgeois public sphere?

The "structural transformation" to which Habermas's title refers was
not an American phenomenon; he draws his evidence from the material
conditions of eighteenth- and nineteenth-century France, England, and
Germany. But the United States becomes more prominent as his analysis
approaches the twentieth century, and parallels to the development of
U.S. capitalism are easily drawn. The rise of corporations and trusts in
the United States was facilitated by a deregulated banking system, and
economic changes were accelerated by the compliance—indeed, the
encouragement—of the state. The government of the Progressive Era
publicly took aim at corporate excesses through antitrust laws, protective
labor legislation, and banking regulations, but it was often lax in the
enforcement of these laws and lenient toward managerial efforts to quell
labor movements. Its usual methods for helping business—whether
through land subsidies, tariff protections, or funds for world's fairs—
proliferated during the 1890s. On the one hand, then, corporations
gained the authority to influence discourse in the public sphere and to
shape public spaces. On the other hand, the state began to administer a
wider range of services than had previously fallen to the public. The consolidation of control over the channels of public discourse in private
hands and the intervention of the state helped transform the function of
publicity itself from "critical" to "acclamatory."

But the chief cause of the degeneration of "critical publicity," according to Habermas, was the massification of culture, its democratization
and standardization. The very principle of inclusivity that served as the
bourgeois public sphere's utopian ideal worked over time and with the
commercialization of culture, he contends, to extend public citizenship

to those unfit to make public use of their reason. On this count, Habermas sounds most like his mentors at Frankfurt.

> To the degree that culture became a commodity not only in form but also in content, it was emptied of elements whose appreciation required a certain amount of training—whereby the "accomplished" appropriation once again heightened the appreciative ability itself. It was not merely standardization itself that established an inverse relationship between the commercialization of cultural goods and their complexity, but that special preparation of products that made them consumption-ready, which is to say, guaranteed an enjoyment without being tied to stringent presuppositions. Of course, such enjoyment is also entirely inconsequential. Serious involvement with culture produces facility, while the consumption of mass culture leaves no lasting trace; it affords a kind of experience which is not cumulative but regressive. (166)

The trouble with consumer culture, in other words, was that it effectively expanded the public sphere at the expense of the public's critical function. Habermas contends that it lowered the entrance requirements not just economically, "for consumers from overwhelmingly lower social strata," but also psychologically, as commodities were "tailored to the convenience and ease of a reception of fewer requisites and weaker consequences" (167). Whereas the appropriation of commodities had always been a necessary precondition for public citizenship, Habermas maintains that their rigorous demands meant that "the 'people' were brought up to the level of culture; culture was not lowered to that of the masses" (166). The critical rationality that had its roots in specific bourgeois institutions and reading practices was diminished, in this account, by the pabulum churned out for profit by book clubs, vaudeville houses, mass-marketed periodicals, and the studios of film, radio, and popular music. In the context of the developing culture industry, then, the bourgeois public sphere could not make good on its principle of inclusivity without undermining its original purpose. "Along with its social exclusiveness," argues Habermas, "it also lost the coherence afforded by the institutions of sociability and relatively high level of education" (132). It became a "pseudopublic sphere" of consumption.

Two currents in the critical conversation about the public sphere hold special promise for a reconsideration of the relationship between race and consumer culture. One involves the question of whether the exclusions on which the bourgeois public sphere was predicated were incidental to or constitutive of its operation. The other troubles a tidy opposition that takes shape not only in Habermas's argument but also in the scholarship on consumer culture more broadly, between consumption and the exercise of critical reason. These are both questions I take up in a specific institutional context in chapter 2, but it is worth pausing here to note their implications.

"Rational-critical debate had a tendency to be replaced by consumption," Habermas claims of the public sphere's transformation. As a result, he argues, "the web of public communication unraveled into acts of individuated reception, however uniform in mode" (161). In its effort to trace the pernicious impact of commercial mass culture on bourgeois publicity and its democratic promise, *The Structural Transformation* misses the extent to which people's public use of their reason survived—or, indeed, was enabled by—the very commodities, institutions, and modes of sociability it denounces. To make this point is not just to accuse Habermas of a typically Frankfurt pessimism; it is fundamentally to reconsider the notion of public citizenship in relation to historical moments in which—and for subjects for whom—the denigrated culture of consumption is not an obstacle to critical publicity but its condition of possibility. Consumption and self-commodification have historically been among the few strategies available to minoritized subjects for miming the privileges of public citizenship, privileges that their "unrecuperated particularity" otherwise foreclosed.[14] There is something tautological about laminating rational-critical discourse so seamlessly onto the institutions and social practices of a particular historical moment (bourgeois Europe) that the transformation of these institutions and practices requires the demise of the democratic energies and intellects they are said to have fostered. The relationship between critical public citizenship and consumption must be more complicated.

Scholars in history and literary and cultural studies have begun this reassessment. Feminist revisions by Nancy Fraser, Joan Landes, and Kathy Peiss, for example, take seriously the attributes of public citizenship that Habermas identifies with bourgeois publicity, but they challenge the premises that produced for analysis only a unified, "official" public sphere; that underplayed its gendered logic of exclusion; and that overlooked consumer culture's role in subverting this gendered logic. By interrogating bourgeois publicity's contradictory investment in people's bodies, such scholars as Michael Warner, Lauren Berlant, and Robyn Wiegman forge a more flexible framework for reading the conditions of public citizenship in a mediatized, commercial public sphere. In *Public Sphere and Experience,* Oskar Negt and Alexander Kluge submit the Habermasian model to a class critique, an alternative to which would account for the reciprocal operations of the official public sphere, the proletarian public sphere, and the public sphere in the realm of production, including commercial publicity and the activity of consumers.[15] Each of these efforts to adapt and revise Habermas's analysis are vitally important because they oppose universalism with an interrogation of historically constituted difference, yet they retain *The Structural Transformation*'s commitment to a critical analysis of the qualitative cultural changes wrought by modern capitalism.

Habermas's critics contend further that the bourgeois public sphere was not merely imperfect in the execution of its democratic tendency toward inclusivity but was in fact founded on a contradiction. The utopian promise of bourgeois publicity was a principle of self-abstraction: particular people could stand in for people in general, mere citizens. But the privileges and protections of abstract citizenship were acquired in exchange for bracketing the socially legible particulars of the person whose body would enjoy those privileges and protections.[16] Minoritized subjects (including women, the propertyless, and bondsmen) were prevented from experiencing themselves as universal, while privileged subjects performed the ideological gesture of mistaking their own particular attributes for universals. "[T]he ability to abstract oneself in public has always been an unequally available resource," writes Michael Warner.

> Individuals have to have specific rhetorics of disincorporation; they are not simply rendered bodiless by exercising reason. And it is only possible to operate a discourse based on self-abstracting disinterestedness in a culture where such unmarked self-abstraction is a differential resource. The subject who could master this rhetoric in the bourgeois public sphere was implicitly, even explicitly, white, male,

literate, and propertied. These traits go unmarked, even grammatically, while other features of bodies could only be acknowledged in discourse as the humiliating positivity of the particular. (382)

For this reason, the rhetorical strategy of personal abstraction has been, as Warner writes, "both the utopian moment of the public sphere and a major source of domination" (382). Thus, *The Structural Transformation*'s question about the public sphere's inclusions and exclusions has been recast as a set of questions about what versions of inclusion were produced at different historical moments. What were the terms in which inclusion was offered? How did the stakes of exclusion from the public sphere vary depending on one's subject position?

Accounts of the role of race in the transformation of the public sphere have considered whether Habermasian categories of value and analysis can be brought to bear on African American history, but they also suggest in turn how discourse on the public sphere and, more broadly, scholarship on consumer culture may be altered by taking race seriously. After all, a great number of African Americans and other nonwhites were systematically denied access to the material conditions on which the public use of critical reason has been said to depend, such as literacy, cultural commodities, and an intimate sphere of bourgeois domesticity. Houston Baker puts the issue as follows:

> Habermas's bourgeois public sphere, *in situ,* is a beautiful idea. It is grounded in a historiography that claims universal men were once golden citizens, rationally exchanging arguments in a realm between the family and the market—regardless of race, creed, color, annual income, or national origin. But insofar as the emergence and energy of Habermas's public sphere were generated by property ownership and literacy, how can black Americans, who like many others have traditionally been excluded from these domains of modernity, endorse Habermas's beautiful idea? ("Critical Memory" 13)

Conceiving the public sphere as a plurality of dominant and oppositional publics instead of a single monolith, Baker answers his question:

> Historically, nothing might seem less realistic, attractive, or believable to black Americans than the notion of a black public sphere. Unless, of course, such a notion was meant to symbolize a strangely distorting

chiasma: a separate and inverted opposite of a historically imagined white rationality in action. Such a black upside-down world could only be portrayed historically as an irrational, illiterate, owned, nonbourgeois community of chattel—legally barred from even establishing conjugal families—sitting bleakly in submissive silence before the state. It would be precisely what white America has so frequently represented in blackface: the "b," or negative, side of a white imaginary of public life in America. Yet it is exactly because black Americans have so aptly read this flip side that they are attracted to a historically imagined "better time" of reason. They are drawn to the possibilities of structurally and affectively transforming the founding notion of the bourgeois public sphere into an expressive and empowering self-fashioning. Fully rational human beings with abundant cultural resources, black Americans have always situated their unique forms of expressive publicity in a complex set of relationships to other forms of American publicity. ("Critical Memory" 13)

Historians Elsa Barkley Brown and Davarian Baldwin have each explored counterpublics that lend depth to Baker's remarks. Barkley Brown demonstrates that a democratic and highly inclusive political public sphere emerged in African American communities in the South soon after the Civil War. Mass meetings often held in churches, mass participation in Republican party conventions, and regular, vocal spectatorship in the galleries of state capitols helped constitute a network of associations from which issued public opinion about such questions as universal male suffrage.[17]

Recasting the terms of *The Structural Transformation,* Barkley Brown's assertion of a form of public citizenship that departed from the liberal ideal of rational-critical debate and that validated emotion and experience as ways of knowing amounts to more than merely a claim of parity, a suggestion that African Americans have public spheres, too. It questions the normativity of bourgeois publicity itself, a normativity that the critical tradition typically leaves unchallenged. Like Barkley Brown, Davarian Baldwin identifies "a Black public sphere" where the critical tradition would not find one, in the shopping center of 1920s Chicago, "The Stroll." As a site of consumption and commercial amusement, "The Stroll" is contaminated by the normative standards of critical publicity, and indeed, E. Franklin Frazier and Charles Johnson claimed at the time that Black Chicago had "no intelligensia" (D. Baldwin 122). Baldwin insists, however, that their inability to see signs of intellectual life anywhere but in gatherings of university-trained professionals and artists prevented them from recognizing it in the consumer marketplace.

> [T]he economic framework is not distinct or separate from the production of arts and ideas, an in fact it was *the* site for a more comprehensive New Negro consciousness. At the center of this New Negro vision of a "city within a city" stood Black Chicago's civic, commercial amusement, and business district, known as "The Stroll." The marginalization of Black people from mainstream sources of education and enterprise made the Black consumer marketplace, in all senses of the term, a Black public sphere, a site of discourse and debate, and, hence, of intellectual production. (123)

If the critical discussion tacitly relies on and reinforces the normativity of a model of publicity generated by a class of racially unmarked, propertied men, this model never has to acknowledge its particularity. Such studies as Baldwin's and Barkley Brown's thus serve to expose and challenge a kind of critical myopia. These are but two of many projects that have begun to engage the discourse of the public sphere through an analytic of race, from Paul Gilroy's *Black Atlantic: Modernity and Double Consciousness* (1993) to Elizabeth McHenry's *Forgotten Readers: Recovering the Lost History of African American Literary Societies* (2002).

Because visibility and corporeality are the conditions of possibility for race, the shift from a discursive, text-mediated public sphere to a visually oriented, spectacle-mediated commercial public sphere suggests the importance of race to an analysis of consumer culture's emergence. Warner has explained that while bodies had previously been bracketed from public discourse ("the anonymity of the discourse certifying the citizen's disinterested concern for the public good"), the public sphere's transformation has increasingly produced "body images everywhere on display, in virtually all media contexts." Warner writes, "To be public in the West means to have an iconicity" (385). Yet this injunction to iconicity did not resolve the founding contradiction of the bourgeois public sphere between a universalizing self-abstraction and a particularizing corporeality. In its turn, consumer culture's rhetoric of visibility has also served as "both the utopian moment of the public sphere and a major source of domination," recasting self-abstraction as self-commodification. As Robyn Wiegman argues, in the context of a mass- mediated public, it is "not that the corporeal abstraction that accrued to white masculinity has been displaced as the universal condition of political entitlement," but "now this abstraction exists in overt contradiction with a visual culture predicated on the commodification of those very identities minoritized by the discourses and social organization of enlightened democracy."

> Under the pressure of contemporary commodity culture, the mythic Habermasian public sphere of open, rational debate, of a decorporealized, supposedly equal citizenship, is filled with bodies hailed in a variety of cultural registers according to, and not in abandonment of, their corporeal specificity . . . [T]he cost of this iconicity is high, not simply because political agency in the realm of identity-as-commodity appears more difficult to grasp, but because the specificities of bodies, while seeming to signify everywhere, still do not signify the same. The minoritized African American subject, for instance, can enter a public discourse previously closed to her, but the differential burden of "blackness" continues to mark and carry its modern double burden: signifying itself, it also anchors the differential meaning of whiteness by lodging it . . . in the epistemology of black skin. (49)

The foundations of the contemporary commodity culture Wiegman addresses here were established between the 1890s and the 1930s, as modern, commercial publicity increasingly relied on spectacle, display, and the use of urban spaces that were neither strictly public nor strictly private. As consumption became a principal modality of public citizenship, the traditional rhetoric of disembodiment associated with bourgeois publicity yielded increasingly to the various embodied forms of "going public."

I turn in chapter 2 to a catalyst of this transition from bourgeois to commercial publicity, the 1893 World's Columbian Exposition, and in particular to the efforts of one fairgoer, Ida B. Wells, to resist paying what Wiegman identified as the high cost of iconicity exacted from minoritized participants in the public sphere of consumption. The argument implicit in the path the present chapter has taken—that consumer culture's emergence was not merely concurrent with but inextricable from the negotiations of race in the Jim Crow era—is nowhere better illustrated than in the 1893 fair's policy of racial exclusion and the attending efforts to challenge it. In this sense, chapter 2 is not only an examination of the articulation between race and consumer culture in the 1890s; it is also the story of one of the earliest contributions to the "reconfigured genealogy" for which the present chapter has called.

2 *"Stage Business"*
as Citizenship

IDA B. WELLS AT THE WORLD'S
COLUMBIAN EXPOSITION

May we not hope that the lessons here learned, transmitted to the future,
will be potent forces long after the multitudes which will throng these
aisles shall have measured their span and faded away?
> —Potter Palmer, president of the World's
> Columbian Commission, October 12, 1892

The personality of Aunt Jemima completely absorbed the identity
of Miss Green. She was Aunt Jemima for the remainder of her life.
> —Arthur Marquette, *Brands, Trademarks, and Goodwill*

VISITORS TO THE 1893 World's Columbian Exposition saw
"Negroes" but few, if any, African Americans. An ethnological display
exhibited the Fon people of Dahomey (now the West African nation of
Benin), but African American endeavors had been scrupulously suppressed. By and large, the only African Americans in the "White City"
were the paying visitors who could afford the price of admission, for
while fair officials prohibited African Americans from producing the
fair, they did not prohibit their consuming it. However, there were a few
who managed to circumvent the systematic exclusion of African Americans, and three such exceptions constitute the framework for this chapter's discussion.

One was Nancy Green. "I'se in town, honey!" she cried daily, breath-
ing life into the Quaker Oats trademark Aunt Jemima at the 1893 fair.
Born into slavery in Montgomery County, Kentucky, Green was a fifty-

nine-year-old Chicago South Sider when she was cast in the part of this southern mammy stereotype (Marquette 144). Chris Rutt and Charles Underwood, white entrepreneurs from St. Joseph's, Missouri, bought a local flour mill in 1889 and marketed their self-rising pancake mix by naming it after a character in the Baker and Farrell minstrel show that had performed in town that fall (Manring 64–67). Four years later in Chicago, Nancy Green's performance of their trademark proved so popular that fairgoers jammed the aisles of the display, bought lapel buttons emblazoned with her likeness, and turned "I'se in town, honey!" into "the catchline of the Fair" (Marquette 146). "On the lookout for a Negro woman who might exemplify southern hospitality, a sufficiently poised and talented actress to demonstrate the self-rising pancake mix," Rutt and Underwood had chosen Green because she was "utterly unselfconscious," as one corporate historian puts it: "she loved crowds and loved to talk about her own slave days, her stories no doubt partly apocryphal but nonetheless entertaining" (Marquette 144–45).[1]

By contrast, another of the few African American women who appeared with some regularity on the fairgrounds, antilynching activist and journalist Ida B. Wells, was quite self-conscious and, in her own words, "not given to public demonstrations" (*Crusade* 80). Wells offers this self-characterization in her account of lecturing in New York's Lyric Hall in October 1892. Recently run out of her hometown of Memphis for her strident antilynching editorials in *Free Speech,* Wells went to Philadelphia to stay with a friend, novelist Francis E. W. Harper, before finding refuge and employment at editor T. Thomas Fortune's *New York Age.* The Lyric Hall event was organized to raise funds for a piece Wells was eager to publish denouncing lynching. Though she had long been vocal in print, Wells writes that this was "the first time I had ever been called on to deliver an honest-to-goodness address," adding, "I had no knowledge of stage business" (*Crusade* 79–80). Nevertheless, the following summer, this author-activist with a self-described aversion to public demonstrations and "no knowledge of stage business" would make an extended public appearance. For three months, she appeared daily in the Haiti Building of the Chicago fair in order to disseminate *The Reason Why the Colored American Is Not in the World's Columbian Exposition,* an eighty-one-page pamphlet written in collaboration with other public intellectuals in response to the fair's systematic exclusion of African

Fig. 1. Advertisement for Aunt Jemima's pancake flour, 1910.
(Courtesy of the New York Public Library; Astor, Lenox,
and Tilden Foundations; Picture Collection.)

Americans. Unbidden and unwelcome, Wells staged what Ann Massa has called "a radical black symposium . . . not on official display" (335).

Downtown, in the newly constructed Memorial Art Palace (now the Chicago Art Institute), a third transgression of the fair's policy of racial exclusion occurred when six prominent African Americans delivered addresses during the weeklong Congress of Representative Women convened by the fair's Education Department. Among the roughly three hundred women who participated, Frances E. W. Harper spoke on "Women's Political Future," Hallie Quinn Brown and Sarah Early on "The Organized Efforts of Colored Women of the South to Improve their Condition," and Fannie Barrier Williams, Anna Julia Cooper, and

Fig. 2. Ida B. Wells, halftone photomechanical print, ca. 1893.
(Courtesy of the New York Public Library; Schomburg
Center for Research in Black Culture; Manuscripts,
Archives, and Rare Books Division.)

Fannie Jackson Coppin on "The Intellectual Progress of the Colored
Women of the U.S. since the Emancipation Proclamation."[2] Historians
disagree about the impact of their addresses. In *When and Where I Enter,*
Paula Giddings characterizes them as having "confront[ed] the issue" of
the character of African American women "that White women rarely discussed in public," with a "frankness [that] undoubtedly shocked the
audiences" (86). By contrast, Hazel Carby argues in *Reconstructing Womanhood* that the larger discourse of black exoticism at the fair placed
these women in "a highly contradictory position": the Women's Congress was "an international but overwhelmingly white women's forum,"
she writes, the African Americans "at once part of and excluded from the

dominant discourse of white women's politics" (3, 6). Carby suggests, therefore, that their status as public subjects and "representative women" was certified by the white frame within which they operated.

On one hand, the Representative Women represented an alternative to the pursuit of publicness through self-commodification. In the nearby Food Building, Nancy Green was emerging periodically from the giant flour barrel that Quaker Oats built to house her, singing songs and telling tales—some drawn from the vaudeville Aunt Jemima song and others from her "memories" of plantation days—a living advertisement for one of the many new "convenience foods" that the fair showcased as part of modernity's "progressive emancipation" of the housewife from "the drudgery of virtual slavery in her kitchen" (Marquette 139). By identifying her own body with the body of a nationally branded trade-mark—by "trading marks"—Green mimed the privileges of a national citizenship that the fair's policy of racial exclusion would otherwise have denied her.[3] On the other hand, like Nancy Green, the Representative Women were also officially endorsed by the fair, and these two versions of producing black women as public subjects may be seen as the poles of an opposition that Wells deconstructed, in effect if not intent. Her inter-vention comes into focus against the backdrop of these two alternatives as a tactic for producing a black, female, public citizen that was neither depoliticized for consumption nor assimilable to a white political agenda. Her appropriation of the commercial public space of the fair served to disarticulate being public from being a commodity.

The Fair and the Pamphlet

At the behest of several of Chicago's well-heeled industrial entrepreneurs and flush with congressional appropriations, architect Daniel Burnham and urban planner Frederick Law Olmsted collaborated in the early 1890s to produce the "White City," a dreamlike vision on the banks of Lake Michigan, composed of neoclassical buildings whose alabaster facades gleamed off of reflecting pools. Adjoining it was the Midway Plai-sance, where the pseudoscience of ethnology merged with Barnumesque display in a panoply of spectacles. The World's Columbian Exposition, which ran from May through October of 1893, was intended to com-memorate (a year behind schedule) the four-hundredth anniversary of

Columbus's arrival in America. Its administration imitated parliamentary procedures, appointing representatives and soliciting displays from every state; the federal government's endorsement provided further legitimacy; and the astonishing array of secondary publicity the fair generated—from continuous press coverage to countless authorized and unauthorized guidebooks—established it as a site of national and international fascination. Hosting an estimated twenty-seven million guests, the fair served as a cultural "pedagogy"—as Alan Trachtenberg writes, "a model and a lesson not only of what the future might look like but, just as important, how it might be brought about" (*Incorporation* 209). A site for producing an imagined community of national citizens, it cast commodity consumption as modern citizenship's primary modality, showcasing, as Trachtenberg put it, "progress" not in the form of "simple matter and things, but matter and things as commercial products" (*Incorporation* 214).

It is difficult to overstate the importance of world's fairs in general and the 1893 exposition in particular in the identification of commodity consumption with "modern" living, national citizenship, and the ascendance of the United States onto the world stage. Though their agendas varied widely, the regional, national, and international fairs and expositions that positively cluttered the calendar around the turn of the twentieth century treated visitors to spectacles of consumer goods to assuage anxieties about the direction in which the society and economy were headed. William Leach depicts this larger process in which the fairs and exhibitions were instrumental.

> From the 1890s on, American corporate business, in league with key institutions, began the transformation of American society into a society preoccupied with consumption, with comfort and bodily well-being, with luxury, spending, and acquisition, more goods this year than last, more next year than this. American consumer capitalism produced a culture almost violently hostile to the past and to tradition, a future-oriented culture of desire that confused the good life with goods. It was a culture that first appeared as an alternative culture—or as one moving largely against the grain of American traditions of republicanism and Christian virtue—and then unfolded to become the reigning culture of the United States . . . [T]he crucial formative years of this culture [were] 1880 to 1930. (xiii)

If Leach's breathless account puts things a bit conspiratorially, it does not exaggerate the kind of effort manufacturers put into their presence at the fairs and expositions. Susan Strasser explains in *Satisfaction Guaranteed: the Making of the American Mass Market*:

> World's fairs offered manufacturers a variety of opportunities to showcase their goods, to enter them in competitions, and to disseminate samples and promotional material. Heinz had three different exhibits at the 1901 Pan-American Exposition in Buffalo: one serving food, one displaying photographs of the workers, and one exhibiting the goods the company produced for the American and British armies and navies. Many companies spent $20,000 to $30,000 at the World's Columbian Exposition in Chicago, and some spent much more. To house its display, the American Radiator Company created a two-room structure supported on Corinthian columns and decorated with pure gold leaf, satin wallpaper, hardwood floors, rare palms, and Turkish rugs. Even small companies spent as much as they could afford on elaborate exhibits, ingeniously designed sample containers, and expensively produced souvenir cards and booklets. (180–81)

Such fairs also reproduced the founding contradictions of bourgeois publicity, downplaying the roles of women, nonwhites, and labor in the development of American industry and culture while offering an iconic spectacle of democratic inclusiveness. "Exhibitions came to function as promissory notes," writes Tony Bennett, "embodying, if just for a season, utopian principles of social organization which, when the time came for the notes to be redeemed, would eventually be realized in perpetuity" (95). If the 1893 fair thus represented the utopian ideal of a particular segment of white America, its exclusion of African Americans "embodied the definitive failure of the hopes of emancipation and reconstruction," Carby writes, "and inaugurated an age that was to be dominated by 'the problem of the color line'" (*Reconstructing Womanhood* 5).

In the spring of 1893, her prominence buoyed by a speaking tour in Great Britain on the atrocities of lynch law in the South, Wells collected chapters for *The Reason Why* from Frederick Douglass, educator I. Garland Penn, and attorney and editor Frederick L. Barnett. "The pamphlet is intended," Wells wrote in its preface, "as a calm, dignified statement of the Afro-American's side of the story, from the beginning to the present

day, a recital of the obstacles which have hampered him; a sketch of what
he has done in twenty-five years with all his persecution, and a statement
of the fruitless efforts he made for representation at the world's fair"
(47). But the project foundered when many black papers refused to
endorse it publicly or to back it financially. Some even cast Wells and
Douglass as self-aggrandizing, impractical, and out of touch with plain
black folks. It was suggested that they express their grievances in a letter
to the president or the people of the United States, which the Associated
Press would gladly carry.[4] Wells was compelled to solicit popular support
and funding by publishing letters to editors, from whom she "beg[ged]
space to say in a few words what we are trying to do."[5] To raise the balance of five hundred dollars needed for publication funds, she turned to
three of Chicago's black churches (Thompson 45–46). It was not until
August 1893, with the fair already "in full blast," Wells writes, that the
"creditable little book" was ready for distribution (*Crusade* 116).

Douglass, who had been the U.S. ambassador to Haiti from 1889 to
1891, was asked by Haitian president Hippolite to oversee the Haiti
Building on the fairgrounds. This site became "one of the gems of the
World's Fair," Wells wrote, "and in it Mr. Douglass held high court" (*Crusade* 116). Douglass gave Wells space in the Haiti Building to distribute
her ten thousand copies of *The Reason Why*. It was a propitious post.

> The peculiar thing about it was that nearly all day long it was crowded
> with American white people who came to pay their respects to this
> black man whom his own country had refused to honor. Needless to
> say, the Haitian building was the chosen spot, for representative
> Negroes of the country who visited the Fair were to be found along
> with the Haitians and citizens of other foreign countries. (*Crusade*
> 117)

Douglass's account of slavery, discriminatory laws, and the convict
lease system comprise the pamphlet's first chapter. Wells then analyzes
lynch law, offering a statistical and descriptive account of lynching, the
rates of which were near their peak in the early 1890s. Penn documents
the "progress of the race" since emancipation, demonstrating population increases, improved literacy rates, the establishment of schools and
churches, and gains made in the arts, labor, and professions. Finally, Barnett recounts the frustration with which African Americans met the fair's

Fig. 3. The Haiti Building at the 1893 Chicago World's
Columbian Exposition. (Courtesy of the Chicago
Historical Society, Photographs Department.)

persistent refusals of their petitions for inclusion. In short, as the United
States put itself on display in Chicago for a multinational audience, the
pamphlet meant to clarify that the absence of African Americans was a
result not of their shortcomings but of the legacy of slavery and a set of
local, deliberate exclusions.

The Reason Why exposes a duplicity on the part of fair officials that constituted what its authors call an international outrage that impoverished
the fair as a whole. The pamphlet explains that by failing to appoint a single African American to the 208-member National Board of Commissioners, U.S. president Benjamin Harrison established "a precedent
which remained inviolate throughout the entire term of Exposition
work" (119).[6] Barnett's chapter in the pamphlet thoroughly documents
the many levels at which efforts by African Americans to secure representation were thwarted. Initially, the fair's director general denied a
petition for a black voice in the direct management of the fair, and the

national directors rejected a suggestion for a Department of Colored Exhibits. The advisability of segregating exhibits by race was debated strenuously among African Americans. In fact, the white directors cited "dissension within the ranks" to justify their denials of African Americans' proposals. But this was merely a convenient excuse, for as August Meier and Elliot Rudwick have shown, the discussion among African Americans over a separate Negro exhibit was less the sociophilosophical debate depicted by the fair administration than a disagreement over tactics: only once all avenues for racially integrated representation had been exhausted did some argue that a separate Negro exhibit would be preferable, which is to say more palatable to fair officials (357). Nevertheless, the fair administration's rationale was serviceable, and it arose repeatedly as African Americans aimed their appeals at the less centralized officers in the fair bureaucracy, including the Board of Lady Managers.

Since several members of the Lady Managers had been active abolitionists, they were thought to be a more sympathetic audience than the central administration had been. Two African American women's organizations were formed to encourage alliances with this board, which was chaired by the influential Bertha Honore Palmer, the wife of one of the fair's leading organizers. However, the two associations failed to agree on which individual African American woman could best "represent the race" on the board and on whether white and black women's work should be exhibited separately. By amplifying the discrepancy between the two associations' agendas, the Lady Managers cast the groups as rivals and cited their fear of internal divisions among the African Americans as a justification for turning them away. It would be impolitic, they claimed, to recognize either "faction." "The promptness which marked [the Lady Managers'] assumption of this position," Barnett wrote in *The Reason Why,* "is fairly indicative of the hypocrisy and duplicity which the colored people met in every effort made" (122).

Even on this most promising of avenues, then, white administrators devised an excuse for excluding African Americans, all the while maintaining a pretense of liberality. Though a black woman, Joan Imogene Howard, was eventually appointed to the New York State Board of Lady Managers, members of the National Board of Commissioners effectively absolved themselves of responsibility for African Americans' inclusion in the fair administration.[7] Bertha Palmer secured a desk job for A. M. Cur-

tis, an African American woman who had served as solicitor for a
Chicago hospital, but Curtis quit the post after less than two months, as
did her successor, Fannie Barrier Williams (Reed 30). Last-ditch appeals
to the U.S. Congress for a two-thousand-dollar federal appropriation for
a "separate Negro exhibit" were denied, despite the fact that ninety thousand dollars in congressional funds went toward the construction of
opening-day floats that, as Barnett notes, "were discarded before they
were finished and never used at all" (*The Reason Why* 128). Though "the
Negro as musician" was an official topic of discussion during the fair's
"Congress on Africa," African American musicians were excluded from
the fairgrounds. When "Hayti Day" was celebrated in July, the all-white
Iowa State Band provided the music, while the preeminent ragtime
musician Scott Joplin, visiting Chicago to see the fair, was compelled to
play just outside the fairgrounds (Reed 70). Even the doctors hired by
fair administrators to perform physical exams on applicants for jobs as
Columbian Guards falsified documents and fabricated physical inade-
quacies in order to disqualify African American men from service (*The
Reason Why* 130–34). A tacit but deliberate policy of exclusion made
itself felt at every turn.[8]

Thus, while there are empirical reasons for the whiteness of the White
City (a mere 1.3 percent of Chicago was black in 1890), its racial
makeup was no demographic accident but the result of a systematic
effort.[9] The authors of *The Reason Why* sought to make this absence conspicuous to white fairgoers. Indeed, we might understand it not simply as
a conspicuous absence but as commercial publicity's reproduction of the
classical public sphere's founding logic of exclusion, that is, as a constitutive absence. More than a mere effect of the biases and practices that
preceded it, the absence of African Americans from the fair served in
turn to facilitate the retrenchment of imperialist social relations in the
emerging forms of publicity. Regardless of what may have been a diversity of opinions among various white fair officials regarding African
American participation, the absence of African Americans became more
than incidental to the fair's function as a public sphere. The resolve with
which this exclusion was pursued turned dark skin into a particular that
could not be abstracted into the general category "American." If, as Bennett writes, world's fairs served as "promissory notes" for modernity,
embodiments of the "utopian principles of social organization" that
would be realized on future redemption, the 1893 Chicago fair

promised the erasure of African Americans and consolidated an equation between whiteness and abstract personhood.[10]

Spectacular Black Womanhood and the Legacy of Slavery

The decision Wells made to produce on the fairgrounds not only a pamphlet but also her body was particularly responsive to the fair's status as a "promissory note" for the emergent racialized, commercialized pseudopublic sphere. It was not self-evident that a black woman could creditably produce herself as a public subject even in the disembodied medium of print, much less as a body in public.[11] We can hear Wells's own discomfort with the antagonism between public, political discourse and spectacular, embodied display in her journalistic and autobiographical writing. The anxieties she expresses show her working through the founding contradiction of the bourgeois public sphere as it was being transformed by commercial publicity—namely, that the utopian promise of self-abstraction through a rhetoric of disembodiment was also the public sphere's chief instrument of domination: bracketing the particularities of one's body was a differentially available resource.

For example, about her speech at the Lyric Hall, Wells writes of her chagrin at having broken into tears at the podium. She had assured herself that despite the keenness with which she recalled the close Memphis friends whom a white lynch mob had recently murdered, she would not cry. Yet as her mind wandered "to the scenes of the struggle, to the thought of the friends who were scattered throughout the country," she writes, "a feeling of loneliness and homesickness for the days and the friends that were gone came over me and I felt the tears coming." Literary historians will note the recourse Wells makes here to a familiar rhetorical device of the nineteenth century, in which crying came to possess a peculiar significance. It was a convention of the sentimental tradition that certified the virtue of the tears' producer and the authenticity of the narrative as an account of interiority. However, Wells goes on to note how "mortified" she felt at having shed tears, and her chagrin is instructive. Such a display undermined her ability, she claims, to express "appreciation for the splendid things" the women in the audience had done. But she also construes her tears as a visible testament to her gendered unfitness for public address, for she adds, "Only once before in my entire life had I given way to women's weakness in public" (*Crusade* 80).

She records her relief that the notables seated behind her on the platform had not seen her tears.

Having previously gone public through the comparatively disembodied print medium, it was at the Lyric Hall that she first had to produce a public body. She regretted that despite her efforts, this body betrayed (what she was compelled to understand as) signs of its gender and its privateness at the moment of intense publicness. This response is informed by a principle of publicness inherited from the bourgeois public sphere—namely, that public discourse demanded a kind of self-abstraction. The conventions of bourgeois publicity placed her in a contradictory relation to her body.[12] On one hand, she was identified with a disembodied public subject that could be imagined as parallel to her private self; a pen name in lights, she was the source of rational, public discourse. Yet she was also the embodied source of incompletely suppressed, private thoughts and desires that manifested as tears. Even as she accessed the kind of negativity that the public sphere's privileged subjects enjoy, a residue of unrecuperable particularity threatened to confirm her minoritized status.

The contributions Wells made to black papers during the fair underscore her discomfort with the perceived antagonism between public discourse and the spectacle of embodiment. She bristled at the comparison editors had begun to draw between her pamphlet and the highly publicized "Colored Jubilee Day," the fair administration's own proposal for honoring African Americans. Her chief antagonist was George Knox, editor of the conservative *Indianapolis Freeman*. Conflating the two projects in an editorial titled "No 'Nigger Day,' No 'Nigger Pamphlet,'" he opposed both for the same reason.

> Both designs, if carried out, while they may add to the evanescent notoriety of certain individuals who may be active participants, and who thrive and grow robust on such things, and are charmed to see their names in print, will only serve to attract invidious and patronizing attention to the race, unattended with practical recompense or reward.[13]

Wells, too, objected to "Negro Day," calling it "a sop to our pride in [a] belated way," whose tacit goal was to fill the fair's anemic coffers (*Crusade* 118). Mindful of the corporate interests backing the fair, she warned

Cleveland Gazette readers that "Negro Day" was a "scheme to put thousands of dollars in the pockets of the railroad corporations and the world's fair folks who thought no Negro good enough for an official position among them."[14] Even more disturbing to Wells than this bald profiteering, however, was the prospect of a physical display of black bodies gathered to consume.

> The horticultural department has already pledged itself to put plenty of watermelons around on the grounds with permission to the brother in black to "appropriate" them . . . The self-respect of the race is sold for a mess of pottage and the spectacle of the class of our people which will come on that excursion roaming around the grounds munching watermelons, will do more to lower the race in the estimation of the world than anything else. The sight of the horde that would be attracted there by the dazzling prospect of plenty of free watermelons to eat, will give our enemies all the illustration they wish as excuse for not treating the Afro-American with the equality of other citizens.[15]

In the discourse of respectability that Wells mobilizes here, such a display of the appetite-driven, "roaming," "munching" class required a more genteel alternative. Thus, Wells's prefatory remark in *The Reason Why*—that it is "intended as a calm, dignified statement of the Afro-American's side of the story"—effectively frames it as the antithesis of "Negro Day." Despite journalists' efforts to yoke the two projects, then, Wells characterized her pamphlet as a more cerebral and therefore more politically promising alternative for African American participation in the fair.

She maintained that it would signal African Americans' fitness for inclusion in the political public sphere because it would observe the bourgeois norm of suppressing the body to approximate an ideal of critical-rational discourse.

Why did Wells not simply publish *The Reason Why* and leave its distribution to more conventional methods? Why risk the humiliation of minoritized public embodiment (the humiliation that she forecast in "Negro Day" and that is borne out in accounts of other appearances of nonwhite people on the fairgrounds) by putting herself "on display"? After all, there were alternatives that avoided this risk. Her remarks in an

April 1893 article in the Baltimore *Afro-American* illuminate her decision. Aware that African Americans' presence at the fair might confirm racist stereotypes, Wells nevertheless maintained that their absence posed the more pressing danger. "The absence of colored citizens from participation in the Fair," she wrote, "will be construed to their disadvantage by representatives of the civilized world." Charles Morris, the African American editor of the Washington, D.C., paper *The Pilot,* argued:

> The World's Fair could do more to raise the negro in the estimation of people at home and abroad as a valuable industrial agent in the future development of this country than anything I know of . . . No class of Americans need[s] the World's Fair as badly as the negro, for the ability of no class has been so universally denied. (18)

Morris clarifies the premise on which Wells's response was based: however inaccurate were the representations of America offered up by commercial publicity, their role as a cultural pedagogy should not be underestimated. A "sham" public sphere like the 1893 fair was not simply a "sham," for it served to enact and naturalize a mode of social segregation and economic and political subordination as much as to reflect an existing one.

Wells's effort to occupy the fairgrounds flouted the widespread opinion among her colleagues that African Americans should abandon the fair that had abandoned them. Morris reported the "wide circulation" being given "to a series of whereases and resolutions of an organization of colored men in this city declaring a boycott against the World's Fair" (17). "We object!" cried the editors of the *New York Age* when they learned of the fair's refusal to appoint an African American woman to the Board of Lady Managers. "We carry our objection so far that if the matter was left to our determination we would advise the race to have nothing whatever to do with the Columbian Exposition or the management of it."[16] Clearly, Wells would not have stood alone had she merely published the pamphlet and boycotted the fair. Moreover, the impact on white institutions of a boycott by black consumers was certainly not lost on Wells, who had recently advocated just such a strategy in Memphis as a response to lynching. Since African Americans were denied a part in producing the fair, a boycott would have in turn withheld from the fair the benefits of their consuming it. However, it was the fair that was boycotting African Americans, and in her determination not only to publish the pamphlet but also to place herself within the fair's circuits of publicity, Wells insisted on the priority of this point. Though a boycott was symbolic, it meant capitulating more broadly to the fair's effort to discipline African Americans.

Racial Semiotics from the Midway to the Women's Congress

In an important sense, Wells's physical presence posed a challenge to the fair that was as vexing as the arguments her pamphlet contained, for she was neither the kind of woman nor the kind of nonwhite that it was producing as a public subject. The fairgrounds were a well-orchestrated sign system, and the fair-going experience was highly managed; in its legibility and its apparent freedom from social conflict, the site at Jackson Park was staged as a better alternative to the surrounding "grey city" of Chicago.[17] Even the size and arrangement of buildings symbolically communicated their relative importance and their relationship to one another.[18] While the White City offered instruction and cultivation, the fair's more frivolous and plainly commercial diversions were found on the Midway Plaisance. The absence of African Americans from the White City obscured, as Wells feared it would, their pivotal role in the material and intellectual progress celebrated there, projecting the illusion of a conflict-free social tableau. The corresponding presence of nonwhites on the Midway served further to consolidate white-supremacist thinking, for there, under the direction of experts in the newly established discipline of anthropology, nonwhites were gathered into communities that ostensibly simulated real life but effectively exoticized their inhabitants, making them testaments to white superiority. From atop the Ferris wheel at the Midway's center, one might see not only the German beer garden, the belly dancers in the "Streets of Cairo," and a simulated destruction of Pompeii but also a Bedouin "encampment," a Javanese "village," and ensembles of scantily clad people from African Dahomey and the South Sea Islands. If the White City defined nonwhites as irrelevant to Western progress, the Midway located them centrally in a field of white fascination and amusement.

Frederick Douglass, in *The Reason Why,* identifies the racism of "exhibit[ing] the Negro as a repulsive savage," and recent historians have argued further that the racialization of the fair's spaces served to confirm white-supremacist thinking and to justify imperialism.[19] It invited whites to understand dark-skinned people as objects at which to gaze and marvel in a process of discovering their own superiority. "The habits of these people are repulsive," one of the fair's many "official" guidebooks observes about the Dahomey villagers, explaining, "They eat like animals and have all the characteristics of the lowest order of the human family" (quoted in Gilbert 116). Another popular guidebook, *The Best Things to Be Seen at the World's Fair,* notes a "barbaric savagery" in the Africans perched on the village's gates "in full war regalia." Its author certifies their abnormality by depicting a perversion of gender roles: he calls the women "savage-looking, masculine in appearance, and not particularly attractive"; he calls the men "small and rather effeminate in appearance" (Flinn 168–69).

The secondary publicity generated by the fair further suggests the disastrous implications for African Americans of this display of Africans. White fairgoers were only too ready to map the racist logic of the Midway onto the domestic context of U.S. race relations. "Blacker than buried midnight and as degraded as the animals which prowl the jungle of their dark land," one popular magazine wrote about the Dahomeyans, "in these wild people we easily detect many characteristics of the American negro." *Harper's Weekly* carried this equation to an extreme in a series of cartoons that caricatured an African American family's visit to the fair. When a fictional Ezwell Johnson pauses to greet a Dahomey villager, his wife scolds him: "Stop shakin' hands wid dat heathen! You want de hull fair ter t'ink you's found a poo' relation!"[20]

Thus, acts of commission and omission forged a racist field of reception for an appearance such as Wells's, but this reception was also bound inextricably to her gender. White women were well represented at the fair, through such vehicles as the Women's Building, the Women's Congress, and the extensive displays of women's artistic productions. To be sure, in and of themselves, these vehicles did little to mitigate the more general patronizing uses to which "woman" was put at the fair, whether as the repository of ideals of domesticity and civic virtue or as bodies for display. Nevertheless, they were more than token gestures, and they reflect the legitimacy white women had secured, however imperfectly, as public subjects—a legitimacy that black women were denied. The dominant assumptions about black women derived from the economic and sexual relations of slavery and specifically from whites' willful misrepresentation of these relations to their own advantage. A typical study of the time, *The Plantation Negro as a Freeman* (1889), by the Harvard-trained writer Philip Bruce, characterized African American women as "morally obtuse" and "openly licentious" (quoted in Giddings 31). Ann Douglas notes that "most whites after the Civil War believed that black women were cut off from any type of moral elevation" and that those women who "wanted to market themselves as exemplars of uplift" commanded an audience that was "not only skeptical, but incredulous and hostile" (264).

We might consider, therefore, how the "exemplars of uplift" in the Women's Congress negotiated incredulity and hostility. On one hand, as Paula Giddings points out, several of the women took it upon themselves to directly address the white presumption of black women's immorality. She notes that Fannie Barrier Williams, one of the few African American members of the Chicago Women's Club, went so far as to assert "that the onus of sexual immorality did not rest on Black women but on the White men who continued to harass them." On the other hand, Hazel Carby contends that the white-orchestrated conditions of the Representative Women's participation rendered it politically problematic (*Reconstructing Womanhood* 3–6). Indeed, in the Williams address Giddings cites, rhetorical gestures that perform an acknowledgment of this white frame compete for attention with the confrontational substance of the claims themselves: "I regret the necessity of speaking of the moral question of our women, [but] the morality of our home life has been commented on so disparagingly and meanly that we are placed in the unfortunate position of being defenders of our name . . . I do not want to disturb the serenity of this conference by suggesting why protection [for black women] is needed and the kind of man against whom it is needed" (quoted in Giddings 86). Such efforts to cast challenging ideas in deferential rhetoric appear to have worked: the president of the National Council of Women remarked approvingly that the African American women had spoken "with temperance and without bitterness [on] the social, intellectual, and industrial status of [their] race" (Sewell 633).

Williams and the other Representative Women advanced a clear, if largely implied, critique of the dominant view of African American women's morality, but they of course could not address the systematic exclusion of African Americans by the fair on whose dais they stood. Their status as public subjects was purchased, in this sense, at the price of a restrained mode of address and was marked by a horizon of interests articulated by the white Women's Congress. Moreover, the Women's Congress itself functioned ambivalently in relation to the fair in general. Its formal ties to the fair were unmistakable—it convened under the auspices of the Women's Branch of the fair's World's Congress Auxiliary— yet only a few of the meetings convened on the fairgrounds proper, and these were the "more informal" gatherings. The majority of the meetings took place downtown at the new Memorial Art Palace (now the Art Institute), and records of the Women's Congress confirm that the African American women represented in its proceedings were among the women annexed from the fairgrounds. Thus, while women's handiwork filled the Women's Building, and "woman" figured prominently as a symbol of domestic and civic virtue, the effect of the congress's annexation must have been to bracket from the business of the fairgrounds the voices of women with extradomestic concerns. The presence of African Americans in the Women's Congress constituted a risk on the part of fair organizers, but one that the terms of their inclusion helped to contain.[21]

A Citizen Where There Should Not Have Been One

I have been suggesting that the version of going public that the Representative Women pursued was incompatible with the demands of publicity on the fairgrounds proper, where instruction was made enjoyable as spectacular display. Nancy Green's Aunt Jemima fulfilled these demands all too well. Posing as an instructor of sorts—"three hundred pounds of affable kitchen wisdom"—Green was not being herself at the fair but was a living advertisement for the nationally branded pancake batter. By identifying her own body with a commercial trademark, Green accessed a new rhetoric of disembodiment, a kind of iconic national citizenship. But her access was predicated on performing a stereotype to soothe and delight white audiences. She served as "domestic consolation" that the "happy darkie" figure lived on despite the drastic changes of modernity (Berlant, "National Brands" 177). In exchange for the sensations of public citizenship that her performance of a national brand afforded, however, Green relinquished the possibility that it would be her own body that experienced these sensations. The Quaker Oats historian puts it literally: "The personality of Aunt Jemima completely absorbed the identity of Miss Green. She was Aunt Jemima for the remainder of her life" (Marquette 147). Rather than occupy an always-already humiliated body whose particulars were unrecuperable in the official public sphere, Green identified herself with a public subject whom she could imagine as parallel to her private person. She exchanged her body for "a better model," one that the emerging commercial public sphere made available in the guise of inclusiveness (Berlant, "National Brands" 177).

Green's version of going public is one Lauren Berlant names the "commercial hieroglyphic," "a body that condenses a narrative whose form seems to assure the impossibility of choosing otherwise, of being something other than a function in a system of conventions" (*Queen* 92). Her appearance both answers and recasts Karl Marx's question about what commodities would say if they could speak. When commodities speak by inhabiting the bodies and voices of black women to whom alternate versions of public citizenship are unavailable, what might black women say and be in public without also signaling their availability to a regime of display and consumption? Wells faced this question implicitly by putting both her pamphlet and her self on the fairgrounds. Presenting not only a critical text but also a black woman, she risked being conflated with the commercial hieroglyphics that shared her space and cried, "I'se in town honey!" But perhaps more pressing still was the risk of being drowned out by that cry. However precarious was her reception, the fair's successful posture as an idealized public sphere made failing to appear there at all a greater casualty. Wells's effort to produce herself publicly at the fair can be understood as a departure from and a challenge to the officially sanctioned versions of public citizenship. The Representative Women avoided becoming merely functions in a system of industrial-commercial conventions. But they, too, paid for their publicness with their bodies, in the sense that the fair partly immunized itself against the political risk that their embodiment signified. Wells's appropriation of space in the White City served to disarticulate publicity from commercial hieroglyphics, being public from being commodity.

Too tidy an opposition between mass culture and authentic citizenship has overorganized the critical conversation on the public sphere.

Examining Wells's work at the fair productively complicates this opposition. Far from treating the fair's pseudopublic sphere as a foreclosure of citizenship, Wells took commercial publicity as the precondition for her intervention, turning it against its intended purpose. The fair's project to bring the public sphere into a seamless alignment with consumption became an opportunity to mime the privileges of the national citizen, whose protections she had been denied. The fair aimed to reconstitute the nation on local grounds and to narrate this reconstituted nation's relationship to other nations and to its own citizens. Wells produced a counternarrative to this reconstituting process and produced a citizen where there should not have been one. But her intervention is not just an illustration of the cultural studies commonplace that the hegemony of the dominant culture always creates opportunities for interstitial resistance. It points up the problem in the discourse on the public sphere with universalizing the value of "critical distance." It problematizes the value of invoking critical distance from the field of commodities and commercial publicity when that critical distance has already been mobilized against you. Wells's intervention underscores the distinction between being excluded from the commercial public sphere and being exempt—through the acts of critical will that scholars tend to valorize—from its effects on collective social life.

3 Thrown into Relief

DISTINCTION MAKING IN
THE AMERICAN SCENE

Henry James noted in *The American Scene* in 1904 that in New York there are "occasions, days and weeks together, when the electric cars offer you nothing else to think of" besides immigrants. "The carful, again and again, is a foreign carful," he continued, "a row of faces, up and down, testifying, without exception, to alienism unmistakable, alienism undisguised and unashamed." On one hand, James meets these faces with imperturbable cosmopolitanism. He suggests an inconsistency in being a nativist in America: "Who and what is an alien . . . in a country peopled from the first under the jealous eye of history?—peopled, that is, by migrations at once extremely recent, perfectly traceable and urgently required." Absolute distinctions strike him as untenable: "Which is the American, by these scant measures?—which is *not* the alien." On the other hand, James is far from the unqualified cultural pluralism that such writers as Franz Boas, Horace Kallen, and Randolph Bourne would soon advocate in the late teens and early twenties.[1] Indeed, he notes that "such a scene as New York may well make one doubt" that immigration is "still urgently required." He insists that there is still a real distinction to be drawn between an American and an alien, a "launched foreign personality." He finds that the inscrutable process of assimilation frustrates his desire to verify the transition from foreigner to American, to glimpse "the dawn of the American spirit while the declining rays of the Croatian, say, or of the Calabrian, or of the Lusitanian, still linger more or less pensively in the sky" (95). In short, the sustaining myth of national assimilation, "the great cauldron of the American character," raised as many questions as it answered.

85

Immigration to America by Italians and Russian Jews reached its peak in 1907,[2] the year James published the aforementioned thoughts in *The American Scene*. The ambivalence he registered there was widespread, for it was not at all clear to many Americans that these swarthy Semitic and Mediterranean people were as susceptible to Americanization as were, for example, their Irish and German predecessors. Nor was their concentration in ethnic enclaves thought conducive to the spread of American values or the propensity for self-government. Moreover, questions of assimilation were inseparable from questions of racial amalgamation. Antimiscegenation laws were on the books to regulate and punish transgressions of the "natural" division between white and black races, but what was the nature of the division between whites and other nonblacks? No one disputed that America was essentially a "white" country, but did white mean Anglo-Saxon or Caucasian? Often conflated today, these terms originated in different discourses, and at the turn of the twentieth century, they were not exactly interchangeable.

Some staked their confidence in the perpetuation of America's essential whiteness on the peculiar absorptive power of the Anglo-Saxon race. Far from being imperiled by amalgamation with other races, wrote Charles Beresford in the 1900 *North American Review,* the Anglo-Saxon race "has had the immense advantage of being constantly invigorated by new blood."

[I]n the United States to-day we see the old principle of incorporation going on; the race ever enriching its blood with that of the best and most enterprising of other nations. It is the extraordinary capacity for absorbing and assimilating the progressive forces of other nationalities that has kept the Anglo-Saxon race moving with the times, and which will long postpone any decadence such as has befallen its predecessors. It is this infusion of fresh blood which has kept alive the fearless energy, sturdy determination, versatile ability, peculiar aptitude for self-government and the unresting spirit of enterprise which characterizes the great Anglo-Saxon people. (804)

Other voices in the mainstream found comfort not in the Anglo-Saxon race's absorptive force but in its continued dominance in sheer numbers. As the title of one *Ladies' Home Journal* article put it in 1903, this is "Why We Are English in Spite of Immigration." The author of the article argues that although the greatest increases in immigration in the previous year had been from Russia and southern Europe, "England also sent us more than she had hitherto sent for many years." "Nor is there yet danger," the author goes on to assure, "of our becoming essentially different in stock or race."

> Seventy-five percent of the foreign born among us are English, Scotch, or Irish, or they are of the German or Scandinavian races, which are first cousins to the English and really belong to the same large and healthy family of men. We are, therefore, essentially English yet; for the English themselves were made up of a mixture of these same races—the Teuton and the Celt. The small admixture of Southern European races has so far counted for little in our composite population. The same race-mingling that made the English is going on again in the United States, making another essentially English people of a later date. (14)

Of course, not everyone was so sanguine. Even if, as Walter Besant put it in 1896, Anglo-Saxons were "a tenacious race . . . a people which if it settles down anywhere, means to go on living as before and to make other people live in the same way," it was clear that not everyone was living in the same way (130–31). Assimilation was also seen to have a reciprocal effect on the native-born. Henry James maintained that "all the hitches and lapses, all the solutions of continuity, in *his* inward assimilation of our heritage and point of view," are "matched on our own side by such signs of large and comparatively witless concession." Regardless of what America would make of immigrants, he wondered, "What, oh, what again, were he and his going to make of us?" (154).

"The opinion . . . that the public schools change the children of all races into Americans" is sheer rubbish, wrote Alfred Schultz in a 1908 polemic, *Race or Mongrel?* Schultz argued: "Put a Scandinavian, a German, and a Magyar boy in at one end, and they will come out Americans at the other end. Which is like saying, let a pointer, a setter, and a pug enter one end of a tunnel and they will come out three greyhounds at the other end" (111). Schultz was not alone in his suggestion of an absolute, irreducible difference among even the European people in the United States, and for like-minded racialists, this difference was more than nominal. There is "a great struggle for survival now going on," John

Denison declared in the *Atlantic Monthly* in 1895, "between the lingering type of Americanism and the alien element that surrounds it." Citing immigrants' complicity in machine politics, he finds "the American type" at the mercy of the immigrant and the "negro" alike.

> The fact remains that by the foreign majority, and its susceptibility to the management of traitors, the American people have been put outside of their own institutions, while those institutions themselves have been turned into an instrument of degrading tyranny. The intelligent are in the power of the unintelligent, and the situation is duplicated in the South, where the possession of the suffrage by the negro has compelled the American population to choose between misrule and practical rebellion against the Constitution of the United States. (16–17)

Thus were expressed, more breathlessly here perhaps than elsewhere, the widespread concerns of people who considered themselves white—concerns that were fed by a demographic shift in immigration, the popularization of racial science, and the contest over African American suffrage.

James's *The American Scene* negotiates these more or less alarmed responses to the question of the future of the white race. It exudes none of the cavalier confidence of the *Ladies' Home Journal* or the smug racial pride of Charles Beresford. James does not indulge their impulse to paper over the conceivable conflicts arising from the claim that one race simply absorbs all others. In fact, *The American Scene* is instructive precisely because of the persistence of its efforts to surface these conflicts, to engage them frankly, to let them rub and irritate—in short, to resist the blithe self-assurance that these other accounts exhibit. Yet neither was James convinced, as were some of his contemporaries, that the Anglo-Saxon race was on the brink of being contaminated out of existence. *The American Scene* reeks of unreconstructed nativism and racism, but white-supremacist ideology was not monolithic at the turn of the twentieth century. As others have noted, to say that James was anti-immigrant and antiblack underdescribes what is actually staged in *The American Scene* as a complex set of identifications and disidentifications. There are "whole categories of foreigners," he contends, "of whom we are moved to say that only a mechanism working with scientific force" could turn into

Americans (98). So jarring is the scene at Ellis Island, he writes, that it is "as if the idea of the country itself underwent [a] profane overhauling" (67). He calls the southern and eastern Europeans at New York's Bowery Theater "representatives of the races we have nothing 'in common' with," irredeemably "alien" (147). They may be "dressed and prepared . . . for brotherhood," but "the consummation, in respect to many of them, will not be, can not from the nature of the case be, in any lifetime of their own." The children of these immigrants, however, lifelong subjects of American social institutions, he calls "another matter." The "colossal" "machinery" of American socialization—"the political and social habit, the common school, and the newspaper"—effectively rears "millions of little transformed strangers." With them, if not with their parents, "the idea of intimacy of relation may be as freely cherished as you like," for "[t] hey are the stuff of whom brothers and sisters are made" (92). Thus, in counterpoint to Schultz's incredulity (surely, Americans are born, as different from others as is a greyhound from a pug) James suggests that they are in fact made. Assimilation, that "queer, clumsy, wasteful social chemistry," is simply the process of "peaceful history," an alternative to "battles and blood and tears" (149).

Nevertheless, something about this account does not sit right for James, and in his discomfort, we glimpse the peculiar crossroads at which racial thinking found itself at the turn of the twentieth century. In *The American Scene,* James asks, "What becomes, as it were, of the obstinate, the unconverted residuum?" (95). What becomes, in other words, of race—the irreducible substance that distinguishes the people of the earth from one another? Transcending culture, how can it fail to survive the process of assimilation? However effective is "the assimilative force," James argues, it nevertheless "has still the residuum to count with." James wishes he could discover where it goes: "you lose yourself in the wonder of what becomes of [it]." The text's frequent, anxious recurrence to this question suggests the high stakes of immigration's volatilization of race in general and of whiteness in particular.

I suggest, though, that what makes *The American Scene* instructive is not just its frank negotiation of the discourses competing for the authority to frame race but also its racialization of the commercialization of America.[3] The text's obsession with consumer culture is unmistakable. Among the first things James notices when he arrives in America is "the air of unmitigated publicity, publicity as a condition, as a doom, from which there could be no appeal" (11). He finds "a society reaching out into the apparent void for the amenities, the consummations, after having earnestly gathered in so many of the preparations and necessities" (13). On the transition from an economy of scarcity to an economy of abundance, he is lapidary: "In the early American time, doubtless, individuals of value had to wait too much for things; but that is now made up by the way things are waiting for individuals of value" (188). "Pecuniary gain," he suggests, is the American's primary goal: "To make so much money that you won't, that you don't 'mind,' don't mind anything—that is absolutely, I think, the main American formula" (176). Even the poor, "one's jostling fellow pedestrians" in the ethnic ghettos, he calls "possible purchasers" (103). Thus, Carolyn Porter has argued that James's late work depicts "a world in which reification has penetrated so deep as to constitute the limits of the knowable" (122). Jennifer Wicke has similarly located in *The American Scene* a "structural analysis of the social conditions in America allowing the advertising society to come into being . . . doggedly alert to the establishment of an image-based economy, a political economy already operating along the lines later discussed by Gramsci, Weber, Barthes, and Debord" (113). Jean-Christophe Agnew suggests that James's texts offer "clues to the ways that feeling and perception were restructured to accommodate the ubiquity and liquidity of the commodity form" (68). Yet such inquiries into this critique of a reified, advertising-driven culture of commodities have seldom linked it to the integral place that race also holds in the text.[4]

Two brief examples from *The American Scene* suggest the importance of making this link, which the rest of the present chapter examines. In Boston, James puts his physiognomic expertise to work on the local Italian immigrants: "The types and faces bore them out; the people before me were gross aliens to a man, and they were in serene and triumphant possession" (172). Later, in Florida, a similarly objectionable "type" confronts him: "As to facial character, vocal tone, primal rawness of speech, general accent and attitude," members of this "type" were "extraordinarily base and vulgar"; they were "specimens of something I had surely never so *indisputably* encountered"; and they "insisted . . . with a strange crudity, on being exactly as 'low' as they liked." The sight of this "type in completely unchallenged possession" leads James to conclude that "a single type has had the game, as one may say, all in its hands." To what race does James say this "personage" belongs? It is not "the Southern negro," who elsewhere provokes similar tirades from James. Here, it is none other than the salesman, "the lusty 'drummer'," "the brawny peddler more or less gorged on the fruits of misrepresentation"; it is, writes James, "the ubiquitous commercial traveler" who "insist[s] on a category of his own" (313, 315). The terms in which James describes and vilifies the salesman are identical to those he uses to identify racial others: their distinct type, specimen, personage, or category expresses itself through qualities that are at once somatic (face, voice, tone, carriage) and behavioral (base, vulgar, crude, indisputable, and unchallengeable).

A second and related example concerns James's recollection that in Newport there had at one time been "a considerable company of Americans, not gathered at a mere rest-cure, who confessed brazenly to not being in business." Instead, they were "the detached, the slightly disenchanted and casually disqualified." Three qualities united them. First, they had "for the most part more or less lived in Europe." Second, they worshiped "the ivory idol whose name is leisure." Third, their leisure produced in them "a formed critical habit." Each of these qualities was exceptional, James maintains, for in America "nobody every criticized," and "the great black ebony god of business was the only one recognized" (165). The opposition between the "ivory idol" of leisure (and its attending critical habit) and the "great black ebony god of business" could be overlooked as mere metaphor with little or nothing to do with race, except that figures throughout the text consistently align commerce with nonwhiteness.

Indeed, the discourse in which the text stages its posture of opposition to consumer culture is thoroughly racialized. *The American Scene* defines and defends the "formed critical habit" that James identifies with whiteness. I suggest that by keying whiteness to something besides skin color—to an oppositional stance toward commerce—James recuperates a version of the white race. This gesture is not equivalent to the ideal of the "100 percent American" extolled by some of James's contemporaries, but I argue that it is equally critical to understanding broad projects of racial formation in the United States during this period. To make this argument, I turn first, in the section that follows, to James's

conflation of race and consumer culture in the idea of "consanguinity";
then, in the subsequent section, I trace three ways in which *The American
Scene*'s responses to nonwhites and consumer culture are mutually rein-
forcing.

*"Colour," Color, and Consanguinity; or,
Who Is at Home if Everyone Is at Home?*

In 1903, the year before James made a return visit to the United States,
Pauline Hopkins's novel *Of One Blood* finished its serialized run. Her title
comes from the words of the Holy Writ, Acts 17:26: "He hath made of
one blood all the nations of the earth." She asks, "Who is clear enough
in vision to decide who hath black blood and who hath it not?" (607).
For Hopkins, miscegenation promises the disappearance of racial distinctions and, consequently, the attenuation of racism. The mulatto in
Hopkins's novel signals the emergence of a universal "brotherhood"
(590). *The American Scene* might have taken the title of Hopkins's novel,
preoccupied as it is with "the recruiting of our race"—the making of one
American blood out of all the nations of the earth—and, further, with
the consequences of this making for what James also calls "brotherhood"
(50). *Consanguinity* is one of the text's most important terms: it names
the shared "blood" of racial descent and the shared "blood" of fraternity.
The American Scene reiterates the letter of Hopkins's question, but not its
spirit. Who indeed is "clear enough in vision," it asks, to make discriminations among bloods? James is as discomposed by the question as Hopkins is emboldened. Her answer—"No man can draw the dividing line
between the two races, for they are both of one blood" (607)—provokes
in James only more questions. "[W]here," asks James in *The American
Scene,* "does one put a finger on the dividing line, or, for that matter,
'spot' and identify any particular phase of the conversion, any one of its
successive moments" (95). The apparent failure of vision to make racial
distinctions becomes a matter of some urgency. "Whom did they look
like the sons of?" James asks, scrutinizing the faces of the young men in
Harvard Yard (50).

James's struggle to make racial distinctions can be understood as an
expression of a much broader struggle his text stages to make all sorts of
distinctions. For him, distinctions are always cast in visual terms. The

United States is "a bad country to be stupid in," he maintains, "none on the whole so bad." "If one doesn't know *how* to look and to see," he argues, "one should keep out of it altogether." He continues:

> But if one does, if one *can* see straight, one takes in the whole piece at a series of points that are after all comparatively few . . . And if one has not learned to separate with due sharpness, pen in hand, the essential *from* the accessory, one has only, at best, to muffle one's head for shame and await deserved extinction . . . If you have luckily *seen,* you have seen; carry off your prize, in this case, instantly and at any risk. Try it again and you don't, you won't, see. (271, 302)

A project in what James calls "restless" analysis, *The American Scene* performs the persistent visual activity of its protagonist. It stands in explicit challenge to the passivity and the failures of discrimination he attributes to Americans. Seeing is the active, distinction-yielding alternative to looking, the passive consumption of views. As Hopkins intends it, the question "[w]ho is clear enough in vision to decide who hath black blood and who hath it not?" is rhetorical; it takes the failure of vision to distinguish between races as a sign that there is no distinction to be made in the first place. For James, however, the short-circuiting of the project of distinction making marks not the end of the need for distinctions but, rather, the failure of the observer to make them. But it is not just that racial distinctions are among those James wishes to make. Rather, the entire distinction-making enterprise itself is inextricable from the question of race.

Naming a close association of fellow feeling, on one hand, and an association based on shared blood, on the other, the dual valence of the term *consanguinity* registers a pivotal transition in racial common sense in the early twentieth century. It was not until the late twenties and early thirties that an insurgent ethnicity-based conception of race displaced the prevailing biological paradigm, which "had evolved since the downfall of racial slavery to explain racial inferiority as part of a natural order of mankind" (Omi and Winant 14–15). On the biological model, race was a matter of heredity, and differences among people could be explained by making recourse to race. By contrast, the ethnicity-based paradigm suggested that "race was but one of a number of determinants of ethnic group identity or ethnicity."

Ethnicity itself was understood as the result of a group formation process based on culture and descent. "Culture" in this formulation included such diverse factors as religion, language, "customs," nationality, and political identification. "Descent" involved heredity and a sense of group origins, thus suggesting that ethnicity was socially "primordial," if not biologically given, in character. (Omi and Winant 15)

During the period of transition to an ethnicity-based paradigm, "highly dissonant terms of descent and origin had become 'semantically interchangeable,'" as Sara Blair has put it. Blair notes that in both the disciplinary and the popular contexts that James's work engages, "categories of descent, such as 'blood,' 'stock,' and 'tribe,' are increasingly overlaid with, and radically confused by, general terms of classification— 'species' or 'kind'—as well as assignments of nation." She contends that James's literary "performances open a lens onto the instability of race— and particularly of whiteness—as a shifting structure of experience and feeling (and of commodification, violence, and repression)" (7). This reading seems exactly right to me. But insofar as *The American Scene* is aware of the racial instability onto which it opens a lens, it is an instability that James's book is far from celebrating or, for that matter, facing complacently. Calling the challenge that immigration poses to racial identity "about as vivid a thing as one can quietly manage," James routinely falters under the pressure of trying to manage it. He makes recourse to a version of whiteness that we could call an ideological "strategy of containment," an intellectual and formal strategy to allow "what can be thought to seem internally coherent in its own terms, while repressing the unthinkable . . . which lies beyond its boundaries" (Jameson, *Political Unconscious* 102, 183–84). What is unthinkable is the disappearance of race tout court. I suggest that *The American Scene* preserves a biological approach to race behind a discourse of ethnicity, by displacing color with "colour."

One of *The American Scene*'s most curious passages seems almost to anticipate James Baldwin's claim that "no one was white until he came to America."[5] Henry James proposes that what Europeans sacrifice when they come to America is their "colour." "'Colour' of that pleasant sort," he notes approvingly, "was what they had appeared . . . most to have" (98). Elaborating, he figures Americanization as a visible whitening: it works to purge every trace of the "colour" that had made Europeans so "pleasant."

> They were all together so visibly on the new, the lifted level—that of consciously not being what they *had* been, and . . . this immediately glazed them over as with some mixture, of indescribable hue and consistency, the wholesale varnish of consecration, that might have been applied, out of a bottomless receptacle, by a huge white-washing brush. (98)

James argues that the unfortunate result of this "feat of making them colourless" is that "the various positive properties" that were "ingrained in generations" are sacrificed permanently. He holds out hope for the contrary: "Isn't it conceivable that, for something like a final efflorescence, the business of slow comminglings and makings-over at last ended, [these properties] may rise again to the surface, affirming their vitality and value and playing their part?" (99). It seems as though James turns nativist white supremacy on its head here, playing out a fantasy of the end of miscegenation yet rejoicing in the restoration of the "vitality and value" not of Anglo-Saxon whiteness this time but of "colour," the "colour" that Europeans have to sacrifice to become American. Of course, one of white-supremacist ideology's most powerful nightmare fantasies was precisely that the latent color in miscegenated Americans would indeed reemerge to subordinate the whiteness that had previously suppressed it and the savagery it betokened. Unlike this white-supremacist narrative, James's fantasy of recalcitrant nonwhiteness "ris[ing] again to the surface" appears to be a source of hope. He openly relishes the possibility that the whitewashing may not last, asking, "[M]ay not the doubt remain of whether the extinction of qualities ingrained in generations is to be taken for quite complete?" (99). Is James revising a white-supremacist script here, preserving its terms but reversing their value so that "colour" comes to look like the overmatched victim of a corrupting whiteness?

Prizing "colour" over "colourlessness" and fantasizing about the reemergence of the "colour" that lies dormant in assimilated Americans, this passage seems on its face to critique a whiteness that James equates with American national identity. That this is not the case only becomes clear once we recognize that he is using "colour" and "colourless" as aes-

thetic designations, not categories of race. The reason this passage is not
a critique of whiteness, in other words, is that it purports not to refer to
race at all. "Colour," like so many other issues for James, is a matter of
manners. It refers, he says, to a pleasantness that Europeans have when
one meets them in their native country, the "element of agreeable
address" that they seem to lose once they arrive in America.

> Here, perhaps, was the nearest approach to a seizable step in the evo-
> lution of the oncoming citizen, the stage of his no longer being for
> you—for any complacency of the romantic, or even verily of the frat-
> ernizing, sense in you—the foreigner of the quality, of the kind, that
> he might have been *chez lui*. Whatever he might see himself becom-
> ing, he was never to see himself that again, any more than you were
> ever to see him. He became then, to my vision (which I have called fas-
> cinated for want of a better description of it), a creature promptly
> despoiled of those "manners" which were the grace (as I am again
> reduced to calling it) by which one had best known and, on opportu-
> nity, best liked him. He presents himself thus, most of all . . . as won-
> deringly conscious that his manners of the other world, that every-
> thing you have there known and praised him for, have been a huge
> mistake. (97)

The "colour" that gets eclipsed by America's "wholesale varnish of consecration," then, is a manner, a kind of grace. Specifically, though, it is a
pleasantness in the way James finds himself addressed. This is a relational question, less a quality that foreigners possess than an effect of
their interactions with him. Still, he goes to great lengths to frame the
change as having occurred in the object itself, in the European turned
American. Decrying their "impudence"—"the way they *become* crude over
here!"—James displaces the experience and prejudices that he brings to
the encounter himself (200). But his project relies for its rich, subjective
suggestiveness on these very experiences and prejudices, so he is not uni-
formly successful at locating the change squarely in the foreigners, and
the relational basis of "impudence" reemerges. He maintains that the
immigrant reaches a "stage of his no longer being for you . . . the foreigner of the quality, of the kind," he had formerly been. The change
James identifies is thus framed as a change in his relationship to these
people, not (as it might be convenient to imagine) a change in the

people themselves. More disturbing than the sacrifice of the grace immigrants possessed as foreigners is the sacrifice of the entire American-foreigner relationship, the construct that authorized James's sense that the foreigner was there "for" him. No longer a "foreigner," the immigrant can no longer be as readily objectified and instrumentalized as he could when met as a foreigner.

In short, what has changed, is nothing more than the Europeans' location but nothing less, therefore, than their status as foreigners, with all of the attending expectations, conventions, and privileges that invited white American gentility to entertain, comfort, and "interest" themselves.

> The Italians, who over the whole land, strike us, I am afraid, as, after the Negro and the Chinaman, the human value most easily produced, the Italians meet us, at every turn, only to make us ask what has become of that element of the agreeable address in *them* which has, from far back, so enhanced for the stranger the interest and pleasure of a visit to their beautiful country. (98)

As it is, James sighs, "the 'American' value of the immigrant . . . is restricted to the enjoyment" of the "luminous discovery" that his former manners were an error. He is no longer valuable, for his value derived from the affective structure of his having been "for you." As an American, James writes, the immigrant can only be "for us": "we must own . . . a tolerably neutral and colourless image" (97). The "tolerably neutral and colourless image" the immigrant presents, then, is not exactly a question of race, in the sense that it refers to an abstract quality of grace and manner. However, this quality of grace and manner already has inscribed in it the very asymmetrical relationship across national borders that constituted turn-of-the-century racial discourse in the first place. So while "colour" and "colourlessness" do not translate into "nonwhite" and "white," they end up referring to race no less directly; they just refer to its basis in asymmetrical social relations rather than skin tone.

Despite James's desire to speak in strictly aesthetic terms, the manners to which he refers when he says "colour" are the product of a national racial imaginary,[6] one that manages the discomfort of James's encounters with "the inconceivably alien" through a series of associations and displacements (66). National difference is understood as racial difference; race is understood as a matter of consanguinity, the sharing of blood; consanguinity is cast in terms of heredity and family. The relationship between people of different nations thus becomes an encounter in the intimate, domestic space of hosts and guests. The passage that sounded at first like a fantasy of the reemergence of nonwhite qualities among miscegenated Americans turns out, to the contrary, to be a fantasy about the reemergence of a consoling subject-object, guest-host relationship, a structure of intimate disidentification. Traveling abroad, James feels most comfortable when he is made to know that he is not actually at home. Foreigners play a crucial role as foreigners: they mediate James's relationship to America and consolidate its intimacy; as immigrant Americans, though, they can no longer play the host and thus no longer serve this mediating function. Nor, for that matter, can they play the guest. After all, as James puts it, "the great fact" about them

> was that, foreign as they might be, they were *at home*, really more at home, at the end of their few weeks or months or their year or two, than they had ever in their lives been before; and that *he* [the American observer] was at home too, quite with the same intensity; and yet that it was this very equality of condition that, from side to side, made the whole medium so strange. (96)

When both are "at home," the structure and its attending pleasures collapse, leading James to see the immigrant as impudent, vulgar, and aggressive and himself as dispossessed, at the mercy of what he calls "the alien presence." He is dispossessed not so much of his home as of the mediating function of the foreigner as foreigner, of the relationship through which James consolidated his intimacy with other Americans.

The idea of being "at home" is critical in *The American Scene*, not just because so much is at stake for James in returning to America after a long absence. As a figure that distills ideas about privacy, domesticity, intimacy, and familiarity and therefore about heredity and consanguinity, the ideal of feeling "at home" is made to do a lot of rhetorical work. It stands in beleaguered counterpoint to the commercial publicity we have seen James denounce as an "unmitigated . . . condition, a doom from which there could be no appeal" (11). In addition to figuring an ideal of prophylactic privacy and domestic consanguinity, being at home guards against too intimate an "alien presence." This figure is the ground on which James stages a disaffiliation, on one hand, and a compensatory identification, on the other. It is a disaffiliation from bourgeois America—its neglect of anything "that is not entirely estimable in more or less greasy greenbacks" (19). But it also enables James's construction of an alternate version of Americanness as whiteness. James's sense of a nation based on consanguinity—the shared blood of a family that courses through the veins of the national body—collides with his sense that Americans are sufficiently different from some foreigners that the idea of a unified national body is seriously compromised. If the American race is to remain viable conceptually, something has to be invented to account for the intimate relationship among Americans that had formerly been conferred by foreigners as foreigners. I think this is where James produces whiteness, not as skin color exactly, but as a robust version of "the American race" that still means consanguinity (that protects the intimacy of that prior historical relationship), rather than the diluted version of the American race that signifies character or culture. In James's text, whiteness is produced in the figure of consanguinity as a position to which the embattled native retreats for consolation in the contest over who is "at home" in America.

"Race" is clearly an idea that James inherits, but "whiteness" is something he arrives at in response to the way the melting pot defies his powers of representation. It puts him in the position of having to represent the intimacy of his relationship with America, a task that the foreigner's status as foreigner had tacitly performed for him. How is James to express a relationship that is, as he puts it, "inexpressibly intimate," "one's supreme relation" (89, 11)? Struck by the efficiency of Americanization, he writes that foreigners "shed [their foreignness] utterly, I couldn't but observe, on their advent, after a deep inhalation or two of the clear native air." But it is precisely this efficiency that makes him uneasy. The "conscientious completeness" with which they shed it leaves him "looking for any faint trace of it," much as he was compelled to wonder "what becomes, as it were, of the obstinate, the unconverted residuum," "those elements in them that are not elements of swift convertability?" (95). If race is invisible, how can it be represented? If it is not susceptible to representation, how can it be verified?

Perhaps the answers lay in a misapprehension of race's true state of matter. In *The Golden Bowl*, James writes of the Italian Prince Amerigo:

"[H]e was somehow full of his race. Its presence in him was like the consciousness of some unexpungable scent in which his clothes, his whole person, his hands and the hair of his head, might have been steeped as in some chemical bath; the effect was nowhere in particular, yet he constantly felt himself at the mercy of its cause" (51). Like an infusion, race is thoroughly affecting yet nowhere in particular. It is figured similarly in a passage from *The American Scene,* as the relationship between the immigrant and the American air is compared to the relationship between a garment and the water in which it is washed.

> [T]he effect I speak of, the rapid action of the ambient air, is like that of the tub of hot water that reduces a piece of bright-hued stuff, on immersion, to the proved state of not "washing": the only fault of my image indeed being that if the stuff loses its brightness the water of the tub at least is more or less agreeably dyed with it. That is doubtless not the case for the ambient air operating after the fashion I here note—since we surely fail to observe that the property washed out of the new subject begins to tint with its pink or its azure his fellow-soakers in the terrible tank. If this property that has quitted him—the general amenity of attitude in the absence of provocation to its opposite—could be accounted for by its having rubbed off on any number of surrounding persons, the whole process would be easier and perhaps more comforting to follow. (98)

What is the "property that has quitted" the immigrant? It is "colour" figured as color, behavior ("amenity of attitude") figured as race. No sooner does the analogy begin than its inadequacy is remarked. Strangely, "colour" does not act like color, fails to "rub off" on Americans, or at least fails to make itself visible. The disconcerting implication of the analogy's inadequacy, however, is not that immigrants fail to infuse Americans with their pleasant amenity of address; it is that whatever made foreigners foreign might disappear without a trace. If only a tint of pink or azure were detectable among the Americans in whose midst the immigrants had been placed, "the whole process would be easier and perhaps more comforting to follow." Instead, James has to contend with the idea that it just drops right out. This raises thorny questions. Race is supposed to work like a closed system: races combine in the "terrible tank" just as they combine in the closed genetic system of sexual reproduction, but they should not just disappear. If one race does, has it merely disappeared from view, not from existence? The first (and only mildly disconcerting) implication of the fact that race can be mixed and disappear from view is that race has no visible evidence. How does one then represent the interracial exchange that James understands immigration to be? More disconcerting still, though, is the prospect that race can be not only mixed but in fact precipitated right out of the solution, disappeared from view because extinguished from existence. The specter this raises is not only the extinction of a white race that is supposed to be irreducible but also a complete overhaul of the closed-system model (the terrible tank, sexual reproduction) for rendering racial exchange intelligible. It requires thinking about the exchange between ostensibly distinct races of people on a model different from the combination of the genes of people of distinct races, and this is a model to which James holds tenaciously. How does one represent the making of the American national body other than as the progeny of "intermarriage," an intermingling that may make race disappear from view but nevertheless preserves its existence (153)?

Of course, these questions were not the exclusive preoccupation of James or even of his patrician class but, rather, emerged because, as John Higham argues, two strands of racial thinking began to coalesce in the late nineteenth and early twentieth centuries.

> Racial science increasingly intermingled with racial nationalism. Under the pressure of a growing national consciousness, a number of European naturalists began to subdivide the European white man into biological types, often using linguistic similarity as evidence of hereditary connection. For their part, the nationalists slowly absorbed biological assumptions about the nature of race, until every national trait seemed wholly dependent on hereditary transmission. This interchange forms the intellectual background for the conversion of the vague Anglo-Saxon tradition into a sharp-cutting nativist weapon and, ultimately, into a completely racist philosophy. (134)

Without reducing James's work to either a record of or instrument for this conversion, we might situate his particular conflation of race and nation within the transformation Higham sketches. It seems important to resist a progressive narrative in which James's historically specific and idiosyncratic racial nativism looks like so much groundwork for later and more virulent forms of racial nativism.[7] But in the particular version of his anxiety about intermarriage, in his layering of an Anglo-Saxon pride that was the legacy of romantic nationalism with a naturalist's genetic and physiognomic approach to racial thinking, and even in his resistance to the more overtly racist implications toward which his assumptions pointed, James stands at the peculiar crossroads of racist nativism at the turn of the twentieth century, a crossroads Higham calls the "fusion—and confusion—of natural history with national history" (134). As pseudoscientific approaches to race were mapped onto the populations of Europe in the 1890s and 1900s, the new southern and eastern European immigrants came to seem to many, including James, like possible limit cases for assimilation and threats to the integrity of the white race, if not to white people themselves.[8]

The Race of Commerce and the Commerce of Race

I have identified two interwoven critiques in *The American Scene,* one of consumer culture and one of nonwhites, but neither critique takes the shape of an argument. Each emerges instead from a series of staged encounters in which the protagonist's effort to reestablish a relationship to his native country is frustrated. These encounters are shot through with undisguised hyperbole, telescopic abstractions, sweeping generalizations, and a deliberate strategy of associative play.

For instance, "the hotel-spirit" is the text's catchall term for the objectionable qualities of a society whose organizing principles are publicity and profit at any cost. But "the hotel-spirit" remains deliberately ill-defined. Elsewhere James calls it "the economic idea" or "the pecuniary interest," suggesting nothing more at many points than mere greed and the priority of market values over aesthetic values (74). At other moments, however, "the hotel-spirit" more specifically names America's "genius for organization." What James finds at the Waldorf-Astoria, for example, is "a social order in positively stable equilibrium."

> Here was a world whose relation to its form and medium was practically imperturbable; here was a conception of publicity *as* the vital medium organized with the authority with which the American

genius for organization, put on its mettle, alone could organize it. The whole thing remains for me, however, I repeat, a gorgeous golden blur, a paradise peopled with unmistakable American shapes, yet in which, the general and the particular, the organized and the extemporized, the element of ingenuous joy below and of consummate management above, melted together and left one uncertain which of them one was, at a given turn of the maze, most admiring. (81)

Here James admires technical mastery even when its effect, as he describes it, is to inculcate false consciousness. He likens this supremely managed state of the hotel to one in which a "high-stationed orchestral leader, the absolute presiding power" pulled the strings on an "army of puppets" yet "found means to make them think of themselves as delightfully free and easy" (82). Sounding a note from Max Weber, James reflects on the hotel that "the whole housed populace move[d] as in mild and consenting suspicion of its captured and governed state . . . beguiled and caged, positively thankful, in its vast vacancy, for the sense and definite horizon of a cage" (325). At still other moments, "the hotel-spirit" names the insidious practice of anticipating, exploiting, and even manufacturing consumer desire. It has a mission "not only of meeting all American ideals, but of creating . . . new and superior ones."

> Its basis, in those high developments, is not that it merely gratifies them as soon as they peep out, but that it lies in wait for them, anticipates and plucks them forth even before they dawn, setting them up almost prematurely and turning their faces in the right direction. Thus the great national ignorance of many things is artfully and benevolently practiced upon; thus it is converted into extraordinary appetites, such as can be but expensively sated. (324)

This passage serves as a proleptic critique of advertising, just prior to its emergence as a national cultural force. Thus, as Mark Seltzer writes, "the hotel-world and the hotel-spirit figure for James throughout as metonyms of the new American society," referencing "that combination of the 'perpetually provisional' and 'the universal organizing passion' that he finds everywhere inscribed on the American scene" (110).

James's use of the term *aliens* is similarly diffuse and evocative. Alan

Trachtenberg identifies the role of aliens in James's text as that of "culturally antithetical carriers of difference" ("Conceivable Aliens" 52). The
term *alienism* refers to the range of "vulgar" behaviors James identifies
with foreigners on U.S. soil, yet it functions as an abstraction that, were
it simply reducible to these behaviors, would do less rhetorical work. In
a text committed to the virtues of impressionistic (rather than conventionally documentary) representation, it is for their utility at conveying
precisely no one thing in particular but, rather, a range of associations
and a sense of immanent energy that James uses terms like "the hotel-
spirit" and *alienism*. Despite what is therefore a studied elusiveness in
James's critiques of commercial publicity and immigration, I suggest
three axes along which to trace them both and thereby suggest their contiguity.

First, both commercial publicity and the immigrant deny observers
any response. Each goes about its business without resistance, silencing
in advance all opposition. By virtue of its sheer presumptuousness, each
compels history to consent to its own desecration. Second, commercial
forces and immigrants are both consistently likened to promiscuous
mothers, irresponsible and monstrous in their reproduction, not so
much sexual as autogenic, either superhuman or subhuman. Finally,
and most crucially for understanding the centrality of race to the text's
critique of modernity, the effect of both commercialization and immigration is to short-circuit the observer's faculties of discrimination. Making distinctions becomes, in and of itself, an oppositional stance in relation to a culture that works inexorably to cloud them. By pursuing each
of these strands in the articulation of race and commerce, I wish to suggest that these social phenomena were experienced in tacit but forceful
relation to one another. I further wish to map out a problematic from
which emerges the alternative version of whiteness that the final section
of this chapter addresses.

James understands himself to be producing value through observation and analysis and, more pointedly, to be producing a distinct model
for value. It is meant as an alternative to the dominant model, which in
his America means "pecuniary value." But just as the effort that novelists
made during this period to shore up a distinction between high and low
culture was precarious, so James's model of aesthetic value bears a similarity to the market model against which it is defined.[9] In the market of

goods, the nonidentity between use value and exchange value makes profit possible. James suggests that aesthetic value is produced by virtue of the nonidentity between a scene's immanent qualities and the qualities the keen observer imputes to it. It was "a question of what one read *into* anything," he writes in *The American Scene*, "not of what one read out of it" (53). In James's *The Golden Bowl*, Adam Verver not only recognizes aesthetic value; he also creates it by paying a high price for his purchase. Likewise, *The American Scene* insists that the value of observations is directly proportionate to the price they exact from the observer, the extent to which they tax his critical and expressive faculties: "It came back again . . . to the quantity to be 'read into' the American view, in general, before it gives out an interest. The observer, like a fond investor, must spend on it, boldly, ingeniously, to make it pay" (274). The strain of observation and analysis required by a scene thus becomes the index of its value, and the capacity of the restless analyst to endure this strain becomes the index of his mastery of aesthetic value making.

Thus, James invokes and reworks a model of marketplace exchange in his representation of the relationship between the observer and the object world. He is concerned that his analysis repay his efforts, that the insights it yields prove valuable, and that a profit can be made on the attention he invests. Like any savvy lender (in this case, a lender of attention), he is motivated by the amount of "interest" a scene creates, and the double entendre is significant even if it is unintentional. Like a merchant, he seeks to create value in the objects of his analysis by paying a high price for them himself, performing the rigors of analysis that testify to the value of the insights they yield. Moreover, the relationship between the observer and his object is cast as an exchange between a producer and a consumer—or, more accurately, between one commodity merchant and another who wishes to buy it and add to its value. Many of the text's ruminations on the susceptibility of a scene to representation stage a negotiation between the source of the raw material, on one hand, and the critical and aesthetic faculties of observation, on the other. While few people are actually quoted in *The American Scene*, the text is alive with competing voices—the assertions, demurring evasions, and elaborate self-justifications that James imputes to people, objects, and images in moments of ventriloquism and mimicry. One voice in particular, "The Refrain of the Hotel," captures "in a few remarkably plain and distinct words" the uncompromising boldness that he comes to identify with both commerce and immigrants. "[I]t is as if every one and everything said to you straight: 'Yes, this is how we are; this is what it is to enjoy our advantages; this moreover is all there is of us; we give it all out. Make what you can of it!'" (299–300). James frames himself as the subject of a peculiar address. Its injunction—to make what he can of conditions that brusquely resist remaking—positions him, first and foremost, as a producer of meaning and value and, second, as poorly treated by his material, for it refuses to cooperate. Ideally the exchange is cordial and mutually gratifying. But on those occasions when the object puts up too much resistance or "demands" to have everything "on its own terms," representation breaks down. This is the problem with both foreigners and spectacles of commercial publicity: "we, not they, must make the surrender and accept the orientation. We must go, in other words, *more* than half-way to meet them; which is the difference, for us, between possession and dispossession" (67). In short, they both drive too hard a bargain.

Commerce and immigrants refuse to accommodate history. In its embodiment in already-existing structures and forms, history receives no accommodation from commerce. In its embodiment in already-existing Americans, history receives no accommodation from immigrants. Indeed, both commerce and immigrants demand accommodation themselves. A dual assault on the "ancient graces," they constitute a regime of the "impudently new" (60). James's impressionistic lament is that "it didn't, the earlier, simpler condition, still resist or protest, or at all expressively flush through," that "it was consenting to become a past . . . with due ironic forecast of the fate in store for the hungry, triumphant actual" (43). The futility of resistance, of making any sort of response, is the primary trope James employs in his reflections on both commerce and immigrants. The terms are equally serviceable to both critiques. In the ostentatious houses on the New Jersey shore, for instance, he finds something unanswerable:

> *the expensive* as a power by itself . . . really exerting itself in a void that could make it no response . . . the air of unmitigated publicity, publicity as a condition, as a doom, from which there could be no appeal . . . no achieved protection, no constituted mystery of retreat, no saving complexity. (11)

It is not just that "the shops, up and down, are making all of this" ancient grace and respectability seem "as if it had never been," but also that they should somehow know better, for they "plead but meagrely . . . for indulgence to [their] tendency to swarm, to bristle, to vociferate." Insufficiently apologetic, commodity "exhibitions" are so unassailable as to seem downright "protected," even "consciously and defiantly protected," "insolently safe, able to be with impunity anything they would." James imagines the commercial world addressing him defiantly, "You must take us or go without, and if you feel your nose thus held to the grindstone by the hard fiscal hand, it's no more than you deserve for harboring treasonable thoughts" (174).

It is in precisely these terms that James identifies the trouble with immigrants. He attributes to them "too crude a confidence," a quality more like "defiance," "insolence," and "presumption." Unwilling to accommodate others and unapologetic in their expectation to be accommodated, immigrants likewise hold the nose of the "native" American to the grindstone by making "us" change without showing adequate willingness to change themselves. To be sure, James relishes "the cheerful hum of that babel of tongues" that characterizes American cities, but he resents that "we, not they, must make the surrender and accept the orientation," that "[w]e must go, in other words, *more* than half-way to meet them" (67). The immigrant ghettos of the Lower East Side and uptown Manhattan were "a quarter of an hour's walk" from Central Park, yet James writes that the immigrants he encounters there—"the fruit of the foreign tree" that had "shaken down there with a force that smothered everything else"—were "as truly in possession . . . as if [they] had had but three steps to come" (90).

Not being met halfway is a crucial figure for being denied the right to collaborate with the object world in the production of meaning. Instead, meaning is handed to him, implicitly but certainly beyond negotiation. Just as the conspicuous display of wealth in architecture insists on an unanswerable impression of "unmitigated publicity," so the alien is held responsible for foreclosing the collaborative process of producing meaning.

If it be asked why, the alien still striking you so as an alien, the singleness of impression, throughout the place, should still be so marked, the answer, close at hand, would seem to be that the alien himself fairly *makes* the singleness of impression. Is not the universal sauce essentially *his* sauce, and do we not feel ourselves feeding, half the time, from the ladle, as greasy as he chooses to leave it for us, that he holds out? (90)

James is discomposed, then, not just by the "singleness of impression" but by the hubris with which immigrants arrogate themselves the exclusive rights to make it. Moreover, as the "rich accretions" of immigrants create increasingly insular ethnic enclaves, each one "may take his time, more and more . . . and he may in fact feel more and more that he can do so on his own conditions." The arrangement is decidedly one-sided: while "the alien is taking his time," the native American "go[es] about with him, sharing, all respectfully, in his deliberation, waiting on his convenience, watching him at his interesting work" (94). It all takes place at the expense of the native American's consent. The very "idea of the country itself" undergoes a "free assault" by immigrants, who "seemed perpetually to insist" on a "readjustment of it in *their* monstrous, presumptuous interest" (67).

The impudence of immigrants is matched only by the impudence of commerce. The hotels and skyscrapers that testify to "the economic idea" (74) similarly overdetermine the process of representation, distilling a stultifying "singleness of impression." "Under pressure of the native conception of the hotel," James writes, "there was often no resisting a vivid view" of the American "genius for organization" (81). Consumerism thrives unchecked in America, which seems to James "a vast clean void expressly prepared for it": "It has nothing either in nature or in man to reckon with—it carries everything before it . . . the perfect, the exquisite adjustability of the 'national' life to the sublime hotel-spirit" (323). In short, the "restored absentee" is cast as embattled and coerced by a dual assault on history. Fascinated by both consumer culture and immigrants, yet silenced by their "unanswerable" performances, James continually stages his own wounded retreat from them. Newly dispossessed, it is not he but they who now "have [their] hands on the whipstock" (86). So an encounter with an Italian, for instance, is an encounter with a "remorseless Italian" (196), and America's "great commercial democracy" is (like the immigrant) "seeking to abound supremely in its own sense and having none to gainsay it" (72).

The second contiguity between *The American Scene*'s treatment of commerce and immigrants is their shared propensity for monstrous reproduction. New York from the Hudson is a "monstrous organism," a body of flinging limbs, hammering fists, and mobile jaws animated by a soul of steel. Its limbs are the bridges, neither measurable nor containable, "subject . . . to certain, to fantastic, to merciless multiplication" (59). This superhuman reproducibility is then put in terms of color.

> [T]he breezy brightness of the Bay puts on the semblance of the vast white page that awaits beyond any other perhaps the black overscoring of *science*. Let me hasten to add that its present whiteness is precisely its charming note, the frankest of the signs you recognize and remember it by. That is the distinction I was just feeling my way to name as the main ground of its doing so well, for effect, without technical scenery . . . [M]emory and the actual impression keep investing New York with the tone, predominantly, of summer dawns and winter frosts, of sea-foam, of bleached sails and stretched awnings, of blanched hulls, of scoured decks, of new ropes, of polished brasses, of streamers clear in the blue air. (59–60)[10]

Whiteness would seem less clearly linked to race here were it not for the fact that "merciless multiplication" is also what James soon attributes to nonwhite people. This passage stages an "investment"—to use his own term for the activity of his memory and impressions—in the whiteness that his representations produce. Under siege, this whiteness is associated with frankness, "candour of avidity," and "freshness of audacity" (59, 60). More important, it is tied explicitly to history, experience, familiarity—the crucial "sign" by which "you recognize and remember" the city. The excessiveness of the city's mechanical reproduction registers here as a threat to its most "charming note," "its present whiteness," which, for its own part, registers as an absence, a lack of the "technical scenery" that animates some European cities. A patient victim of "black overscorings," the "thin, clear, and colourless" absence that characterizes the "ambient air" is a "permitting medium." It awaits an occupying presence, mustering not even the feeblest resistance to the city's inexorable "will to grow" and provoking in James the exasperated question "What would it ever say 'no' to?" (43).

Identified with an idealized whiteness, the version of the city James holds dear is a violated mother, subject to the irrepressible advances of a masculinized "science" and conscripted in a project of perpetual repro- duction. Her monstrous offspring is a quasi-mechanical "loose limb[ed]" creature, to whom she adds by "binding" it with "stitches" that must always "fly further and faster and draw harder," "all under the sky and over the sea" (59). This passage's discomfort about modernization is not exactly an allegory of the perceived threat of sexualized black men to vir- tuous white women. But its close association with this anxiety, which underwrote fears of and laws against racial miscegenation, is evident in James's idiom and figure. The one-drop rule controlled when race claims were adjudicated, and here it emerges in "the unredeemed com- mercialism that should betray his paternity," the "black overscorings" of a rapacious father "science" (52).[11]

Intoxicated by "the hotel-spirit," American civilization cannot say "no" to consumer culture's racialized sexual advances. She becomes the "gre- garious state," "the whole immense promiscuity"; and "the promiscuity carries . . . everything before it" (79). The Pullman train, like the hotel with which James equates it ("Pullmans are like rushing hotels and the hotels like stationary Pullmans") is identified with promiscuous mater- nity (300). Just as "some monstrous unnatural mother might leave a fam- ily of unfathered infants on doorsteps or in waiting rooms," so the Pull- man leaves a trail of disfigured nature behind as it passes through the country (341). Indeed, James tires of the frequency with which he must "all pensively suffer" being shown "the American social order in the guise of a great blank unnatural mother, a compound of all the recreant individuals misfitted with the name" (318). It is a burden to keep wit- nessing the desecration of virtuous white motherhood at the hands of commerce, a burden from which, as I shall elaborate, James feels he deserves relief.

Like the consumer culture to which they are analogized, nonwhites in *The American Scene* never fail to raise the specter of mass production— "mass" in both its excessive quantity and in the identity of each of its products. As Sara Blair and Jonathan Freedman have argued separately, the Jew in particular "consistently stands for that 'portentous' too much, 'too many,' to which the 'brooding critic' always 'come[s] back with the gasp' of refused or controverted mastery" (Blair 189). For James, it is the Jew who most embodies the logic of mass reproduction, "whose power to forge a new America 'make[s] the observer gasp with the sense of isolation'" (Blair 189). Freedman similarly notes that James's *The Golden Bowl* identifies Jews with "unchecked sexual reproduction" and "cultural reproduction." In *The American Scene*, "a Jewry that had burst all bounds" arises from New York's Lower East Side. Representing this "flood" of humanity as the result of excessive reproduction, James is struck by both the quality and the quantity of the evidence.

> There is no swarming like the swarming of Israel when once Israel has got a start, and the scene here bristled, at every step, with the signs and sounds, immitigable, unmistakable, of a Jewry that had burst all bounds. That it has burst all bounds in New York, almost any combination of figures or of objects taken at hazard sufficiently proclaims. (100)

So self-evident is the excessiveness, in other words, that even an arbitrary canvas of the scene reveals it. Having "burst all bounds" in New York, the Jewish flood may expand without restraint: "I remember how the rising waters, on this summer night, rose, to the imagination, even above the housetops and seemed to sound their murmur to the pale distant stars" (101).

However gently deployed, the flood is a common anti-immigrant trope, but it is worth remarking here because of the peculiar type of agency it suggests. Anticipating the more sharply anti-Semitic nativism of Madison Grant in *The Passing of the Great Race* (1916) and Lothrop Stoddard in *The Rising Tide of Color against White World Supremacy* (1927), James's account in *The American Scene* locates the Jew's threat in no particular quality of ethnic character or malice other than a propensity to reproduce. Excessive reproducibility fails to alarm James in the way it will Grant and Stoddard, suggesting instead, "in its far spreading light and its celestial serenity of multiplication," the more benign vision of a "New Jerusalem on earth" (101). Yet it is the Jew's seemingly infinite capacity for multiplication that most strikes him.

> It was as if we had been thus, in the crowded, hustled roadway, where multiplication, multiplication of everything, was the dominant note,

at the bottom of some vast sallow aquarium in which innumerable fish, of overdeveloped proboscis, were to bump together, for ever, amid heaped spoils of the sea. The children swarmed above all—here was multiplication with a vengeance; and the number of very old persons, of either sex, was almost equally remarkable. (100)

Twin testaments to excessive reproduction, children are everywhere in evidence, and the elderly, for their part, proliferate as well. Like the city's own mode of reproduction, the Jewish "race" multiplies itself in a bestial, autogenic fashion.

[I]s it simply that the unsurpassed strength of the race permits the chopping into myriads of fine fragments without loss of race-quality? There are small strange animals known to natural history, snakes or worms, I believe, who, when cut into pieces, wriggle away contentedly and live in the snippet as completely as in the whole. So the denizens of the New York Ghetto, heaped as thick as splinters on the table of a glass-blower, had each, like the fine glass particle, his or her individual share of the whole hard glitter of Israel. (100)

The propagation of the Jews is so superhuman that they deserve little credit or blame themselves—"it could only be the gathered past of Israel mechanically pushing through" (101). James absolves the Jews of agency, but only by recasting their ubiquity as irrational—"they were all there for race, and not, as it were, for reason" (101). Though James calls the Jews "an intellectual people," their irrational quality is figured by turns as "mechanical" and animal—he finds "irresistible" the similarity between the fire escapes "with which each house-front bristles" and a "cage for the nimbler class of animals" in a zoo: "it seems to offer a little world of bars and perches and swings for human squirrels and monkeys" (102). Thus, if Jews are cast in James's work as peculiar among nonwhites in their link to the market and their retention of ethnicity despite diasporic dislocations, they join other nonwhites in *The American Scene* in a spectacle of infinite reproducibility, a spectacle in which their collaborator is "the whole immense promiscuity" of the hotel, the Pullman, and industry's "black overscorings" of "thin, clear, and colourless" "present whiteness."

In a later and more popular critique of American mass culture,

Dwight MacDonald's *Against the American Grain* would disparage postwar America for the way it "mixes, scrambles everything together, producing . . . homogenized culture." "Mass culture is very democratic," he continues, for "it refuses to discriminate against or between anything" (12). The terms of this indictment and its tone of sweeping generalization are anticipated in James's earlier lament in *The American Scene,* where America looks hopelessly mixed, scrambled, and homogenized; where its democratic ideal amounts to "the jealous cultivation of the common mean only, the reduction of everything to an average of decent suitability" (325). But it is MacDonald's assertion of the consequent impossibility of making distinctions, of discriminating against or between anything, that most precisely reiterates the concern James voices in *The American Scene.* There are two agents of the decline of the possibility for making distinctions, two agents of the collapse of natural differences into a muddled mix: commerce and foreigners. To be sure, James insists that an ideal social order is characterized by heterogeneity, but it is a legible heterogeneity, one that is properly grasped by making distinctions and keeping distinct elements in productive tension. These critical practices are imperiled by the "promiscuous" mixing that is performed inexorably by America's "commercial democracy," on one hand, and its melting *"pot au feu,"* on the other (50). In America, "the parts of life and the signs of character have . . . been lumped together . . . indistinguishably sunk in the common fund of mere economic convenience" (71). In America, unlike Europe, "every one is, for the lubrication of the general machinery, practically in everything" (79). Of all the reciprocities between consumer culture and race in James's problematic of modernity, this challenge to distinction making is the most important. It goes most directly to the need to produce an alternative account of whiteness.

On one hand, James is concerned with grouping, with noticing similarities that coalesce into types, as is indicated by his question about the Harvard men, "Whom did they look like the sons of?" But the corollary to grouping is making distinctions, an exercise that has been pointedly linked to the preservation of class hierarchies by Pierre Bourdieu. In *Distinction,* Bourdieu suggests that "the whole language of aesthetics is contained in a fundamental refusal of the facile . . . that 'pure taste,' purely negative in its essence, is based on the disgust that is often called 'visceral' . . . for everything that is 'facile'" (486). As James strings together abstract, synecdochic categories of value in the following passage, we hear the revulsion to which Bourdieu refers. It is a refusal of "the usual" that takes the form of an insistence on distinction making, on noticing deviations from the standard, whether in goods or people.

> [T]here are no such pleasure-giving accidents, for the mind, as viola-
> tions of the usual in conditions that make them really precarious and
> rare. As the usual, in our vast crude democracy of trade, is the new,
> the simple, the cheap, the common, the commercial, the immediate,
> and, all too often, the ugly, so any human product that those elements
> fail conspicuously to involve or to explain, any creature, or even any
> feature, not turned out to pattern, any form of suggested rarity, sub-
> tlety, ancientry, or other pleasant perversity, prepares us for a recog-
> nition akin to rapture. (53)

Thus, to stake out his own difference—and critical distance—from America's "crude democracy of trade," James asserts the primacy of the faculties of observation that make distinctions.

Commerce and immigrants are cast as "vulgar," and as Bourdieu writes, " 'vulgar' works are not only a sort of insult to refinement, a slap in the face to a 'demanding' (*difficile*) audience which will not stand for 'facile' offerings; they arouse distaste and disgust by the methods of seduction . . . which they try to use, giving the spectator the sense of being treated like any Tom, Dick, or Harry who can be seduced by tawdry charms which invite him to regress to the most primitive and elementary forms of pleasure" (486). The difficult task of distinction making, then, is itself a mark of one's own distinction. "The refusal of what is easy in the sense of simple, and therefore shallow, and 'cheap,' because it is easily decoded and culturally 'undemanding,' " writes Bourdieu, "naturally leads to the refusal of what is facile in the ethical or aesthetic sense, of everything which offers pleasures that are too immediately accessible and so discredited as 'childish' or 'primitive' (as opposed to the deferred pleasures of legitimate art)." Thus, rather than ingest the facile offerings that other Americans consume, James takes satisfaction in having delib-erately "starved" his aesthetic appetite. This satisfaction itself serves both to constitute and to compensate for his sense of hunger: "These lonely ecstasies of the truly open sense make up often, in the hustling, bustling desert, for such 'sinkings' of the starved stomach as have led one too often to have to tighten one's aesthetic waistband" (53). Rejecting vulgar, facile satisfactions, the project of distinction making is its own reward, compensation through deprivation.

So resilient are the obstacles to distinction making that documenting the observer's persistence in spite of them becomes itself one of *The American Scene*'s central concerns. "I grope for their features and seek in vain to discriminate between sorts and conditions," James writes of his effort to represent the hotel patrons, but their "scant diversity of type . . . left me short, as a story-seeker or picture-maker" (335). The capacity to make distinctions becomes itself the mark of distinction among a staggeringly uncritical public. Over against a "nation [that] is almost feverishly engaged in producing . . . an intellectual pabulum after its own heart," James produces an alternative to the pabulum, an account that not only makes distinctions but, in so doing, also seeks to render indispensable the high culture with which distinction making is equated.

Where James discusses distinction making as a matter of exercising one's critical faculties, his figures consistently invoke color. Specifically, they turn on whiteness and the difficulty in America of differentiating among its various appearances. He pronounces it "the genius of the American land and the American people to abhor, whenever may be, a discrimination." He contends that Americans make discriminations "as lightly and scantily as possible" (225–26). This failure to discriminate is as much the deficiency of the physical landscape—in which James finds a "criminal continuity"—as of Americans themselves (342). As James struggles to "dissociate" his memory of his trip from Philadelphia to Baltimore "from anything else in the world," he develops an earlier figure. He calls this scene's failure to distinguish itself "only another case of the painting with a big brush, a brush steeped in crude universal white, and of the colossal size this implement was capable of assuming."

> Gradations, transitions, differences of any sort, temporal, material, social, whether in man or in his environment, shrank somehow, under its sweep, to negligible items; and one had perhaps never yet seemed so to move through a vast simplified scheme. The illustration was once more, in fine, of the small inherent, the small accumulated resistance, in American air, to any force that does not simplify. (226)

The size of the brush and the crude universal quality of the white forbid internal distinctions. Both Patricia McKee and Alan Trachtenberg have argued that the power of American whiteness in James is precisely this absorptive inclusiveness—its capacity to be, as McKee claims, the embodiment of inclusivity; simultaneously, in Richard Dyer's formulation, "everything and nothing at all"; or, as Trachtenberg claims, an identity whose basis in an act of identification, rather than fixed heredity (consent rather than descent), serves to eliminate color distinctions.[12]

But like many of his more xenophobic contemporaries, James has not made his peace with this "crude universal" version of whiteness. He goes on to figure the foreclosure of distinctions that is brought on by commercialization as a threat that one version of whiteness poses to another: "The spread of this single great wash of winter from latitude to latitude struck me in fact as having its analogy in the vast vogue of some infinitely-selling novel . . . with as little possibility of arrest from 'criticism' in the one case as from the bleating of lost sheep in the other" (226). Earlier, the crude and universal whitewash of assimilation masked real distinctions and required James's recovery of whiteness for "authentically" white Americans. Here, that "false" whiteness is refigured as the single great wash of winter that—barring the intervention of the same critical faculty that opposes mass culture—threatens to obscure the bleating sheep.

The market collapses distinctions, James suggests, by reducing everything to a logic of equivalence among commodities—some more expensive and some less, but all equally measurable in terms of money. The distinct cultural "forms" from which one might read a society become merely temporary vessels for what he characterizes as a fluid movement of capital. In a declaration that anticipates late capitalism's global commodity flows and flexible accumulation, James calls the market "an interested passion that, restless beyond all passions, is for ever seeking more pliable forms" and a "perpetual passionate pecuniary purpose which plays with all forms, which derides and devours them, though it may pile up the cost of them in order to rest a while, spent and haggard, in the illusion of their finality" (61, 85).[13] Thus, the goods in the shops that line the corridor of a Florida hotel, for example, are indistinguishable from one another according to the logic of equivalence, a logic that extends even to the shops' patrons.

[T]he elements of difference, whatever they might latently have been, struck me throughout as forcibly simplified by the conditions of the place; this prompt reducibility of a thousand figures to a common denominator having been in fact, to my sense, the very moral of the picture. Individuality and variety is attributed to "types" in America, on easy terms . . . so that what I was most conscious of, from aspect to aspect, from group to group, from sex to sex, from one presented boarder to another, was the continuity of the fusion, the dimness of the distinctions. (333–34)

By contrast, James observes that in Washington, D.C., for once "in our vast commercial democracy," "nobody was in 'business'" (252). Instead, "the force really in possession . . . consist[ed] but of a small company of people engaged perpetually in conversation" (251). Much like the participants in the bourgeois public sphere of Habermas's account, who are said to have performed through conversation their abstraction into a self-conscious public, "it is about herself *as* the City of Conversation precisely" that Washington "incessantly converses" (253). Also like the eighteenth-century bourgeois public, Washington society is characterized by the illusion of its exemption from and opposition to the "vulgar," "vociferous" mass market. This exemption "was the only way in which, over the land, a difference *could* be made," and the only way in which any difference "acquires prodigious relief"—the kind of relief of which the bleating sheep are deprived by the "single great wash" of occluding whiteness (254).

It is for some "relief," then, in both senses of the term, that James pursues the strategy of containment I take up in the next section of this chapter. Writing an alternative version of whiteness in response to consumer culture and immigrants, he seeks relief from the difficulty they pose to his project of distinction making. He also seeks to throw into relief a racialized group of people (bound by consanguinity) who would otherwise disappear like sheep in a snowstorm.

Whiteness as Consolation and Compensation

In their recent work on whiteness, George Lipsitz has examined the material effects of white Americans' "possessive investment in whiteness," and Cheryl Harris has made the case for whiteness as property.[14] Having sketched the terrain that produces James's desire for "relief," I turn now to a set of local encounters along the eastern seaboard in order to develop the idea, following Lipsitz and Harris, that whiteness is reconstructed in *The American Scene* as consolation and compensation.

Reflecting on his visit to Ellis Island, James writes, "[My] sense of dispossession . . . haunted me so, I was to feel . . . that the art of beguiling or duping it became an art to be cultivated" (67). Tricking himself out of feeling dispossessed, he makes recourse to a version of American whiteness that may not be visible or traceable but is there nonetheless. To represent it, he is compelled to render it through such visual metaphors as the ones I have noted, but these metaphors necessarily break down, because he is not really talking about color. One example puts a finer point on it. The visit of "any sensitive citizen" to Ellis Island, James writes, "shakes him—or at least I like to imagine it shakes him—to the depths of his being; I like to think of him, I positively have to think of him, as going about ever afterwards with a new look, for those who can see it, in his face, the outward signs of a new chill in his heart. So is stamped, for detection, the questionably privileged person who has had an apparition, seen a ghost in his supposedly safe old house" (66). It is interesting that the effect is "a new look, for those who can see it, in his face," but much more significant is James's professed willfulness: he imagines, he likes to think of, and he positively has to think of the questionably privileged person as newly stamped. More important than the fact that this "new look" is figured as a change in the face is the injunction James feels to recast the native visitor with a new stamp. The art he has been compelled to "cultivate" is "the art of beguiling or duping" his "sense of dispossession," not resolving it so much as evading it.

Dana Nelson writes, "What white men are symbolically promised by national/white manhood"—that is, "a space where men can step out of competitive, hierarchically ordered relations and experience rich emotional mutuality of fraternal sameness"—"is almost never what they get" (19). *The American Scene* advocates neither sameness nor the leveling of social hierarchies, yet the promise of the "rich emotional mutuality" and escape from the competitive structure of market relations that Nelson identifies everywhere mark James's nostalgic, idealized version of white manhood. In the course of examining what she calls "fraternal practices and imaginings," Nelson "repeatedly discovered that white men seem able to achieve the equalitarian reassurance of unmediated brotherhood only with dead or imagined men" (x). The texts in her study are "melancholic echo chambers, disrupted by the repeating claims of national manhood's others, crisscrossed by ungrievable losses" (179). *The American Scene* is just such an echo chamber. Since "there was no escape" for James "from the ubiquitous alien into the future, or even into the present" ("there was an escape but into the past"), he, too, finds the consolation of unmediated brotherhood only with dead or imagined men (68). The text is an elegy to an imagined national fraternity that offers refuge from the market but that can only be posited retrospectively, as a loss. Along with "unity" and "equality," the third "great continental condition" James identifies is not fraternity but "prosperity," and Americans have paid for this prosperity, he avows, with their fraternity, their "consanguinity" (286). What they are left with is "a necessary vicious circle of gross mutual endurance," consanguinity's antithesis (175).

James's recollection of two encounters—one with Italian laborers in New Jersey and another with an Armenian in New Hampshire—leads to his most self-reflexive engagement with what he admits is an idealization of America, "some close and sweet and whole national consciousness" (66). Specifically, it is the impossibility of conversation that provokes him. But his account of both encounters makes clear that conversation stands in here for something far less concrete and far more affective than mere talk. His desire to interact with the laborers was foreclosed, he recalls, by the lack of "mutual recognition, founded on old familiarities and heredities, and involving, for the moment, some impalpable exchange." Since the men were "Italians of the superlatively southern type," James writes, "any impalpable exchange struck me as absent from the air to positive intensity, to mere unthinkability" (91). It is not the absence of conversation itself that James bemoans, in other words, but a specifically "impalpable exchange," an unspoken affinity rooted in something prior to the conversation but that the conversation would express and represent.

Two dimensions of this nonexchange are worth emphasizing. First, it is keyed to "type," which is cast in the genetic terms of "familiarity" and "heredity": what makes the foreclosed exchange impalpable is its dependence on shared race. Second, the absence of an exchange is so intense as to take on a positive quality. This is the paradoxical logic of whiteness not only in *The American Scene* but also—Toni Morrison and Richard Dyer have argued—in a great deal of American cultural representations: how to represent an absence with such intensity that it takes the form but not the substance of racial presence and particularity. A difference that is understood as racial short-circuits the exchange with the Italians. What its failure gives shape to is James's own (non)race, which emerges in its contrast with the Italians' "superlatively southern type." Faced with "aliens in the first grossness of their alienism," his American whiteness is a "void that could make it no response" (92, 11).

Having lost his way during a "ramble among the New Hampshire hills," James has an equally troubling nonexchange with a deceptively American-looking young man, whom James asks for directions.

> [H]is stare was blank, in answer to my inquiry, and, seeing that he failed to understand me and that he had a dark-eyed "Latin" look, I jumped to the inference of his being a French Canadian. My repetition of my query in French, however, forwarded the case as little, and my trying him in Italian had no better effect. "What *are* you then?" I wonderingly asked—on which my accent loosened in him the faculty of speech. "I'm an Armenian," he replied, as if it were the most natural thing in the world for a wage-earning youth in the heart of New England to be. (91)

What is so jarringly denied in both New Jersey and New Hampshire is the consoling fiction of the "imagined fraternity of white men," a racialized identification meant to transcend and compensate for difference and antagonism. James longs for the "vague warmth" of the days when "any honest man" could count on "a social relation with any encountered type" (91), which is only to say no particular type at all, a nonparticularity that characterized whiteness in this context. Gone is that "space where men can step out of competitive, hierarchically ordered relations," as Nelson puts it, "and experience rich emotional mutuality of fraternal sameness" (19). In *The American Scene,* James was to find this "social relation" "drop out again and again." Visiting Ellis Island was said to provoke in the observer a new look in the face and new chill in the heart. In New Hampshire, it was "rather a chill, straightaway, for the heart, and rather a puzzle, not less, for the head," to find this "social relation with any encountered type" "so suddenly dropping out, in the land of universal brotherhood" (91). It is to take off the chill and to keep the puzzling at bay, I am suggesting, that James makes recourse to the consoling explanatory power of American whiteness.

Why did James not just dispense with the idea of a united American race altogether? After all, immigration's "too-defiant scale of numerosity and quantity" strains his notion of "American" as a singular racial identity. The tenacity with which James and his contemporaries held fast to this identity is an index of their possessive investment, however inadvertent, in whiteness. The resilience of the family as the paradigm for the nation prevents him from reformulating national identity in other terms. "The sense of the elements in the cauldron—the cauldron of the 'American' character," he writes, "becomes thus about as vivid a thing as you can at all quietly manage." While this unmanageability "is not directly adverse to joy," it is troubling insofar as "the question settles into a form which makes the intelligible answer further and further recede." The resolutely settled form that the question of American identity takes suggests that the limits of white American identity have been reached—or, if not reached, finally glimpsed—and that its principle of inclusiveness has been finally pressed to its limit. James puts it to himself in earnest, "What meaning . . . can continue to attach to such a term as the 'American' character?—what type, as the result of such a prodigious amalgamation, such a hotch-potch of racial ingredients, is to be conceived as shaping itself?" (93). What type indeed, for it cannot exactly be called white—it includes too much; yet neither, evidently, can America be reimagined as something other than white. American whiteness already subsumes too many types to deserve the designation "white," as James has known it, and it tends only toward subsuming more. So where might he draw the distinction?

In this form—its only, irreducible form—the question of white American identity prompts James frankly to take occasional refuge. Acknowledging that a truly tireless observer would pursue such questions relentlessly, James admits his own fatigue and, unable to formulate the questions otherwise, invokes the luxury of turning away.

The challenge to speculation, fed thus by a thousand sources, is so intense as to be, as I say, irritating but practically, beyond doubt, I should also say, you take refuge from it—since your case would otherwise be hard; and you find your relief not in the least in any direct satisfaction or solution, but absolutely in that blest general drop of the immediate need of conclusions, or rather in that blest general feeling for the impossibility of them. (92–93)

The "too-defiant scale of numerosity and quantity" becomes, in itself, a solution to the problem posed by the "hotch-potch of racial ingredients." On one hand, they make it impossible to discern a singular American type; on the other hand, they justify abandoning the task of asserting a positive and general definition for whiteness. The inability to say becomes itself a kind of luxury. The deferral permits James to obscure the contradiction he has surfaced: how to preserve the viability of whiteness yet recognize the "amalgamated" racial status of the "American" character.

It is more than a comfort to him, truly, . . . this too-defiant scale of numerosity and quantity—the effect of which is to multiply the possibilities, so to open, by the million, contingent doors and windows: he rests in it at last as an absolute luxury, converting it into a substitute, into *the* constant substitute, for many luxuries that are absent. He doesn't *know*, he can't *say*, before the facts, and he doesn't even want to know or to say. (93)

Making a virtue of necessity, James sees the impossibility of distinguishing an American type not as a challenge to the very notion of an American type (for that would obviate the entire task of representation he has appointed himself) but, rather, as an inducement to relieve himself of the responsibility of representing it in positive terms. The ever-multiplying contingencies forbid such a generalized representation. It is simply an imagined fraternal sameness projected onto the past.

The consolidation of a national American whiteness—specifically one that compensates for the difficulty of understanding the nation as an intimate family—is forcefully dramatized in the chapters on the South. For James, the South is romantic, its old order nobly bearing the burden for its former deluded reliance on slavery (that "so fallacious presumption") and for its defeat in the Civil War (276). Richmond seems to him an invalid—"a patient who has been freely bled" (287)—and Charleston a "sick lioness who has visibly parted with her teeth and claws" (307). "One understood at a glance," writes James, how the "Southern black . . . must loom, how he must count, in a community in which . . . there were comparatively so few other things." In fact, "all the voices of the air" conspired to tell him "that the negro had always been, and could absolutely not fail to be, intensely 'on the nerves' of the South" (276–77). The southern black is not only on the minds but on the nerves of southern whites—not simply in their midst, but an intimate presence.

It is blacks' intimacy that short-circuits James's representation of America as a social whole. In fact, his recollection of two groups of "tatterdemalion darkies" in particular poses an obstacle to the project (276). Sounding frighteningly like a marksman on safari, James first recalls that a "formidable question" "rose suddenly like some beast that had sprung from the jungle" when, at a train station in Washington, D.C., "an African type or two . . . lounged and sunned themselves within range" (276). He leaves the question unstated, but it is the same question white patricians asked and answered obsessively, from Jefferson in *Notes on the State of Virginia* to the early twentieth century's so-called experts on "the Negro question": namely, what is to be done with freed people? To James, the group in Washington was the integrationist's nightmare, for they "represented the Southern black as we knew him not, and had not within the memory of man known him, at the North," and "to see him there, ragged and rudimentary, yet all portentous and 'in full possession of his rights as a man,' was to be not a little discomposed, was to be in fact very much admonished" (276). What exactly James feels admonished for is not entirely clear, whether for the state's having denied African Americans these rights in the past or, to the contrary, for the state's having recently granted them. What is clearer is how much less certain America's future looks and how little it is likely to resemble its past. The redrawing of the boundaries of citizenship to include such "ragged and rudimentary" "darkies" marks a change in America unprecedented in "the memory of man."

But this is only because, as I have argued, James casts citizenship as an intimate relation—indeed, as "one's supreme relation." At no other point in American history did African Americans and Anglo Americans come into such intimate contact as during slavery, yet their post-emancipation encounters in public spaces count, for James and many of his white contemporaries, as intimate. Or to use James's own term for this intimacy, it is when African Americans appear "at home" in public. This impression of their being newly "at home" is what the second group of African Americans leaves. He recalls having walked on "a wide, steep street" in Richmond, "a place of traffic, of shops and offices and altogether shabby Virginia vehicles," and having noticed that the vehicles were "in charge of black teamsters." What this sight "emphasized . . . with every degree of violence" was "that already apprehended note of the negro really at home" (278). The immediate effect of this apprehension is not simply to introduce an uncomfortable wrinkle in James's idea of America but to destabilize it utterly. Newly conscious of the impossibility of stabilizing "America" and of the evasions it would require, he gropes about the object world for something he can call "a definite fact." He worries, of what does "the American picture" consist?

> [I]t melts away, with a promptitude of its own almost . . . ; and though the restless analyst has arts of *his* own for fixing and saving it—as he at least on occasion fondly flatters himself—he is too often reduced to wondering what it can have consisted of in a given case save exactly that projected light of his conscience. Richmond—*there* at least was a definite fact—is a city of more or less nobly precipitous hills. (278)

The city's name and its topography become the only refuge for representation, the only reliable facts. This is a meager version of representation indeed for an artist so committed to pressing beyond the journalist's mere enumeration of facts. Yet it is what James resorts to in the face of the realization—prompted by the sight of "the negro really at home"—that he cannot say certainly and without the possibility of distortion what the American picture "can have consisted of in a given case." He makes recourse to flat-footed empirical claims, recalling finally "no intellectual consequence whatever" of his visit to this avenue "but the after-sense of having remounted it again on the opposite side"—a conspicuously unembellished account of a hilly walk (278). In short, what turns out to have been "admonished" is James's very faculty of representation itself.

From an intimate encounter with African Americans that "discomposed" and "admonished" him and another that prevents him from "fixing" his American picture without excessive artifice, James finds solace in national white manhood. When the son of a Confederate soldier ("a gallant and nameless, as well as a very handsome, young Virginian") speaks to him at the Confederate Museum in Richmond, the figure of "the Southern negro" becomes the target for an imaginary violence, a fantasy that produces a white manhood in which both James and the Virginian can take part. The Virginian recalls his father's wartime exploits; he "related, felicitously, some paternal adventures of which I have forgotten the particulars, but which comprised a desperate evasion of capture, or worse, by the lucky smashing of the skull of a Union soldier" (285). Having complimented the Virginian on the precision of his account of the smashing of the skull ("these old, unhappy, far-off things"), James found the Virginian's "candid response charmingly suggestive": " 'Oh, I should be ready to do them all over again myself!' And then, smiling serenely, but as if it behoved even the least blatant of Northerners to understand: 'That's the kind of Southerner *I* am!' " This is an account of violence between white men, a Confederate and a Union soldier. But James immediately displaces it with the soothing recognition of a racial solidarity that transcends and imaginatively heals the sectarian division between North and South. The solidarity is forged from white violence—or, more accurately, white fantasies of violence—toward blacks.

> I allowed that he was a capital kind of Southerner, and we afterwards walked together to the Public Library, where, on our finally parting, I could but thank him again for being so much the kind of Southerner I had wanted. He was a fine contemporary young American, incapable, so to speak, of hurting a Northern fly—*as* Northern . . . [T]hough he wouldn't have hurt a Northern fly, there were things (ah, we had touched on some of these!) that, all fair, engaging, smiling as he stood there, he would have done to a Southern negro. (286)

A proud son of the Confederacy, the Virginian would not really have hurt anything northern, James thinks, dismissing his claim as an idle threat. But the proposed violence toward "a Southern negro," the "things he would have done" that the text gestures toward but refrains from naming, seem certain. The Virginian would not duplicate his father's act by braining another Northerner, but he would certainly, happily, do violence to "a Southern negro."

In this narrative of national racial history writ small, the fantasy of racial violence becomes the currency of an important exchange. Reconciling North and South on the basis of a national whiteness, it transcends and unifies regions divided along political lines by asserting the priority of race. James celebrates the rechanneling of southern resentment over the defeat of the Confederacy into fantasies of violence against blacks, in which not only southern but northern whites too can participate. This is why the Virginian is not simply a Southerner but also "a fine contemporary young American"; in his invitation to participate in a white manhood that is consolingly national, he is precisely "the kind of Southerner" James "had wanted" (286).

The South of *The American Scene* is thus no less "imprisoned in" and "overdarkened by" the "intimate presence of the negro" than during slavery. Around an imagined shared peril and imprisonment, whites consolidate the intimacy of the bond of whiteness. This intimacy proves to be the effect of the perceived imposition of nonwhites. This is clear even in the North, where James finds that perfect consanguinity has, in one case, been attained. The perfect consanguinity of Philadelphia, he contends, is the result of its having eliminated immigrants. But as his account unfolds, it becomes clear that it is the result of having eliminated them from view yet preserved them as a perpetual threat, a constitutive outside that is felt always on the verge of intruding. Philadelphia can be called "a society" in a way that New York and Chicago cannot, James writes, for the latter are subject to "alteration, extension, and development," and their neighborhoods are one-third empty and one-third "objectionably filled" (206). Since James's premise is that "what makes a society [is] the number of organic social relations it represents," Philadelphia is the consummate society, "representing nothing *but* organic social relations." In fact, James notes, "every individual was as many times over cousin, uncle, aunt, niece, and so on through the list, as poor human nature is susceptible of being" (206). Realizing James's ideal, Philadelphia "wasn't a place, but a state of consanguinity, which is an absolute final condition" (206). "Society" is conceived on the model of the family. But family proves to be a euphemism for race, since it is the absence of "the grosser aliens" that renders the place "solely and singly Philadelphian . . . covered *all* over by perfect Philadelphians." James observes that the "sharp note of the outlandish, in the strict sense of the word," which he "had found almost everywhere so disconcerting" was "soothing[ly] . . . absent" (208). In short, what was "required" to "consummate" James's image of Philadelphia as "intimate with that intimacy" he "had tasted, from the first," was "this elimination of the foreign element" (217, 209).

However, it is not just the *elimination* of immigrants that confers intimacy and self-identity on this society, but rather a currency of fear of "the foreign element." Were nonwhites truly absent (not just out of sight, but out of mind), the fear that facilitates white racial identity would be obviated. In this sense, though immigrants are absent from immediate view, they are importantly present. James insists that "we" might "still distinguish" "the common arks by which these companies" of Philadelphians "are known"—these "fragments and ghosts of old social orders"—even "through their bedimmed condition." What is that "bedimmed condition" if not the nonwhite threat that also "overdarkens" the South? What, if not shared race claims, are the "common arks" by which the residents could be "known," the traces of "old social orders"?

As I have been suggesting, this is a lexicon of whiteness in the process of emerging—less a euphemistic language than a groping to name. It seems symptomatic of a distinctively turn-of-the-century convergence of concerns prompted by a demographic shift in immigration, the popularization of racial science, and the vexed citizen status of African Americans. More instructive still, its articulation is occasioned by a distinctively turn-of-the-century culture of "publicity." "There is the sense for everyone of being in the same boat with everyone else," James notes of Philadelphia, "a closed circle that would find itself happy enough if only it could remain closed enough." His text engages questions of how open American society could be to what seemed like radical alterity yet still "remain closed enough" and of what would serve to close the circle. It proves not to be an immanent quality shared by its constituents but, rather, a mutual fear of everyone outside. James writes, "The boat might considerably pitch, but its occupants would either float merrily together or (almost as merrily) go down together, and meanwhile the risk, the vague danger, the jokes to be made about it, the general quickened sociability and intimacy, were the very music of the excursion" (211). The logic that confers identity and intimacy is a logic of disavowal, a shared sense of the "vague danger" lurking outside. It takes hold despite the internal difference and strife among those on board and despite the possible price (going down together) to be paid for maintaining it. But the consolation for feeling so perpetually imperiled—the compensation that makes it tolerable, even "merry"—is that out of the trial comes whiteness, less a destination than "the very music of the excursion."

4 Race-changes
as Exchanges

THE AUTOBIOGRAPHY OF AN
EX-COLOURED MAN

REFLECTING ON HIS TRAVELS by Pullman coach at the end of *The American Scene,* Henry James imagines a race-change. He speculates that his perceptions would be altered dramatically were he "red" instead of "white," a Native American rather than a "native" American. He scolds the railroad itself: "If I were one of the painted savages you have dispossessed, it wouldn't be to *you* I should be looking in any degree for beauty or for charm. Beauty and charm would be for me in the solitude you have ravaged, and I should owe you my grudge for every disfigurement and every violence, for every wound with which you have caused the face of the land to bleed" (341). Out of sympathetic identification with another "type," he elaborates this critique of the Pullman's social significance, its defilement of "the great lonely land." But he soon comes to a startling realization about his imagined race-change. He notes how the critique it allows him to generate is materially reliant on precisely his not being a Native American: "[I]f I had been a beautiful red man with a tomahawk I should of course have rejoiced in the occasional sandy track, or in the occasional mud-channel . . . Only in that case I shouldn't have been seated by the great square of plate-glass through which the missionary Pullman appeared to invite me to admire the achievements it proclaimed" (342). Transparent yet impenetrable, the plate glass of the Pullman window serves here as both a medium for his vicarious experience and a reminder of the exclusive white privilege of holding that seat in the train car. It simultaneously marks the color line, makes possible an

129

imaginary traversal of the color line, and constitutes that traversal itself
as unequally available.

In an anonymous account of racial "passing" that appeared in *The
Independent* in 1913, the black narrator's light skin enables him to do
exactly what James's red man could not.

> I am a sort of Dr. Jekyll and Mr. Hyde. I can ride in Pullman cars in the
> heart of the South, have my lunch in the best restaurant on my route,
> and stop for the night, as I have done, at the Piedmont hotel, or the
> Desoto, or the Heritage, and then when I am tired of being among
> strange folks I can go down on Auburn avenue in Atlanta, or Lawton
> avenue in St. Louis, and be a negro just as long as I choose. Sometime
> I shall possibly decide to be one or the other for all time, but just now
> the game is too interesting. ("Adventures of a Near-White" 376)

Like James, this narrator identifies the Pullman with the trappings of the
good life that consumer culture promoted. Also like James, he draws the
color line between the quasi-public interior spaces of that consumer culture—its comfortable conveyances, restaurants, and hotels—and the life
"on the avenue." Through the exclusion of life "on the avenue," these
spaces of consumer culture acquire their racial specificity.

In her 1928 novel, *Plum Bun,* Jessie Fauset offers a differently gendered account of this same color line through another fair-skinned black
character. For Mrs. Murray, passing for white affords access to pleasures
of consumption and spectacle that are not merely idle and fleeting but
nearly indispensable.

> It pleased her to stand in the foyer of the Great Hotel or of the Acad-
> emy of Music and to be part of the whirling, humming, palpitating
> gaiety. She had no desire to be of those people, but she liked to look
> on; it amused and thrilled and kept alive some unquenchable instinct
> for life which thrived within her. To walk through Wanamaker's on
> Saturday, to stroll from fifteenth to ninth street on Chestnut, to have
> her tea in the Bellevue Stratford, to stand in the lobby of the St. James
> fitting on immaculate gloves; all innocent, childish pleasures pursued
> without malice or envy contrived to cast a glamour over Monday's
> washing and Tuesday's ironing, the scrubbing of kitchen and bath-
> room and the fashioning of children's clothes . . . Much of this plea-

sure, harmless and charming though it was, would have been impossible with dark skin. (15)

While James and the narrator in *The Independent* use their white bodies to access the all-seeing, mobile, commanding privileges of white masculinity, Mrs. Murray's surrogate body is an alternative to the gender and racial identity that relegate her to domestic labor.

Mrs. Murray's privilege is echoed in Irene Redfield of Nella Larsen's 1929 novel *Passing*. When Irene tires of shopping for her two sons out on the "scorching cement" of the Chicago streets, Larsen writes, she simply "lifted a wavering hand in the direction of a cab parked directly in front of her," and "the perspiring driver jumped out and guided her to his car." As he "helped, almost lifted," her in, she "sank down on the hot leather seat," telling him: "'I guess it's tea I need. On a roof somewhere.'" He suggests the Drayton Hotel ("They do say as how it's always a breeze up there"), and when she steps out of the elevator, she is "led to a table just in front of a long window whose gently moving curtains suggested a cool breeze." Irene thinks this is "like being wafted upward on a magic carpet to another world, pleasant, quiet, and strangely remote from the sizzling one that she had left below" (146–47). Needless to say, as Fauset puts it, this pleasure "would have been impossible with dark skin."

By citing these excerpts together, I do not mean to imply that racial passing always raised questions of consumer culture or that questions of consumer culture always raised questions of race. But in their shared reflection on what is only possible with light skin, the race-change passages from James, *The Independent,* Fauset, and Larsen suggest how deeply ideas about race were informed by emerging consumer culture and how deeply consumer culture's emergence embedded the asymmetries of racial marking. Clearly, the passing narratives that proliferated in the late nineteenth and early twentieth centuries are vital sites for an inquiry into contemporaneous processes of racial formation. The narrative on which I focus in this chapter, James Weldon Johnson's *The Autobiography of an Ex-Coloured Man* (1912), is particularly instructive for its striking representation of a mutually constitutive relationship between race and consumer culture. Before turning to Johnson's text, it will be useful to make some general remarks about the culture of segregation, a culture that conditioned the possibility for—and even required—the racial passing that it policed.

The Historical Moment of the "Ex-Coloured Man"

Race relations between 1900 and World War I were arguably as divisive—and antiblack sentiment about as high—as at any point in U.S. history. The turn of the twentieth century saw the decimation of the black franchise and the proliferation of Jim Crow codes and practices. When the poll tax, property clause, and literacy test were implemented among Louisiana voters at the turn of the century, for example, the number of registered black voters plummeted from 130,334 in 1896 to a mere 1,342 in 1904 (Vann Woodward 85). While the majority of southern states initially applied Jim Crow laws only aboard passenger trains, segregation was extended in the decade after 1900 to waiting rooms and other modes of public transport, to workplaces and state institutions, and to recreation sites and other locally delimited arenas too numerous to name here. The elaborate caste system of Jim Crow not only turned race into a critical axis of public life but also comprehended a broad range of so-called Negroes ("black," "quadroon," "octoroon," "high yellow," "dicty," etc.) and other insufficiently white ethnics within a single, subordinate legal designation: "colored." Nor was segregationist ideology confined to those southern states that were putting the increasingly rigid and convoluted laws on the books. "It was quite common," C. Vann Woodward writes, "to find in the *Nation, Harper's Weekly,* the *North American Review,* or the *Atlantic Monthly* northern liberals and former abolitionists mouthing the shibboleths of white supremacy regarding the Negro's innate inferiority, shiftlessness, and hopeless unfitness for full participation in the white man's civilization" (70). Within a few short years, Vann Woodward writes, "the extremes to which caste penalties and separation were carried in parts of the South could hardly find a counterpart short of the latitudes of India and South Africa." "It is well to admit, and even to emphasize," he adds, that even these laws "are not an adequate index of the extent and prevalence of segregation and discriminatory practices in the South," for "the practices often anticipated and sometimes exceeded the laws" (101).

By keeping races separate, segregation induced and justified the racial antipathy that it was ostensibly meant to deflect. There was a wide-spread perception among southern whites, for instance, that they shouldered an undue financial burden for educating African Americans, even though, as *The Independent* pointed out in 1910, only one-tenth of the money spent on educating white Americans went to black schools ("Burden of the White Taxpayer" 538). In employment, segregation was more commonly de facto than de jure, as "the written or unwritten policies of Jim Crow unionism made segregation superfluous by excluding Negroes from employment" in many trades (Vann Woodward 98). As *The American Scene* showed, the "intimate presence of the Negro" felt by many whites was less the product of any new proximity of association than of the ubiquity of methods to monitor the color line, to transgress the color line, and to punish its transgression. Professor John Spencer Bassett of Trinity College is among those whom Vann Woodward cites as having felt in the first decade of century that "there is today more hatred of whites for blacks and blacks for whites than ever before"; John Temple Graves of Georgia claimed that "the races are wider apart, more antagonistic than in 1865"; and in the same year that W. E. B. DuBois called "the problem of the color line" the defining problem of the coming century, novelist Charles W. Chesnutt contended that "the rights of the Negroes are at a lower ebb than at any time during the thirty-five years of their freedom, and the race prejudice more intense and uncompromising" (Vann Woodward 96). The years around World War I would bring roughly half a million rural, southern blacks to northern, urban areas seeking employment in war-related industries. Despite the immediate outbreaks of racial violence that this tremendous demographic shift precipitated in the late teens, it would in time alter race relations decisively. But prior to 1915, practices of segregation were aggressively pursued, meagerly opposed, and thoroughly naturalized.[1]

As a result, there was a tremendous appeal—some would say an imperative—for light-skinned African Americans to try to "pass," to conceal their African ancestry and live as whites.[2] Novelists from disparate backgrounds were drawn to the related themes of race mixing and passing: while such writers as George Washington Cable, Albion Tourgee, Mark Twain, Frances E. W. Harper, Pauline Hopkins, and Charles Chesnutt used the figures of the mulatto and the "passing" black to explore the violence perpetrated by segregation or to expose the arbitrariness of racial distinctions,[3] such white patricians as Thomas Nelson Page and Thomas Dixon cast these figures as threats to white dominance. Of course, many African Americans who could pass for white chose not to, and passing novels commonly valorize this decision as a gesture of race solidarity or, as Robert Bone puts it, "a symbolic rejection of the . . . unconscious desire to be white" (98). In "Why I Remain a Negro," Walter White estimated that "every year approximately 12,000 white-skinned Negroes disappear—people whose absence cannot be explained by death or emigration."

> Nearly every one of the 14 million discernible Negroes in the United States knows at least one member of his race who is "passing"—the magic word which means that some Negroes can get by as whites, men and women who have decided that they will be happier and more successful if they flee from the proscription and humiliation which the American color line imposes on them. (14)

Though White was writing in 1947, the statistics he cites are less important than the spirit of his statement. Johnson's *The Autobiography of an Ex-Coloured Man* marks an important transition between turn-of-the-century passing narratives and those of the so-called Harlem Renaissance.[4] The first novel published by an African American in the first person, *The Autobiography*'s light-skinned African American narrator-protagonist tells a story of having abandoned his ambition to become a credit to his race in favor of the comforts of a white life. Ambivalent about having deserted his "true" race, the narrator speaks at once to exculpate himself via the reader and to give white Americans a glimpse behind what DuBois had recently called "the veil of race."

The ex-colored man changes his race four times in the course of *The Autobiography*'s narrative, the plot of which is readily summarized. Born shortly after the Civil War, he is the illegitimate son of a wealthy white Georgia man and a "quadroon" seamstress. He is raised by his mother and sees his father seldom as a child and only once, by chance, as an adult. His light skin and fine hair allow him to pass for white, though his partial African ancestry makes him black by custom and by law. He takes himself (and his mother) for white until, at age ten, his teacher reveals what we are to understand as his true race. After recovering from the initial shock, he resolves to become a credit to his race. He briefly attends a black university, pursues several careers in which he is taken to be a Negro, and achieves such notoriety as a ragtime piano player that he secures himself a white patron, whom Johnson also keeps nameless. So dedicated is this patron that he makes a companion and showpiece of the protagonist, who accompanies him on an extended tour of Europe. Here, he finds temporary relief from the strain of living alternately as a fraudulent white and a subordinate black in the United States. At one European performance, however, he is inspired by the prospect of turning ragtime into classical music; he recommits himself to his childhood goal to become a race leader and, defying his patron, returns to the United States to record the black folk culture of the rural South. Here, he is black when it is convenient to be black, and white when it is convenient to be white. Ultimately, however, he finds that his upbringing, his education, and his European refinement have unfit him to live as a subordinate to white Americans. He also witnesses a lynching, which makes him feel ashamed to be black and hastens his move to embrace whiteness once again. Despite his childhood ambition to become a race leader, he avails himself of his light skin privilege and becomes, once and for all, the "ordinarily successful white man" that he is as he narrates (211). As the narrative closes, his racializing process is extended through a domestic retrenchment: he graduates from business school, makes his fortune in real estate, marries a white woman, and raises two white children, of whose African ancestry only he is aware.

The novel reflects on what black and white mean at the turn of the century and offers an incisive critique of white-supremacist ideology and the binary logic of race that supports it. More important, by framing race as a thing that some people get to choose, the novel manages to clear some space to consider what constitutes race in the absence of such visible guarantees as skin color. By suspending biological assumptions about race, it invites readers to think in terms of projects of racial formation and of the many agents such projects involve. What especially interests me is the novel's representation of race as a product of existing relations of consumption and exchange, a product that is enlisted in turn to help reproduce these economic relations. Recent scholarship in labor and social history has challenged the perpetuation of white skin privilege by specifying the historical construction of white subjects. Building on these arguments, I want to suggest that the ex-colored man's abjuration of blackness says as much about processes of white racial formation and white privilege as it does about the experience of blackness in America to which the text is usually supposed to speak.

Race as Performance

Because they are in ignorance of his African ancestry, many of the people who encounter the protagonist of *The Autobiography of an Ex-Coloured Man* do not understand him as black. More interestingly, there are also a number of characters in the novel who know of his African ancestry and nevertheless maintain that he is not black. To begin analyzing the performativity of race, I want to look briefly at three of these latter claims, each of which mobilizes a different account of racial identity.

The first is made by the ex-colored man's mother in response to his having realized, for the first time, that he is black. Though she is the source of his "black blood," his mother is herself passing for white in the Connecticut town in which she raises her son, so until age ten, he is led to believe that he is white. His realization otherwise comes when the school principal enters his classroom and "for some reason" says, "I wish all the white scholars to stand for a moment." Of course, to remain seated would never have occurred to the protagonist, but when he stands, his teacher asks him to "sit down now, and rise with the others." How she alone knows her students' "true" race is a question Johnson leaves unexplained, perhaps assuming that our desire to know how the protagonist will respond to his "fall" from whiteness supersedes our desire for narrative probabilism. In any event, it is framed as an utterly destabilizing "conversion" from one race to another. It requires a total evacuation of the white subject before the black subject can be constructed, sui generis, in its place: "I sat down dazed. I saw and heard nothing. When the others were asked to rise, I did not know it. When school was dismissed, I went out in a kind of stupor" (16). There is no extraracial category of experience to which he can make recourse to mitigate his disorientation, nor is there any longer a unified subject. Bereft of his racial identity, the newly colored man temporarily loses his self.

His classmates immediately move to fix his racial indeterminacy: "A few of the white boys jeered me, saying: 'Oh, you're a nigger too.' I heard some black children say: 'We knew he was colored'" (16). In the haste with which the rigid binary of racial classification is mapped onto the protagonist, we may gauge the investment—among whites and blacks alike, however different their reasons may be—in restoring the "fraud" to his proper race. The text underscores precisely the inadequacy of this system of classification—the incoherence of a single racial category to comprehend everyone of African ancestry, as well as the falsity and violence of the white-supremacist assumptions that authorize this practice. Thus, when the protagonist buries his head in his mother's lap and cries, "Mother, mother, tell me, am I a nigger?" Johnson closely attends to his confusion over her responses. "No, my darling, you are not a nigger," she consoles him, emphasizing, "You are as good as anybody." Her statement significantly makes "nigger" a category of virtue or social prestige rather than simply of race. "If anyone calls you a nigger, don't notice them," she advises, but her advice serves as tacit confirmation that he cannot dispute the label itself.

It is no wonder, then, that the protagonist finds, "the more she talked, the less I was reassured." Having failed to make his race make sense from this approach, he starts over from the other side of the opposition, asking: "Well, mother, am I white? Are you white?" Tellingly, his mother takes the second question first: the logic of hypodescent dictates that answering "I am white" would not necessarily mean "You are white, too," but answering "I am not white" would be tantamount to "You are not white either." She answers "tremblingly," "No, I am not white." As if to prevent her response from also serving as an answer to the first question, the one about himself, she immediately qualifies it: "But you—your father is one of the greatest men in the country—the best blood of the South is in you" (18). Maintaining that his father is not only white but also one of the "greatest" and "best" of whites, his mother's trembling qualifier looks to forestall the force of the one-drop rule. She makes recourse to the quality of his "white blood," when law and custom dictate that only its quantity can matter. The point of the exchange, then, is that an understanding of race as binary and keyed to hypostasized quantities of blood denies her the language to represent him.

Later in the narrative, the ex-colored man's white patron offers a competing account. This account suggests that while the one-drop rule may control socially, there is no reason it should determine the protagonist's self-perception. It arises when the protagonist threatens to abandon the patron in Europe and return to the United States to live as a black man, a proposal the patron opposes strenuously. "My boy," he explains, "you are by blood, by appearance, by education, and by tastes a white man" (144). The claim is instructive in its attempt to anchor the ex-colored man's whiteness in these attributes. It suggests the range of qualities that constitute racial identity. It suggests that while race cannot be verified in and of itself, what can be verified are the blood, appearance, education, and tastes through which race is supposed to express itself. It raises the question of whether his race is therefore reducible to the qualities through which it is expressed, whether these qualities are not merely necessary but sufficient to constitute the ex-colored man as white. The patron goes on to call the narrator's decision to return to the United States "this idea you have of making a Negro out of yourself." "What kind of a Negro would you make now?" he asks (145). The premise seems to be that the protagonist would be compelled to become a Negro if he were to return to the United States, not just to be one again. Framing racial identity as something one can take on, inhabit, and even discard, rather than something one is, the patron's argument seems almost to treat race as a matter of performance: why become black when you are so convincing a white? It turns out, though, that the patron is not offering a strictly performative account of race; he is arguing that whiteness has just as legitimate a biological claim on the protagonist as does blackness. Besides the protagonist's acquired qualities ("white" appearance, education, and tastes), it is his "white blood" that secures his claim to whiteness in the mind of the patron. This inherited quality underwrites the other, acquired qualities—appearance, education, and tastes—turning them into an authentic expression of the protagonist's race rather than a series of effective but nonetheless fraudulent masks over it. What the patron has done, then, is not so much undermine the one-drop rule but invert it. He considers the narrator's "black blood" less significant than his "white blood" and posits, on this basis, an essential whiteness for the protagonist that is authentically expressed in but not reducible to a performance. Like the mother, the patron works within a biological discourse of authenticity, he just proposes turning the one-drop rule on its head rather than continually bumping up against it.

The patron's argument suggests that since the narrator must have a racial identity (he cannot fail to have one at all), it may as well be white as black, since, in strictly biological terms, an equally compelling case can be made for his whiteness. Such a case should be made, if only to point up the brutal arbitrariness of the one-drop rule. Nevertheless, reading the narrator as white for this reason (that he has a legitimate biological claim to whiteness) enables only a limited critique. It challenges assumptions of white supremacy, but it reproduces the assumption that race is a natural, blood-borne phenomenon. Reading the ex-colored man as white might be a provocation to generate more race categories to account for a racially complex citizenry, it might be an insistence on a more supple understanding of existing race categories, or it might even be a suggestion that the kinds of similarities and differences that transcend race matter more than do racial differences. But because it reproduces race itself as natural and whiteness as something essential, reading the narrator as biologically white does not acknowledge the social construction of race. Nor does it acknowledge that race, as a concept and system of marks, is inherently rac*ist*—that race is always an interested way of organizing social bodies, or as Omi and Winant put it, a way of referring to these bodies that "signifies and symbolizes social conflicts and interests" (54–55).

One of the earliest, most incisive performative accounts of race in the United States, Gunnar Myrdal's *An American Dilemma* (1944), instructively stops short of taking its observation of racial performativity to its plausible conclusion. Myrdal, a Swedish economics professor, recounts a story about traveling in the South with an African American colleague who had "some unmistakable Negro features." Though this colleague ordinarily had to haggle with white hotel clerks when he went to meet Myrdal in his room, he found this was not necessary if he acted white.

> He just walked straight in, kept his hat on his head and behaved as a normal white person of the educated class. Nobody bothered him. My explanation is that the ordinary white Southerner, if he sees a man walking into a hotel and carrying himself with assurance and ease, actually *does not see his color*. He, literally, "does not believe his eyes." Behind the Southern whites' not seeing my friend, might also—unconsciously—be the realization of all the trouble it would mean for them to effectuate the caste rules, if they recognized facts, and the great risk they incurred if they were mistaken. (684)

Myrdal advances a provocative hypothesis about racial performativity. He concludes that whites "accustomed to seeing all Negroes in a sub-servient caste role and living in a society where the inconvenience and risk involved in telling a person that he is a Negro are so considerable, will have greater difficulties in recognizing a Negro who steps out of his caste role." But even the thoroughgoing constructivism Myrdal exhibits here has its limits. By saying that the hotel clerk does not see his col-league's color, Myrdal means that he sees white—that is, that he first sees a member of the white race and then consequently understands the somatic features of a white person. Since we do not conventionally disas-sociate race from color, the temporal sequence of the move Myrdal describes—seeing a race, then seeing its corresponding "color"—ordi-narily happens in reverse. Instead of reading race off of behavior and then "color" off of that race, racial apperception ordinarily feels like a recognition first of "color" and then consequently of race.

Thus, when Myrdal writes that the white observer "does not believe his eyes," he actually means that the observer believes them only too well. The point is precisely that the observer's eyes see a whiteness of behavior that prevents them from seeing anything but a corresponding whiteness of somatic features. Somatic whiteness can then be imagined to confirm retroactively the person's status as member of the white race. Yet Myrdal's own account suggests that the observer's eyes fooled his brain. Had it not been for the optical illusion his colleague had mastered, the observer could have known (in the sense that Myrdal himself knew) that the man walking by was black. Thus, even as Myrdal's antiracist project is to disassociate race from color, a move that invites the more radical pos-sibility that race is strictly a performance, he makes recourse to a con-cealed racial essence. Recognizing the performative elements of white-ness does not lead Myrdal to reduce whiteness to a performance. Some performances are optical illusions, his anecdote suggests, while others are authentic expressions.

Reading the ex-colored man as white may give us some rhetorical footing from which to critique tacit but tenacious white-supremacist assumptions, but it seems destined to reproduce the assumption that race is a coherent idea and a naturally occurring phenomenon. At the end of the novel, however, a third account of the ex-colored man's white-ness is articulated, this time from the narrator himself, and this account seems to me to open onto a compelling reading of the novel as a whole. "I am an ordinarily successful white man who has made a little money," he declares on the novel's last page (211). The line is ironic, of course; we know that according to law and custom he is black, however convincingly his light skin enables him to pass for white. Still, I am interested in the implications of reading the line straight. On what basis might we read the ex-colored man as white, but not white in essence? What critical problems and possibilities emerge if we take his claim to whiteness seriously?

One immediate drawback to reading him as the "ordinarily successful white man" he claims to have become is that it undermines a politically important historical investment, especially among nonwhite readers, in understanding him as black. Given the prominent place of the novel in the history of African American literature, I am reluctant to claim the ex-colored man on behalf of some reified version of the white race. But by reading race in this text as a matter of performance, I mean to call attention to its implication in concurrent economic relations of exchange, consumption, and display. Such a reading need not evacuate race of "real" meanings, reducing it to a mere illusion that we would do well to discard, but could instead better position us to notice the novel's suggestion that these meanings—no less real in their effects for having no basis in nature—are made via material processes.

In today's critical moment, we may take the indeterminacy of the narrator's race (either black or white) and make it the basis of a performative reading that was not historically available to Myrdal or to the white patron in Johnson's novel.[5] What would it mean that a black man would have to "make a Negro out of [him]self"? On one hand, the narrator claims a Negro "birthright"—those ties of race that, at the novel's end, he feels he may have sold "for a mess of pottage" (211). On the other hand, the patron suggests that the situation is not that the narrator is a Negro but that he must make himself one. The contradiction is clear: the narrator is supposedly faced with a choice about whether to make himself what he already is. The point, then, is not whether the narrator is black or white—whether he lies or tells the truth about what he is—but that each identity involves a project of making. The incoherence of race is not that you cannot become something that you are not; it is that you cannot become something you already are. Johnson's novel suggests that race is not material but, rather, needs to be materialized; that legal and social fictions operate to constitute the material differences that they name. By showing that the protagonist's race attains its false stability through a "forcible reiteration of regulatory norms," the novel exposes the performativity of race more broadly (Butler 2).

To call race performative is not to say that racial identity is voluntary (and to the extent that it is voluntary, such identificatory mobility has ordinarily accrued to the race that is the cultural dominant). Nor is it to deny somatic differences. But it is to recognize that the peculiar salience and even visibility of certain somatic differences and the groups into which they are supposed to coalesce naturally are effects of the legislation, scientific discourse, and social practices of societies structured by dominance. It is to recognize, further, that the maintenance of these groups requires not just an act—a single act of will or law, for example— but persistent activity.[6]

In one sense, a performative account of race undermines the traditional interpretation of Johnson's project. Henry Louis Gates, Jr., writes in the introduction to the 1989 Vintage edition that *The Autobiography*'s importance is that it "shows in precise detail that racial identity in America is arbitrary, that it is a matter of convention" (xvii). It pursues this antiracist project by revealing just how convincingly a black man can pass for white. Passing is considered subversive because it gives the lie to white supremacy: unencumbered by dark skin, the black characters passing for white reveal their equality with whites in every other respect besides their race designation. Their success at passing suggests the absence of any invidious distinction between races and the lack, therefore, of any basis for white supremacy. But the absence of invidious distinctions that passing implies does not mean that the basis for racial distinctions disappears. To the contrary, the logic of passing presupposes the presence of racial distinctions, however noninvidious. To speak of passing for white, one posits the existence of a blackness that transcends skin color. Otherwise, light-skinned black people would not be passing at all. They would not be black people exploiting their light skin in a color-stratified society; they would just be white people like any others. In other words, the phenomenon of passing—even and especially in its implications for revealing the "conventional" quality of race in America—depends, for its coherence, on a belief in racial differences that preexist and cause other differences, including skin color. Contrast this understanding of race with the view that so-called racial differences are effects—effects, that is, of differences that were constructed juridically and socially but that took on an air of natural inevitability. If one holds this latter view, there is no passing, strictly speaking. Anyone who succeeds at passing becomes—and thus is—the thing for which he or she passes. Passing is subversive insofar as it reveals how convincingly black people pass for white yet still remain black. Otherwise, they are no longer passing but, rather, performing effectively the behaviors that code as race. Passing itself rests on an assumption of racial authenticity that Johnson's novel can be read to challenge.

In advancing a performative reading of race in the novel, I am mindful of the political importance of the strategic essentialism that has historically read mixed-race characters as black. After all, there is a strategic essentialism to the narrator's own self-characterization as black. On it hinge the claims the novel makes, unprecedented in American fiction at the time, about the complex interiority of African Americans and about the richness and sophistication of African American culture, claims that urgently needed to be made in 1912 and arguably still need making. Nevertheless, an essentialism—strategic or inadvertent—that comprehends the protagonist as black is worth pressuring, because it does not help us notice the novel's commitment to particularizing whiteness as well as blackness, to flushing whiteness out of its comfortable unself-consciousness. Early in the narrative, the narrator uses "we" and "them" to identify the young version of himself with his white schoolmates, some of whom cast themselves as the black students' antagonists.

There were some black and brown boys and girls in the school, and several of them were in my class . . . Some of the boys often spoke of them as "niggers." Sometimes on the way home from school a crowd would walk behind them repeating:

"Nigger, nigger, never die,
Black face and shiny eye."

On one such afternoon, one of the black boys turned suddenly on his tormentors and hurled a slate; it struck one of the white boys in his mouth, cutting a slight gash in his lip. At sight of the blood, the boy who had thrown the slate ran, and his companions quickly followed. We ran after them, pelting them with stones, until they separated in several directions. (13–15)

The narrator will soon become incapable of using "we" unself-consciously. Later in the narrative, speaking of his passage by steamship back to the United States from Europe, he makes his acquired self-consciousness explicit. After he introduces himself to a "tall, broad-shouldered, almost gigantic, coloured man," the two discuss "different phases of the Negro question." He continues, "In referring to the race I used the personal pronoun 'we'; my companion made no comment about it, nor evinced any surprise, except to raise his eyebrows slightly the first time he caught the significance of the word" (150–51). If the narrator can no longer say "we" around whites, in what sense can he say "we" around blacks? Is the ex-colored man black in the same sense that his companion on board the ship is black? Unlike the ex-colored man, the companion never has been and never will be taken to be white. Yet because they are equally subject to—and subjectivated by—the law, they come to seem equal to the narrator. Thus, he marks his fall from whiteness as the defining event in his life. We are meant to understand it as the moment at which he realizes that he *is* black, "the miracle of my transition from one world into another" (20). Nevertheless, it seems to me that strategically essentialist readings make a kind of tacit peace with the legal construction of blackness. We might briefly note the political ambivalence in the way these readings have been deployed.

In the preface to the 1912 edition published by Sherman, French, and Company, the editors read the protagonist as black and praise *The Autobiography* as an indictment of passing; they contend that Johnson diagnoses a serious social ill. However, what turns out to most trouble the editors about the phenomenon of passing is not the racism that prompts whites to police the color line. It is the desire among light-skinned blacks to pass for white and thus "require" such policing. The editors denounce the "unsuspected fact that prejudice against the Negro is exerting a pressure" on blacks to pass. But the conclusion they draw from the fact of this prejudice implicitly reinscribes a sanctity of the white race. They conclude that race prejudice "is actually and constantly forcing an unascertainable number of fair-complexioned colored people over into the white race." One has the sense that passing is being condemned as much for its effects—the production of fraudulent whites—as for its causes, its roots in white-supremacist thinking. Which alarms the editors more, the fact that passing is occurring in "unascertainable" numbers or the "prejudice" that provokes it?

The Sherman, French editors appeal to the detective in their readers. More accurately, they construct readers as detectives. In this respect, they are following the lead of the narrator, who figures reading explicitly as a process of detection in the opening paragraph: "I feel that I am led by the same impulse which forces the un-found-out criminal to take somebody into his confidence." This formulation sheds light on the ontology of race informing Johnson's writing. The criminal is a criminal, the narrator suggests, whether or not he acts like one and is therefore revealed to be the criminal that he already was. By the logic of the one-drop rule, which is the historically inescapable logic of the narrative, the mixed-race subject is a Negro, whether or not he acts like one. Whether the ex-colored man is uncolored because he is not yet black (which is how we are to understand the young protagonist) or because he is no longer black (which is how we are to understand him as an adult), his blackness is always already established in the same way that the "un-found-out criminal" is always already a criminal. Johnson writes that the criminal's impulse to divulge the fact of his crime is so irresistible that he must "take somebody into his confidence, although he knows that the act is likely, even almost certain, to lead to his undoing" (3). We are told that the narrator is "led by the same impulse." For him, the act of narrating his life to a detective audience is almost certain to lead to undoing the whiteness that he had secured before he began narrating.

The ex-colored man has often been read not only as black but as a representative of the race, the embodiment of black experience. On *The Autobiography*'s republication in 1927, the prominent white patron of black art, Carl Van Vechten, expressed his confidence that "new readers . . . will examine this book with interest: some to acquire through its mellow pages a new conception of how a coloured man lives and feels, others simply to follow the course of its fascinating story" (xxxviii). This idea that the ex-colored man is typical of his race has substantially shaped the way the text has been read. "It reads like a composite autobiography of the Negro race in the U.S. in modern times," writes Van Vechten (xxxiv). His reference to the composite—a photo technique for producing the appearance of an average from an aggregate of individual images—echoes *The Autobiography*'s 1912 editors. They note that every previous black author took "some one group of the race or another to prove his case" and that "[n]ot before has a composite and proportionate presentation of the entire race . . . been made" (xil). Johnson improved on the work of Washington in *Up from Slavery* and DuBois in *The Souls of Black Folk*, Van Vechten contends in *The Autobiography*'s 1927 edition, because "no limitations" were imposed on the subject matter—the narrator "either discusses (or lives) pretty nearly every phase of Negro life, North and South and even in Europe, available to him at that period" (xxxv–vi). Critic Sterling A. Brown would echo this claim in 1966, calling *The Autobiography* "rather more a chart of Negro life than a novel" (82). Claims of representativeness hinge on an interesting contradiction, one that Johnson's protagonist seems to be deployed to resolve. On one hand, they insist on the ex-colored man's ordinariness, his capacity to have the experiences that other African Americans share. On the other hand, as a "composite" who accounts for "pretty nearly every phase of Negro life," the ex-colored man is exceptional, a figure that distills into one life a vastness of experience that comprehends yet exceeds the lives of each individual African American.

In the late 1950s, Robert Bone's influential study *The Negro Novel in America* would resolve the protagonist's racial indeterminacy by arguing that it is unimportant. Bone advances a reading that assimilates the narrative to the race-transcending genre of tragedy.

> While in one sense the racial identity of the protagonist is the central fact of his existence, in another, it is almost irrelevant. The protagonist faces a series of situations from which he flees; his flight into the white race is merely the crowning instance of his cowardice. To be sure his tragedy is heightened because there are good objective reasons for his final flight, but these reasons in no sense constitute a justification. The focus of the novel is not on the objective situation but on the subjective human tragedy. (48)

The narrator's "flight into the white race" is read here as a symptom of a generic tragic flaw: cowardice. The "objective situation" that provokes his flight—his presence at the scene of a lynching and the attending shame he feels at being black—is comparatively insignificant. "He becomes," Bone writes, "a symbol of man's universal failure to fulfill his highest destiny" (47). By universalizing the protagonist's experience, assimilating it to the transracial genre of tragedy, Bone turns the ex-colored man's racechange into a "mere" manifestation of "man's" weakness for pursuing the path of least resistance.

This move to assimilate the ex-colored man to a narrative of "universal" themes was politically progressive, even radical, in 1958—a challenge to the conventional white wisdom of the irredeemable particularity of black experience. Still, there is never any question in Bone's reading that the protagonist is, in essence, black. Echoing the claims about the protagonist's representative blackness, Bone reads the novel as "a series of episodes which runs the gamut of Negro life in America": in the dramatic classroom episode, the protagonist "learns through a traumatic experience that he is a Negro," and while he can authentically "resolve . . . to become a great Negro composer," his essential blackness prevents him from having anything but "ironical success as a white businessman" (46–47). In short, the distinction between the ordinary black experience of never having imagined one was white and the extraordinary experience of falling out of whiteness remains submerged.

Armed with the lessons of racial constructivism over thirty years later, Henry Louis Gates makes a similar dual critical gesture to universalize the ex-colored man yet read him as black. In his introduction to the 1989 Vintage edition of *The Autobiography,* Gates calls the text "a classic of American literature," in order to counterbalance his attention elsewhere in the introduction to *The Autobiography*'s specifically African American commitment to investigating race. On the text's engagement with race, Gates writes that Johnson is "intent upon unfolding the layers of veils that mask black culture from white Americans" (xxiii). This unmasking constitutes the novel's broad humanist project: Gates claims that Johnson sought to draw back the "layers of veils" to expose difference but was "is equally intent upon establishing a commonality of the human condition, shared at a most fundamental level by every human being, however alienated" (xxiii). Elsewhere, in a more historicist but equally universalizing turn, Gates reads the ex-colored man as anticipating high-modernist ambivalence about commerce. He writes that the ex-colored man "more than anything else embodies the alienation charac-

teristic of modernity, as the solace of 'getting and spending' displaces all
ambitions of artistic creation" (xix). Although Gates assimilates *The Autobiography* to a genre with no explicit race affiliation ("modernist prose"),
he also notes Johnson's debt to the slave narrative and makes clear that
for his purposes, the ex-colored man is black. "Concerned that black
individuals escape the racism implicit in characterizing one person by
the stereotypes said to be shared by an entire ethnic group," Gates writes,
"Johnson created the first-person black novel, the fictional autobiography, as a way of rendering in fiction the range of sensibility and consciousness of a black character" (xvi).

To be sure, reading the protagonist as black has an ongoing strategic
importance. The novel's demonstration that, as Gates puts it, "even the
most race-conscious character experiences the world on a daily basis as
does every other human being" has not lost its urgency (xxii). Nevertheless, it seems politically important now to question an assumption on
which these accounts rest: namely, that a transracial character and a
black character amount to the same thing; or, to put the assumption
another way, that since passing characters are useful, in so many ways, for
dramatizing racist hypocrisy, they therefore are black—they serve the
project that a black character would if he could. Gates is too thoroughgoing a constructivist to simply call the ex-colored man "black"; elsewhere, he calls him "mulatto" and even "a character who is white *and*
black" (xvii, xviii). But what is "white *and* black"? Is it synonymous with
"mulatto"? Does it designate a particular version of "mulatto," perhaps
one who is especially resourceful or capable of changing races, as Gates
puts it, "at his whim and by his will" (xiii)? In this case, why is Gates's
phrase not "either white *or* black," rather than "white *and* black," since
the ex-colored man is never taken to embody both races simultaneously?
For that matter, why not "*neither* white *nor* black"? Indeed, this designation would seem to be the most sensible one for Gates, who reads *The
Autobiography* as a lesson about the arbitrariness of race categories and
often puts quotation marks around the terms *white* and *black* to mark his
awareness of their descriptive inadequacy.

The ex-colored man has been seen to literalize the figure of double
consciousness that DuBois uses in *The Souls of Black Folk* to describe
blacks' experience of social subordination. DuBois's description of this
condition, a "sense of always looking at oneself through the eyes of oth-

ers," anticipates the ex-colored man's statement that his racechange gives him new eyes. One is always "measuring one's soul," DuBois writes, "by the tape of a world that looks on in amused contempt and pity. One ever feels his twoness,—an American, a Negro; two souls, two thoughts, two unreconciled strivings; two warring ideals in one dark body, whose dogged strength alone keeps it from being torn asunder" (3). It is tempting to map Johnson's protagonist onto DuBois's formulation. In contrast to the white man, Johnson writes,

> an additional and different light must be brought to bear on what [the coloured man] thinks; and his thoughts are often influenced by considerations so delicate and subtle that it would be impossible for him to confess or explain them to one of the opposite race. This gives to every coloured man, in proportion to his intellectuality, a sort of dual personality; there is one phase of him which is disclosed only in the freemasonry of his own race. (22)

For that matter, Johnson writes explicitly about "twoness," an irreconcilable split between the ex-colored man's desire to be a credit to the black race and his desire to be financially stable, which in this novel's terms amounts to an aspiration to whiteness. Moreover, Johnson's reference to practices of partial disclosure across the color line echo DuBois's ideas about life behind the "veil" of color. But in Johnson's ex-colored man, there is an important difference from the subjects of double consciousness in DuBois's metaphor, a difference that these otherwise compelling correspondences hide. DuBois writes about a struggle that takes place within "one dark body." I do not wish to construe "dark" too narrowly; it may be that "dark" refers to race as an idea separate from and irreducible to skin color. But DuBois is clearly writing about people who had been and, as far as they could tell, always would be considered black. This characterization does not fit Johnson's ex-colored man. His experience of crossing the color line virtually unimpeded seems to me to mark a crucial difference from the people whose experiences concern DuBois. The ex-colored man's success at passing for white seems at least to require something more than, if not entirely different from, the terms DuBois offers. The prospects for a person with "one dark body" at the turn of the century were significantly different from the prospects for a person with a light body but "dark blood." The elision of this distinction seems neither logical nor sufficiently resistant to the historically racist practice of equating transracial subjects with "black" subjects.

To elide this distinction requires a selective reading of *The Autobiography*, which consistently dramatizes the difference between people who determine whether they appear white or black, on one hand, and people who can only identify and be identified as black, on the other. The principal difference it emphasizes is a difference in geographic mobility. In Johnsons's text, whites (including those who signify as white despite their African ancestry) move about more quickly and readily than do blacks. Being black in his text is a geographically circumscribed existence, with explicit and implicit prohibitions against moving through physical spaces. There are no such prohibitions for whites. When the protagonist arrives in Atlanta to attend college, the black Pullman porter assures him, "of course, you could go anywhere in the city; they wouldn't know you from white" (57). Later, having taken up with a rough crowd of black gamblers in New York, the narrator similarly links blackness and immobility. He says, "my New York was limited to ten blocks."

> I look back upon the life I then led with a shudder when I think what would have been had I not escaped it. But had I not escaped it, I should have been no more unfortunate than are many young colored men who come to New York. (113)

The protagonist contends that this circumscribed existence, common among black men, enervates their "will and moral sense" (114). The text suggests, moreover, that many concrete effects follow from the fact that skin color determines physical mobility—effects on social mobility, education, employment, and, consequently, blacks' ability to challenge assumptions about their "natural" inferiority.

Gates calls the protagonist "a 'black' man who can become 'white' at will" and "a 'white' man who can become 'black'" (xviii). His formulation suggests the impossibility of determining the direction in which the protagonist is passing. It suggests that, at least formally, an equally viable claim can be made that the narrator passes for black as that he passes for white. In fact, at those moments in which his experience is so thoroughly shaped by his whiteness and so remote from the experiences of other African Americans, it makes more than just formal sense to consider him a white man passing for black. At one pivotal point in the narrative, some white men in the unnamed southern village in which the protagonist has taken up temporary residence lynch a black man. It is after eleven o'clock when the protagonist hears "hurrying footsteps on the silence of the night," the gallop of horses, and men muttering about "some terrible crime" that has been committed (184). Antiblack violence was at its peak at the turn of the twentieth century, when the narrative takes place. Yet what the protagonist feels is not fear, the threat of violence, but, rather, a "tense excitement" that propels him outside to join the crowd. He acknowledges, "Perhaps what bravery I exercised in going out was due to the fact that I felt sure my identity as a coloured man had not yet become known in the town" (185). Only a person whose whiteness felt secure indeed would venture out under such conditions, much less remain there once he noticed, as the ex-colored man does, that the crowd was all white and "steadily arriving . . . from all the surrounding country."

The narrator's description of his "first sight of coloured people in large numbers" also suggests that we might understand him as white passing for black. It makes clear that if black is an experiential category, he has no claim to "being" black.

> I had seen little squads around the railroad station on my way south, but here I saw a street crowded with them. They filled the shops and thronged the sidewalks and lined the curb. I asked my companion if all the coloured people in Atlanta lived on this street. He said they did not and assured me that the ones I saw were of the lower class. I felt relieved, in spite of the size of the lower class. The unkempt appearance, the shambling, slouching gait and loud talk and laughter of these people aroused in me a feeling of almost repulsion. Only one thing about them awoke a feeling of interest; that was their dialect. I had read some Negro dialect and had heard snatches of it on my journey down from Washington; but here I heard it in all of its fullness and freedom. (56)

Passages like this one insist on the distinction between the protagonist's experience and the experience of people who could never pass for white. It is not that whites have exclusive rights to feeling "almost repulsed" by lower-class blacks. If anything, Johnson suggests that the experiences of the black elite approximate those of upper-class whites more than those of other blacks. But the passage seems to me to make it impossible to avoid asking, What is the difference between a person with no African ancestry who identifies as white and a person who has hidden his African ancestry, successfully identifies as white, and exhibits the signs and values of this success, such as a fascinated disdain for African Americans? It makes us ask, in other words, why not understand the pro- tagonist as white?

One reason is that, historically, the white person with no discoverable African ancestry courts none of the risks of the black person who passes for white, who is always subject to the punitive mechanism of the law even if he or she is not fully subjectivated by it. However, from another perspective, to understand the ex-colored man as white would be to chal- lenge the essentialism that accrues to the minoritized character and to see race instead as a matter of performance mastery. Recently, such scholars as Samira Kawash, Walter Benn Michaels, and Gayle Wald have made this case about Johnson's narrator. None of them dispute that "blackness continues to determine the narrator's consciousness in a way whiteness does not," as Kawash puts it, that his "whiteness is a state of per- petual anxiety, in a way blackness is not" (71). But each maintains, as I have here, that the novel undermines the logic of authenticity on which claims to race identity are based and suggests that *all* race identity is the product of passing. Where I depart from these readings is in my sugges- tion that, as strange as it sounds, the ex-colored man may be more typi- cally white than these performative accounts have suggested. Kawash writes that "rather than being 'both black and white,' he is in fact neither black nor white" (70). While it is well to remark that he is neither race "in fact," the fact that neither race exists "in fact" in the first place makes this formal claim about performativity feel very a priori. After all, we are talking about not what is true in fact but what is true in fictions—in his- tory's legal and social fictions. Taking this claim as a starting point, then, rather than a conclusion, I suggest that there is a nonontological basis for reading the ex-colored man as white and that we illuminate more in so doing than if we settle for reading him as "both black and white" or "neither black nor white."

A Representative White

The protagonist of Johnson's *The Autobiography of an Ex-Coloured Man* eventually decides to "stay" white. This decision resolves (at least to his own satisfaction) the contradiction into which he has been placed by historical accident. He retains this white identity through his adult life, passing to everyone (including his children) except his white wife. Johnson conveniently kills her off, leaving the narrator to declare, finally, "I am an ordinarily successful white man who has made a little money" (211). It sounds more like a glib flourish than an assertion, but we should take it seriously—not because whiteness has the primary ontological claim on him, but because the pressures of racial self-fashioning to which he is subjected do exemplify those of "an ordinarily successful white man." The process by which he is ex-colored actually speaks as interestingly to the question of why white people want to be white and how they do it as it does to the question of why black people want to be white and how they do it. It turns out that his indeterminate racial status does not unfit him for an analysis of white people's racialization but, to the contrary, positions him to illustrate what it means (even and especially for light-skinned people with no known African ancestry) to assume and embrace whiteness. As paradoxical as it sounds, we might read the ex-colored man not as an exceptional white man but as a representative one.

At the risk of sounding disingenuous, we might ask what has caused people in the United States to want to be white. Historically, this has also been a question of what has caused people to resist being black. It has primarily been social and economic subordination—both legal and extralegal—and their attending deprivation and humiliation. The ex-colored man clearly articulates his reasons for pursuing whiteness. He says that more than anything else, more than "discouragement or fear or search for a larger field of action and opportunity," he wants to be white because of the "shame, unbearable shame [of] being identified with a people that could with impunity be treated worse than animals" (191). Like other whites, the narrator prefers to identify with those administering such violence than with their victims (even as he criticizes white supremacists). Like other whites, the narrator seeks to preserve the whiteness of his family lineage at all costs. Of his children he says, "There is nothing I would not suffer to keep the brand [of color] from being placed upon them" (210). Like other whites, the narrator pursues whiteness instinctively because the alternative feels like unbearable financial struggle, if not financial suicide. "I had made up my mind that since I was not going to be a Negro," he says, "I would avail myself of every possible opportunity to make a white man's success; and that, if it can be summed up in any one word, means 'money'" (193).

But the most interesting quality that the narrator shares with other whites may be his disavowal of any agency in the performances that racialize him. He resolves to "let the world take me for what it would" (190). This gesture—which shifts the responsibility for determining his race from himself to his society—rings a little hollow. He knows, as other whites know, that as long as he lets "the world take me for what it would," it will see only his chromatic and somatic whiteness. His standard English, his carriage, and the experiences he articulates will seem to confirm the "visual evidence." His disavowal of agency in the performances that racialize him is tantamount to an active embrace of whiteness; despite its appearance of equanimity, it is indistinguishable in effect from a deliberate pursuit of whiteness. He arrives, in other words, at a realization that has long driven other ambiguously raced people toward whiteness, the same realization that has kept those whites whose race has always felt self-evident bound to their whiteness: namely, that "it was not necessary for me to go about with a label of inferiority pasted across my forehead" (190).

The history of what George Lipsitz calls the "possessive investment in whiteness" in the United States helps elucidate the idea that the ex-colored man's white racialization is not exceptional but exemplary. Though his becoming white is figured as an anomaly, it is anomalous mainly in the explicitness with which it dramatizes white racialization; that is, he encounters self-consciously the problems and performances that self-evidently white whites can afford to leave largely unexamined. Whiteness is a dynamic category whose complex and contradictory history belies the biological arguments that have been marshaled to stabilize and naturalize it. These arguments have served to produce and maintain whiteness even as they have assumed that it is natural rather than cultural. Lipsitz writes:

> More than a product of private prejudices, whiteness emerged as a relevant category in American life largely because of realities created by slavery and segregation, by immigration restriction and Indian policy, by conquest and colonialism. A fictive identity of "whiteness" appeared in law as an abstraction, and it became actualized in every-

day life in many ways. American economic and political life gave different racial groups unequal access to citizenship and property, while cultural practices including wild west shows, minstrel shows, racist images in advertising, and Hollywood films institutionalized racism by uniting ethnically diverse European-American audiences into an imagined community—one called into being through inscribed appeals to the solidarity of white supremacy. ("Possessive Investment" 370)[7]

Many Americans commonly thought of today as white (or its variant, "white ethnic")—including the Irish, southern and eastern Europeans, Czechs, Slavs, and Jews—were not always white. Americans in each of these groups chose and often struggled to forge a precarious white status alongside so-called native American whites. Each group's pursuit of whiteness in turn shaped popular and legal definitions of whiteness, rendering it more supple, on one hand, and inoculating it against subsequent boundary assaults, on the other.

The history of new (and not so new) Americans' claims to whiteness is also a history of self-distancing from African Americans. It is a history of discovering, as the ex-colored man puts it, how to make it "not necessary for me to go about with a label of inferiority pasted across my forehead." In "On Being 'White' . . . and Other Lies," James Baldwin writes, "No one was white until he or she came to America." Historian David Roediger notes that while Baldwin's claim is not strictly true (e.g., a sense of whiteness developed among workers in some European cities with a significant black population), "in its broad outline Baldwin's point is hardly assailable. Norwegians, for example, did not spend a great deal of time and energy in Norway thinking of themselves as white. As the great Irish nationalist and antiracist Daniel O'Connell thundered to Irish Americans who increasingly asserted their whiteness in the 1840s, 'It was not in Ireland you learned this cruelty'" (186).

It almost goes without saying that the ex-colored man's equivocation about his race is inseparable from his equivocation about choosing a job. Labor history shows that the economic and cultural alliances and antagonisms forged through work were crucial to the development of whiteness. Drawing on histories of longshoremen and industrial workers, for instance, John Higham writes that in all regions of the United States, "native-born and northern European laborers called themselves 'white men' to distinguish themselves from the southern Europeans whom they worked beside" (173). They could thereby assuage the fear "that they would be cast as 'white niggers' and their jobs as 'nigger work'—an anxiety that the white working poor seldom escaped" (Roediger 191). One physician testified at the turn of the twentieth century: "[T]he Slavs are immune to certain kinds of dirt. They can stand what would kill a white man" (quoted in Roediger 191). His claim not only shows a Slav's place in the racial hierarchy; it also explains their motivation to "grasp for the whiteness at the margins of their experiences," as Roediger puts it, rather than to focus on the experiences that they shared with African Americans. Their shared experience of oppression produced hostility toward whites, but this hostility competed with a strong desire to receive better treatment from whites. Thus, such stereotypes as the one that Slavs could endure "what would kill a white man" did more than declare them nonwhite.

> [It] gave free rein to employers hiring them as laborers . . . to place them in the dirtiest and most unhealthy jobs. In such positions Slavic workers would be said to be 'working like niggers' and would, like the most exploited Jews, Sicilians, or Louisiana creoles elsewhere, face further questioning of their whiteness based on the very fact of their hard and driven labor. (Roediger 191)

White was clearly not what you were but what you did, including crucially how you worked. Thus, the whiteness of even light-skinned immigrants was far from self-evident and in fact mattered little in the face of the "evidence" that they did exactly what blacks did. To pursue whiteness by distancing oneself from the "niggers" among whom one worked, then, was a choice that must have felt not much like a choice but instead like a compulsion.

The compulsion among not-yet-white ethnics to pursue whiteness derived its force not only from competition in the labor market but also from nativism in public discourse. When arguments raging over immigration threatened their status in America, not-yet-white ethnics availed themselves of a racist rhetoric (Who is white?) in order to displace a nativist one (Who is foreign?). If the argument was about foreigners harming Americans' opportunities, immigrants could not win. But if the terms were changed and the issue became "defending 'white man's jobs' or a 'white man's government,'" Roediger writes, "the not-yet-white ethnic could gain space by deflecting debate from nativity, a hopeless issue, to race, an ambiguous one" (190). Nativist rhetoric employed and served to strengthen the existing equation between white and American. During Reconstruction, whites across the United States had responded to the abolition of formal subordination of blacks by forging a sense of whiteness that transcended local differences through a "community" of race. Later, the sense of whiteness that immigrants helped native-born whites to forge served similarly to transcend differences of class and national origin.

Becoming white in the United States has always meant taking a place within a historically specific set of economic relations.[8] During Reconstruction, for example, whites in Mississippi initially saw the Chinese who came to work on the Delta as black: like African Americans, the Chinese started there as sharecroppers (Davis 115). However, many Chinese soon left the cotton fields to become grocers, and their economic success in the next several decades temporarily upset the binary system of racial classification. A "third term" had to be locally produced to account for these neither black nor white people. Thus, in the 1930s and 1940s, there was a "triple segregation" system, with separate buildings for whites, blacks, and Chinese. But the departure from racial binarism was fleeting, for by the 1950s, with Jim Crow legislation still in effect, Chinese were admitted into white public facilities, including schools. Thus, the once-black, precariously whitened Chinese were reincorporated into the binary system of racial classification, this time at the white pole instead of the black one. It is important to notice that their protracted shift between black and white did not hinge on skin color (Mexicans sharecropping in the Delta shared a racial designation with African Americans, not with the Chinese). Nor was it a matter of one's individual will to be white. Rather, Davis writes, "the Delta Chinese could not have assumed the role of a middle minority if a special niche had not opened up in the structure of compulsory segregation in the sharecropping system."

The whites did not want to sell groceries to blacks or do the manual labor of unloading wagons and stocking shelves. Most of the former slaves had no experience in small business . . . The delta Chinese were able to seize the rural opportunity when it opened up because they were on the land when the economic gap occurred . . . Although there were tensions, and white opposition to their rise in group status, they avoided overt conflicts. (115)

What determined whether people were white was not exactly skin color but a dynamic relationship between skin color and the material conditions through which people reproduced their lives. Myrdal anticipated this point. He speculated that light-skinned southern blacks would have trouble passing for white because they had been rehearsing nonwhiteness all their lives. It was "a great subjective and objective barrier" to passing, he wrote, "that Negroes in the South are trained to appear and behave in a very different way from white people" (683). Like Davis, Myrdal emphasized that light-skinned blacks stayed black not because of their skin color so much as because of the performances of race that the material conditions of their existence had determined.

Obscured from Myrdal's claim is the sense that the white appearances and behaviors in opposition to which blacks were "trained" were themselves the product of efforts to appear and behave nonblack. In other words, if blacks were "trained" not to be white, there was no less racial training involved for whites, who fashioned whiteness in opposition to the very "black" appearances and behaviors to which Myrdal refers. It was within this matrix of mutually determining, antagonistic performances of race that people like the "delta Chinese" of whom Davis writes forged their whiteness.

[T]hey developed a lifestyle visibly different from that of the black sharecroppers, being careful to speak, walk, and even dance more like the whites. They established homes away from the stores, became acquainted with white ministers, bankers, and wholesalers, and slowly persuaded the white community to open its schools, hospitals, and other white facilities to them. (116)

Davis's discussion shows that whiteness must be understood as a function first and foremost of one's position within a historically specific set of economic relations, such that it then becomes possible to fashion a racial identity that is legibly distinct from blackness.

In *The Autobiography of an Ex-Coloured Man,* Johnson foregrounds the dynamic economic relations of the turn of the twentieth century. The ex-colored man positions (and repositions) himself in an economy that is increasingly dependent on consumption and leisure. In general, the narrator represents himself as choosing between two competing race claims, the difference between which is merely serial and syntactic. Occasionally, however, he acknowledges that race-changes are not exactly autonomous, free-market choices but are in fact conditioned by the legal and economic status of whiteness. He notices the "tendency" among blacks to look whiter and to marry light-complexioned spouses and calls this tendency "an economic necessity" (154). He assures readers that it should not be construed as "a tacit admission of coloured people among themselves of their own inferiority judged by the colour line." "After all," he argues, it is "most natural" if we consider that "the United States puts a greater premium on colour, or better, lack of colour, than upon anything else in the world." Designating whiteness "an economic necessity," the narrator would seem to challenge the claim, made by readers and elsewhere by the narrator himself, that his race-changes occur "at his whim and by his will." In her work on whiteness as property, Cheryl Harris similarly contests the model of voluntary agency.

> The economic coercion of white supremacy on self-definition nullifies any suggestion that passing is a logical exercise of liberty or self-identity. The decision to pass as white was not a choice, if by that word one means voluntariness or lack of compulsion. The fact of race subordination was coercive and circumscribed the liberty to self-define. Self-determination of identity was not a right for all people, but a privilege accorded on the basis of race. The effect of protecting whiteness at law was to devalue those who were not white by coercing them to deny their identity in order to survive. (117)

Taking the words of both Harris and the ex-colored man himself as our cue, then, we could question the model of the autonomous, rational subject that is suggested by the phrase "at his whim and by his will." Instead, we might notice that, far from exemplifying "the black race" in any unproblematic way, the ex-colored man's racial performances may make him a representative white. His implication in consumer culture puts a finer point on this idea.

Consumer Culture and the Color Line

In 1932 ,an African American economist at Fisk University named Paul K. Edwards published a pioneering volume of market research called *The Southern Urban Negro as a Consumer.* Among the worst casualties of segregation, Edwards writes, was the restriction to whites of most new commercial sites of leisure and amusement, those we associate today with the emergence of urban mass culture in the United States. According to Edwards, these sites "condition intellectual development and motivation"; thus, he finds their absence from the lives of most African Americans a severe setback for the race. Inverting a prevalent anxiety about the adverse effect of commercialism on spiritual life, he argues that the proliferation of these sites of leisure and amusement designated "for whites only" had the unintended (and in his view unfortunate) result of propelling African Americans to church. To support this claim, he cites a 1926 "scientific survey of Negro life" written by the Mayor's Interracial Committee in Detroit.

> The Negro has been humiliated in so many public and privately owned institutions and amusement places that he has resorted to the church as a place in which he can be sure of peacefully spending his leisure time. To a large extent it takes the place of the theatre, the dance hall, and similar amusement places, and fills the vacancy created by the failure of public and commercial places of recreation and amusement to give him a cordial welcome. (10)

Hopeful about the civic benefits of commercialized leisure, Edwards casts the black church in a weak, compensatory role. Of course, his account neglects the fact that the black church had been a vital public and political institution long before the arrival of "the theatre, the dance hall, and similar amusement places." Still, according to this odd version of historical causality, church was something African Americans had resorted to in the absence of anything better, and had it not been for segregation, this better thing could have been consumption.

The last race-change of the protagonist in *The Autobiography of an Ex-Coloured Man* recalls Edwards's argument. This is the point at which the protagonist decides to become white for good, and in an important sense, it is the point at which he begins to turn himself into the "ordinarily successful white man" who tells the story. What is the first thing he does upon making this decision? "I went to Coney Island and the other resorts," he proclaims, "took in the pre-season shows along Broadway, and ate at first-class restaurants." Sounding almost systematic, his approach recalls the passing moments I cited at the outset in James, *The Independent,* Fauset, and Larsen. Previously, the racialized conventions of leisure had made a commodity of him: the patron "told him that he would give me lots of work, his only stipulation being that I should not play engagements . . . except by his instructions" (119). Having removed himself from these conventions, his first white gesture is to enlist them to his own purposes. He turns immediately to the amusements, resorts, shows, and restaurants that were fueling the emergent culture of consumption. But consumption not only figures here as a way to express his whiteness; it also serves to confer whiteness upon him. To be sure, he already has light skin, which gives him access to these public and commercial sites of leisure and amusement. But since race is not just a matter of subjective affiliation but also a social designation, he is only white insofar as his whiteness can be consolidated publicly. Thus, the precariously white protagonist exercises the privileges that reinforce his whiteness, that make it feel like a permanent, natural, and necessary part of his identity. His participation in the culture of consumption that Coney Island, Broadway, and the first-class restaurants represent is, in other words, not only a result of his whiteness but its cause.

W. E. B. DuBois was once asked why he continued to use the term *black* if he did not believe in biological race distinctions. He replied, "I recognize [blacks] quite easily and with full legal sanction: the black man is a person who must ride Jim Crow in Georgia" ("Superior Race" 477). His formulation reverses the commonsense causality: it is not that a person rides in the "colored" car because he is black but that riding there makes him black. A polemical effort to move race from a biological to a social register, it takes the fact that people can misrepresent their race as requiring an epistemological shift. Black and white are not therefore meaningless for DuBois; they are just better understood as the effects of practices of ordering social bodies than as the cause or precondition of these practices. In Johnson's novel, the practice in question is the orchestration of consumer culture's representations and pleasures, which is not simply restricted to whites but acts in turn to confer whiteness on its practitioners. Johnson does not announce that the reason his protagonist immediately pursues commercial leisure is because it is the most effective way to consolidate his whiteness, but he does not have to. By omitting any particular reason for the protagonist's decision about what first to do with his new whiteness, he suggests the obviousness of the choice.

A protagonist who is an agent in determining his race rather than simply a vessel for carrying it enables the novel to examine the nature and the limits of that agency. The novel suggests that the protagonist's decisions are never symmetrical: they are not freely made choices between races whose difference is merely formal; rather, they come structured by racialized relations of economic exchange. This tension between agency and structure is inscribed in the narrator himself. On one hand, he concedes that whiteness exerts a pull whose force is only partly conscious. The narrative even supplies a kind of primal scene. His most vivid memory of his white father is of his shiny shoes, gold chain, and great gold watch and of a gift he gave the narrator, a ten-dollar gold coin with hole drilled through the center. He says, "I have worn that gold piece around my neck the greater part of my life, and still possess it," but he adds, "more than once I have wished that some other way had been found of attaching it to me besides putting a hole through it" (6). What his father leaves him, we might say, is a damaged version of the inheritance to which he would be entitled were it not for his mother's blackness. It is currency without exchange value. While he calls it a necklace, it works more like a yoke, for it seems to condense an implicit historical narrative: white signs of wealth (shiny shoes and gold chains and watches) are backed by real wealth, while black signs of wealth (the gold necklace) are conspicuous display. As a necklace, the coin represents wealth, but it can no longer be wealth once it has been punctured out of circulation. This scene is represented as structuring the protagonist's racial unconscious. Its excavation by the narrator suggests that no matter how much agency is conferred by his light skin, the mobility of his identifications is partly determined.

On the other hand, the narrator works elsewhere to shore up a fantasy of complete identificatory mobility. He would have readers see him as an autonomous subject, one whose light skin and African ancestry allow him to choose freely between two formally equivalent race claims. But the narrator's fantasy of autonomous, rational subjectivity is belied by the consistent presence of social and economic structures. If he changes race voluntarily, these changes nonetheless require him to navigate circuits of commodified exchange and display. Specifically, it is a culture whose traffic in representations preserves the color line, reproduces itself by proliferating new contexts in which to inscribe the color line, and turns the act of traversing the color line into a marketable commodity. I conclude this chapter by examining three factors that condition the possibility for the protagonist's ongoing project of racial formation: the contradictory demands of contemporary circuits of publicity, where race leadership means embodied blackness but embodied blackness means being susceptible to physical violence, social surveillance, and economic commodification; the text's differentiation between northern industrial and southern agrarian societies; and the protagonist's relationship to spectatorship and codes of reception.

We are told that the protagonist's initial popularity as a musician derived from his talent at "converting" white music into black performance. With the "first ragtime transcriptions of familiar classical selections" as his repertoire, he becomes the best ragtime player in New York and single-handedly raises the number of "slumming visitors" to the club at which he performs. Anticipating Fitzgerald's descriptions of the guests at Gatsby's parties, Johnson represents these white audiences explicitly in terms of conspicuous consumption: "These were people—and they represented a large class—who were ever expecting to find happiness in novelty, each day restlessly exploring and exhausting every resource of this great city that might possibly furnish a new sensation or awaken a fresh emotion, and who were always grateful to anyone who aided them in their quest" (118). An ambitious, demonstrative set of desiring creatures, they work on a quickened cycle of planned obsolescence. In this context, black exoticism intersects with a desire for novelty and physicality, and inflecting classical pieces with black accents pays the protagonist "more than playing Beethoven and Chopin could ever have done." "It was a pleasure to me," he declares, "to watch the expression of astonishment and delight that grew on the faces of everybody"; and it secures him a white patron.

Yet if his initial success comes from blacking up white music, it is the inverse gesture—to make ragtime classical—that later presents real promise. His inspiration for this new project comes from a European in the crowd for whom he has been playing ragtime overseas.

> [A] big bespectacled, bushy-headed man seated himself at the piano, and, taking the theme of my rag-time, played it through first in straight chords; then varied and developed it through every known musical form. I sat amazed. I had been turning classic music into rag-time, a comparatively easy task; and this man had taken rag-time and made it classic. (141–42)

In the prospect of performing ragtime in a classical register, he sees a chance to "carry out the ambition I had formed when a boy": to be known as a race leader. His rise to prominence, he decides, will be to popularize black creativity by elevating it, as he sees it, to the status of a European form. He decides to forsake his patron and head for the Deep South. "I made up my mind to go back to the very heart of the South," he says of his last days in Europe, "to live among the people, and drink in my inspiration firsthand. I gloated over the immense amount of material I had to work with" (142).

The patron sees this decision as an imprudent abandonment of the white privilege the protagonist has enjoyed in Europe. He warns the protagonist that it would mean a return to blackness; it would mean, he says, "going home and working as a Negro composer." But it seems to me the patron does not get it right, for it is the narrator's whiteness that he reclaims as he makes classical music from black cultural production. When he performed classical pieces as ragtime (his first type of exchange), it was his access to black conventions of performance that conferred value. Conversely, his performance of ragtime as classical music derives its value from his mastery of white performance conventions. The patron implores the protagonist not to "make a Negro out of [him]self" by returning to the United States, but, far from an abdication of the protagonist's whiteness, this return is an opportunity to realize its profitability. So he puts it to work in the project of making value out of black popular culture.

The idea that the narrator's return to the United States is not an abdication but an embrace of whiteness is underscored in a passage that assesses the virtues and the limitations of black performers. The narrator remarks that what makes great ragtime players great is a natural, God-given gift for music (rather than, say, a lifetime of practice). When he first heard the "barbaric harmonies" and "audacious resolutions" of ragtime, he tells us, he pursued the performer only to find "that he was just a natural musician, never having taken a lesson in his life" (99, 101). This discovery causes him to wonder what someone "with such a lavish natural endowment" could have done with some technical training. But he concludes:

> Perhaps he wouldn't have done anything at all; he might have become, at best, a mediocre imitator of the great masters in what they have already done to a finish, or one of the modern innovators who strive after originality by seeing how cleverly they can dodge about the rules of harmony and at the same time avoid melody. It is certain that he would not have been so delightful as he was in rag-time. (101–2)

Training not only would have failed to improve this natural talent but would have destroyed what made the player so "delightful" to audiences in the first place. The black ragtime performer is great, in other words, precisely because of his lack of training, not despite it. It is this very lack of training that marks his difference from white musicians, and it is this difference that enables him to be "delightful." With training, the black musician might remain nominally black, but he will have ceased simply to be black and will have begun instead to perform blackness. If what makes a black performer black (and not just a performer of blackness) has less to do with his skin color than with his lack of formal training, we can see just how far the narrator's return to the United States is simply a return to being a "Negro composer."

While he would have us believe that the benefits that will accrue to him personally are merely incidental, his efforts to legitimate his project end up emphasizing what he seems to disavow—its dimension of cultural expropriation, the complicity of "love and theft."[9] By figuring himself as the pivot point in an antiracist project of cultural mediation, he entitles himself to its attending profit and acclaim. Since (as he says) "the Negroes themselves do not fully appreciate these old slave songs," the protagonist becomes the necessary lubricant for exchanges through which blacks will begin to fully appreciate their work and through which their work will fully appreciate in market value (182). In an important sense, then, the project that brings him back to the United States is not a foreclosure of his whiteness but, rather, depends on his continued ability to trade on it, to master the economic relationships and conventions of performance that were foreclosed to nonwhites. His access to blackness and whiteness is not merely formal, nor is it accomplished "at his whim and by his will." It is embedded firmly in the traffic in commodities and specifically in the traffic in racialized culture as a commodity. "If some white artist could go among the Negroes and live with them much beautiful stuff might be got," the white writer Sherwood Anderson would remark in his 1926 *Notebooks,* adding: "The trouble is that no American white man could do it without self-consciousness. The best thing is to stand aside, listen and wait. If I can be impersonal in the presence of black laborers, watch the dance of bodies, hear the song, I may learn something" ("Note 23," reprinted in *Black Images in American Literature* 97). The ex-colored man may well be the white artist Anderson imagines, one whose awareness of his African ancestry minimizes his self-consciousness.

But if the move of *The Autobiography*'s narrator to the rural South is a gesture to reclaim whiteness, it is not exactly being white that holds the thrill and promise of consumer culture. The novel shows the vast privilege attending membership in the white race, but being white is not exactly the protagonist's project. (Nor for that matter does the thrill and promise of consumer culture lie in being black—though blackness could be exploited in some contexts, as the protagonist's New York ragtime success testifies.) Rather, it is the capacity to cross the color line that is figured as most thrilling and value making. What inspires him is the prospect of mediating what he understands to be authentic black folk culture into marketable high culture. Removing it from its original conditions of production and reception, he seeks acclaim for himself and for the black race by reproducing it according to the conventions of classical music. His whiteness lies in this identificatory mobility, this capacity to turn race-changes into exchanges. Gayle Wald writes: "American literature and culture, especially in the twentieth century, is rife with examples of legally white subjects who have taken advantage of their privileged racial mobility to experiment with modes of racial signification as a means of political expression, personal exploration, cultural theft, or self-critique. Yet such ludic or strategic border-crossing is far less available to subjects whose identities, conceived as inferior, deviant, or threatening to the norm, have historically been more stringently policed" (139). The whiteness of the ex-colored man is not his biological whiteness but his exercise of what Wald describes as the uniquely white privilege to cross the color line and cross back with relative impunity. However "black" he becomes, his whiteness, like the whiteness of legally white subjects, is always available.

The Autobiography is often read as a challenge to the color line. But what its narrator effectively does, like the culture of consumption in which he is implicated, is produce a color line that can then be crossed for profit. What seems most significant, therefore, about the relationship between the color line and consumer culture in the novel is not the commodification of white versions of blackness. This is what we hear in the protagonist's zeal for "jotting down in my notebook themes and melodies, and trying to catch the Negro in his relatively primitive state" (173). More provocative is the novel's suggestion that the possibility of a profitable participation in the traffic in commodities is conditioned by the protagonist's capacity to perform whiteness—in particular, to perform it despite the supposed fact that he is black. It suggests, in other words, that value can be made through a continual movement across the color line—a thing that does not simply preexist him but that he, however inadvertently, also helps to produce.

This chapter has focused on one literary text and advanced a fairly formalist reading at times. But its claims have fascinating historical corollaries in the early years of the twentieth century. One might point, for example, to the exchange between the African American composer Harry T. Burleigh and the Czech composer Antonin Dvorak, with whom Burleigh studied and to whom he introduced the Negro spirituals that Dvorak incorporated in the *New World* Symphony. Another African American who studied with Dvorak, the composer and violinist Will Marion Cook, is credited with having combined elements of white classical and black vernacular music in ways that later inspired the Gershwins' opera *Porgy and Bess*. It was Cook who collaborated with poet Paul Laurence Dunbar on a musical sketch comedy called *Clorindy; or, The Origin of the Cakewalk* (1898) and who published *A Collection of Negro Songs* in 1912, the year *The Autobiography of an Ex-Coloured Man* appeared. However, the most interesting historical referents for the phenomena I have been discussing in Johnson's novel may well be Tin Pan Alley and vaudeville.

In Tin Pan Alley, a wildly popular sheet music and recording industry came about through the immersion of a number of young, Lower East Side, immigrant Jewish men (e.g., Irving Berlin, né Israel Isidore Baline) in the black vernacular music they were hearing in the streets and the backrooms of downtown cafés. These men in turn interpreted that music on the instruments and according to the rhythms that were indigenous to their eastern European backgrounds. As immigrant Jews whose families were often quite poor, they would have been considered neither black nor white in the years around the turn of the century, and it was in no small part because of this racial ambiguity that they served as pivot points between black and white culture. As Tin Pan Alley and vaudeville grew popular and were incorporated into the commercial channels of mainstream American music and mass culture, two important and related things occurred: their original associations with African American vernacular forms grew fainter, and the racial status of these Jewish men grew less ambiguous. The irony, to paraphrase Michael Rogin's argument about how Jakie Rabinowitz becomes Jack Robin in *The Jazz Singer* (1927), is that it was only by putting on blackface that the poor, immigrant Jewish performer shed his racial particularity and joined the great white way.[10] The color line between black and white was, as I noted already, not only a generative condition of possibility for culture as a commodity in these years but also one of consumer culture's products, effectively resolving the contradiction that the Jew's ambiguously raced body represented in the black-white taxonomy. In the chapter that follows, then, I turn from close textual analysis to examine the racial dynamics of an emerging cultural institution.

5 A Black Culture Industry

PUBLIC RELATIONS AND
THE "NEW NEGRO" AT
BONI AND LIVERIGHT

> We are witnessing the beginning of a new era in the
> treatment of colored writers.
>
> —Floyd Calvin, editor, *Pittsburgh Courier* (1924)

> What you all doin', white folks? What's all dis? What you all lookin'
> at me fo'? What you doin' wid me, anyhow? . . . Is dis a auction?
> Is you sellin' me like dey uster befo' de war?
>
> —Eugene O'Neill, *The Emperor Jones* (1920)

THE SAME YEAR that Boni and Liveright published Jean Toomer's
Cane (1923), which many took as a signal of the maturation of a new generation of black writers, a book entitled *Publicity* appeared, outlining the
subtle new tactics of promotion that were bolstering the new industry of
public relations. This chapter examines how the transformation of the
book business after World War I through advertising and public relations cultivated demand for African American fiction and informed its
reception. My argument is that the commercial and visual discourses of
advertising and public relations were not necessarily consonant with—
and were sometimes dramatically at odds with—the intentions of the
authors and the implicit arguments of their books. The firm Boni and
Liveright focuses this discussion for two reasons: its life span (1917–33)
was roughly coextensive with this transformation in the publishing
industry and with the Harlem Renaissance, and it was a vital institution
in both of these developments.[1] Book historian John Tebbel writes of
changes in publishing between World War I and the Great Depression

that were so dramatic as to constitute a "revolution," and he calls B&L "the epitome of the period" (136).

   Tebbel is correct in that the firm exemplified the period's dramatic push toward advertising and publicity and its effort to challenge the genteel Victorianism that had characterized book publishing before World War I.[2] But B&L was unusual in the risks it took, including in the investment it made in African American authors. There is a major discrepancy in the scholarship about this firm—a symptom, I think, of the continuing relegation of African American literature to special-interest status. On one hand, scholars of African American literature routinely invoke B&L as a principal agent of the Harlem Renaissance. George Hutchinson goes so far as to call Horace Liveright one of "the most important and fearless publishers of the Harlem Renaissance" (372). On the other hand, book historians have without exception overlooked this aspect of B&L's role in literary history.[3] Ultimately, however, my interest is not in setting the historical record straight about one firm but, rather, in using this firm's peculiar situation at the crossroads of the Harlem Renaissance and the commercialization of the book to examine consumer culture's agency in racial-formation projects of the period.

   Focusing on one firm, as I do here, is not to suggest that it was more important in an absolute sense than its contemporaries. In fact, such questions about the priority and influence of individuals or specific organizations have limited the discussion of African American fiction during this period. They should be integrated with an inquiry into the broader network of capitalist social relations that Bourdieu calls the "field of cultural production." Bourdieu notes,

> [W]hat "makes reputations" is not . . . this or that "influential" person, this or that institution, review, magazine, academy, coterie, dealer or publisher; it is not even the whole set of what are sometimes called "personalities of the world of arts and letters"; it is the field of production, understood as the system of objective relations between these agents or institutions and as the site of the struggles for the monopoly of the power to consecrate, in which the value of works of art and belief in that value are continuously generated. (78)

Thus, I have here tried to consider two broad questions: what were the existing institutions and discourses that conditioned book publication, distribution, and reception; and what translations of racial meaning were required to mediate among them and perform the cultural work of reproducing race?

Much of the scholarship on this period has obscured these questions by focusing instead on individual authors, patrons, and texts. These accounts have told us a great deal about how such writers as Langston Hughes, Zora Neale Hurston, James Weldon Johnson, and Walter White negotiated the asymmetries of racialized social power, forging conflicted and, at times, contentious relationships with members of the white literary establishment. These analyses prompted a welcome reassessment of the motives of white editors, patrons, and promoters and of the influence they exerted on black cultural production. Primitivism, the fetish for the exotic, the "vogue in all things negro," as Hughes put it, are now central to our understanding of modernism in many forms, including and especially the Harlem Renaissance.[4] While my discussion in this chapter is indebted to this critical conversation, I hope to suggest one of its limitations. All of these people, regardless of their intentions and influence, were also participating in some dramatic changes in the publishing industry, changes that exceeded the grasp of any one individual or group. While we cannot discount the role of such people as Carl Van Vechten, Fanny Hurst, Nancy Cunard, and Charlotte Osgood Mason in shaping literary history and should not stop asking questions about their motives and their impact, we can productively resituate them within this volatile transition in U.S. consumer culture, one in which books played a vital role.[5]

Scholars of modernism have already begun to trace the relationship between the emergence of advertising and public relations and the work of European and American modernists.[6] One of the ironies this scholarship reveals is that the same firms that were established around the war years and that pursued a more aggressively commercial course than their predecessors—such firms as Ben Huebsch (1911), Alfred A. Knopf (1915), and Boni and Liveright (1917)—were also the firms that invigorated a literary modernism that was deeply critical of the commercial basis of modernity. Many modernists sought to carve a space for cultural autonomy and authenticity in response to what they felt was the homogenizing force of mass culture. The stable at B&L was full of authors decrying the sterility of modern bourgeois society and the artificiality of

the belletristic tradition. In fact, it has been argued that precisely this critique of modernity drew white writers to write about African Americans
and in turn drew such publishers as B&L to African American authors.[7]
Unlike Henry James, who (as I argued in chapter 3) figuratively
identified blackness with commercialism, the primitivists and cultural
pluralists of the interwar years inscribed African Americans with value as
recalcitrant pockets of genuine humanity within a rapidly standardizing
industrial-commercial society. In turn, however, the African American
writers in whom such firms as B&L invested found themselves and their
blackness implicated in an institutional field that was increasingly commercial and driven by publicity concerns. The publication of their work
was shaped not only by the fiat of downtown's Negrophiles and the conviction of uptown's civil rights champions, as others have demonstrated,
but also by the book business's embrace of advertising and public relations and the concurrent endorsement by influential academics of
African American writing as quintessentially American writing.

Conflicting Imperatives: The Status of "Stereotype" in Public Relations and "New Negro" Discourse

By the 1920s, book distribution had undergone dramatic changes since
the turn of the century, when it had been carried out primarily by "general" bookstores or stationers, by religious bookstores, and by the rare
and secondhand book dealers. As early as 1894, *Publisher's Weekly*
lamented a trend in publishing, "as in other trades, toward overproduction, without regard for capacity for consumption." The result, the editorial continued, was "a congestion that has entailed unnumbered hard-
ship on the bookseller, has rendered the public apathetic, and is
beginning to react on the publisher" (quoted in Borus 199). Department stores provided an important new outlet, and by the twenties, they
accounted for about half the retail total (Tebbel 312). Still, some maintained that the full market for books remained untapped. Helen Woodward, a publicist who had made her mark publicizing O. Henry and
Robert Louis Stevenson, delivered an address to the Women's National
Book Association, excerpted in a 1920 issue of *Printer's Ink,* in which she
exhorted publishers to think more like other manufacturers. Compared
to the sales of such luxury items as silk stockings, perfume, and automo-

biles, she noted, the sale of books had risen relatively slowly. Publishers were to blame.

> It is preposterous to think that in this country today there are only about 30,000 who buy the work of three English novelists who, with one exception, are perhaps the greatest living writers in the world. *There are several million people in this country ready to buy books if someone tells them about them in the right way* . . . It seems to me that there is a possibility for the publisher to build up a huge clientele for at least some of his writers if he would approach his product as a manufacturer would, and merchandise it and advertise it in similar fashion. My suggestions, therefore, are three: First, that the publisher advertise books for what is in them rather than some literary measure of forty years ago; second, that publishers appeal to a new public; and third, that publishers invest in an author with the same foresight which a soap manufacturer might invest in soap. (Quoted in Tebbel 315–16)

Publishers were already responding. In 1920, a group of thirty-five publishers launched a collaborative advertising campaign, including promotional posters appearing monthly and bearing such slogans as "Buy a Book a Week" and "Why Not Books?" No fewer than thirty-four articles devoted to the subject of book advertising and publicity appeared in the pages of *Publisher's Weekly* between 1918 and 1923.[8] In other words, publishers started doing what other manufacturers were so eager to do in the twenties: expand and nationalize their ad campaigns, cultivate brand recognition and brand loyalty by creating trademarks, stimulate interest in the "newsworthy" aspects of their products, and avail themselves of the promotional possibilities of film and commercial radio. It worked: by 1923, book printing and publishing had become the seventh-largest industry in New York.[9] Nationwide, the number of works of fiction published each year nearly tripled in the decade between the war and the stock market crash.[10] There were other contributing factors besides advertising and public relations. As Janice Radway notes, the library movement of the first decades of the century fostered a favorable bookselling environment, and literacy rates rose markedly during the same years, as the number of students enrolled in high schools increased 650 times between 1900 and 1920 and as college attendance tripled in the century's first three decades. "For a population newly taken with the value and possibilities of higher education," Radway writes, "the noblest books evoked" "a mixture of awe, fear, desire, and promise." Radway observes that though few people pursued book-related careers, "the book itself became a symbol of all that they had acquired through their education" (161). Thus, advertising and public relations were able to capitalize on the association, forged in other cultural arenas, of book reading (and, more specifically, book owning) with self-improvement and social prestige, to cultivate an unprecedented demand for books.

If authors and their publishers routinely construe the meaning and the cultural significance of authors' work differently (as even a casual acquaintance with the book business will suggest), public relations officers have still a different view. This is not to say that one perspective is definitive or more authentic or that one is unaffected by the others. But the difference is more consequential than is usually noted, for while the work, the author, and the publisher are generally looked to (in that order) as shapers of the work's reception by its readers, the public relations officer exerts a profound influence on the public reception of the work and may even be said to constitute that audience in the first place. Edward Bernays, onetime chief public relations officer for Boni and Liveright, wrote of his own perusal of his firm's list: "I read them, not for purposes of literary evaluation but to mine them for raw material, ideas—to further the public's interest in them. I looked for ideas in the flow of contemporary thought that could be dramatized and publicized" (*Biography* 280). We do not need to believe in an ideal of "literary evaluation" uncontaminated by history or ideology to see the issues raised by Bernays's statement. There is no such thing as a disinterested or decontextualized reading of a literary text, but not all interests and contexts are equivalent. The interests Bernays articulates and the use to which he puts his reading practice seem distinct from other popular interests in literary texts and the reading practices performed on them. The question is, whose reading becomes authoritative? In other words, to what extent is the reception of literary texts (or, for that matter, their selection for publication in the first place) a function of the generalization of the readings produced by the reading practice of public relations officers? If it is difficult to answer this question empirically, it is still important to provide local responses. It becomes especially important in relation to the reception of work by "ethnic" and subaltern writers at his-

Fig. 4. Advertisement of the Association of American
Booksellers' "Year-Round-Bookselling Campaign,"
from *Publishers Weekly*, March 31, 1923.

torical moments when the stakes of representation are high and questions of authenticity have much currency.[11]

The importance of "paratextual" elements in constituting the meaning of African American literary texts at this time is best illustrated by two advertisements.[12] The first, an advertisement for Jessie Fauset's novel *There Is Confusion*, appeared in the *New York Times Book Review* and the *Literary Review* in April 1924. The second is an advertisement for Alain Locke's edited volume *The New Negro* in the February 1926 issue of the NAACP journal *The Crisis*.

According to Floyd Calvin, editor of one of the country's leading black newspapers, the *Pittsburgh Courier*, the spring of 1924 marked "the beginning of a new era in the treatment of colored writers." He was reacting to the publication of *There Is Confusion*, the eagerly awaited first novel by Jessie Fauset, literary editor of *The Crisis*. But it was not Fauset's novel itself that interested Calvin; it was the publicity surrounding it.

Calvin observed: "It was well received. Generous reviews appeared in
New York Times Book Review, and in the *Literary Review.* Boni & Liveri
the publishers, purchased liberal space in the two notable publicatic
Calvin went on to quote the ad copy in its entirety.

> A few weeks ago a dinner was given at the Civic Club in New Yoi
> honor of Jessie Redmon Fauset, which the intellectual leaders o:
> metropolis attended. They were celebrating the birthday of a new
> of book about colored people—no lynchings, no inferiority (
> plexes, no *propaganda*—the birthday of a fine novel about Negro
> the upper classes of New York and Philadelphia—as impressive
> vital in their special environment as the upper class whites w
> Edith Wharton or Archibald Marshall love to write about . . . *Yes,*
> *something new under the sun and it is* <u>There Is Confusion.</u>

The ad suggests that the black upper class is a new subject for a re
public grown weary of social protest literature, dismissed here
thetically inferior "propaganda." However, for Calvin at the *Co*
was not Fauset herself that ushered in the "new era" so much as h
lishing company. Calvin noted that Boni and Liveright's public
unusual for black writers.

> Heretofore they have received no such encouragement whe
> work was accepted for publication and but scant notice w
> appeared. We dare say comparatively few of either race ki
> DuBois' "The Quest of the Silver Fleece," and James Weldoi
> son's "The Autobiography of an Ex-Coloured Man." And there
> Ovington's "The Shadow" and all of Charles W. Chesnutt's
> They were and are good books, well worth reading. Unfortu
> they came ahead of the times. But it is heartening to see this n
> tude. We trust the reception of Miss Fauset's book will make t
> even easier for other literary aspirants who choose to follow. (:

On one hand, Calvin was exactly right to see the investme
advertisements require as an index of progress. The capital that
tising required was important in itself, but it was more important
the "guarantee" of the white publisher's conferral of his "accun
symbolic capital," bringing the writer into a "cycle of consecrat
The black writers who had published with white firms in the previ

Fig. 5. Advertisement for *There Is Confusion,* by Jessie R. Fauset,
from the *New York Times Book Review,* April 13, 1924.
(Courtesy of the New York Public Library; Astor, Lenox,
and Tilden Foundations; General Research Division.)

decades were not only few and far between; they were also poorly promoted. Calvin identified the implicit racism of a publishing industry that
considered these books inferior and of a reading public whose interests
the industry was anticipating.

On the other hand, by equating publicity with social progress, Calvin
flattened out a complex and contradictory path that was being forged for
these writers. In the early twenties, publicity was rapidly developing into
a vast network of advertisements and reviews, posters and press releases,
staged news events and book-jacket blurbs. It was multilayered and
ambivalent in its implications. While writers and artists challenged white-
supremacist assumptions and traditional imagery, commercial publicity
played a vital role in naturalizing racist idiom and caricature and in
reproducing racial thinking more broadly. What did the emergence of
the black writer as the subject of commercial publicity augur for the
social inequities to which Floyd Calvin pointed?

The New Negro, a collection of prose, poetry, stories, and artwork by a
set of predominantly young artists and intellectuals, is in many ways the

definitive document of the literary Harlem Renaissance—not o〉
commitment to self-determination for African American artis〉
an Africanist aesthetic, but also in its frank elitism. Published ir
Albert and Charles Boni, who had recently parted ways wit
Liveright, the volume was edited by Howard University's Al
whose introductory essay was a kind of manifesto. On one 〉
readers on notice that a change had occurred in the ps〉
spirit of African Americans since the turn of the centur〉
hand, it seems polemically aimed to bring about the very change it
announces as a fait accompli—aimed, that is, to galvanize the energies of
Harlem's creative leaders and intellectual elite and to deliver on the
promise of the "New Negro" ideal. Locke writes of African Americans
"achieving something like a spiritual emancipation" by "shedding the
old chrysalis of the Negro problem" (4). He relegates racist stereotypes
to the past, claiming that the reality of African Americans' lives was too
obviously at variance with these stereotypes to sustain them.

> [T]he Old Negro had long become more of a myth than a man . . . His
> has been a stock figure perpetuated as an historical fiction partly in
> innocent sentimentalism, partly in deliberate reactionism . . . The day
> of "aunties," "uncles," and "mammies" is gone. Uncle Tom and
> Sambo have passed on, and even the "Colonel" and "George" play
> barnstorm roles from which they escape with relief when the public
> spotlight is off. The popular melodrama has about played itself out,
> and it is time to scrap the fictions, garret the bogeys and settle down
> to a realistic facing of facts. (3, 5)

As much as Locke's claims were borne out by the work collected in *The
New Negro,* the way readers received and understood this work was
inevitably also shaped by messages communicated by the publicity for
the volume. These messages complicated Locke's stated intentions.

In the February 1926 issue of *The Crisis,* an advertisement for *The New
Negro* shares space with another Boni brothers book, *Mellows,* by R.
Emmet Kennedy. The advertisement calls *Mellows* a book of "Negro spirituals, work songs and street cries," and while there is nothing inherently
demeaning about publishing such folklore, the ad copy continues as follows: "Beautifully bound in a special bandana cloth, with intimate pictures of house servants and field hands of old slavery days and scenes of
Louisiana. Many of the songs are here printed for the first time. Price

$5.00" (203). Clearly, when it came to *Mellows,* it was very much the "Old Negro" that the Boni brothers were marketing. Locke sounded the death knell for "aunties," "uncles," and "mammies" in the text of his essay, but such "paratexts" as this advertisement confirmed that the "Old Negro" doggedly pursued the "New Negro" in the popular imaginary of race, even among readers of *The Crisis.* In the logic of the advertisement, there is evidently no contradiction in pairing one work expressing—indeed, embodying in its bandana-cloth binding—a nostalgia for the plantation tradition and its stock racist stereotypes with another work repudiating this tradition and set of figures. Not only were readers of *The Crisis* introduced to these texts side by side, but the order form implicitly discourages readers from ordering one without the other, inviting them instead to check off the request to "please send me *The New Negro,* and *Mellows.*"

The New Negro eulogized "aunties," "uncles," and "mammies," featuring, by contrast, Aaron Douglas's drawings of lithe-limbed figures in profile, heads raised—evoking an Africanist nobility amid a jagged iconography of the modern city. But advertisers were still having a field day in 1925 with "Nigger-Head" tobacco, "pickaninnies" at the mercy of alligators, and retreads of the stock Uncle Tom and Mammy figures. Moreover, the racism of print advertisements lay as much in their acts of omission as in those of commission, for the few nonwhites who were represented in print ads were invariably the subordinates of the whites who solicited the viewer's identification.[14] In this context, a public relations officer who was dutifully performing his job of assessing the "mental equipment," as Bernays put it, of the targeted audience would have little trouble identifying "stereotypes" that could be "tapped" when publicizing work by African American authors (*Crystallizing* 61–63). The real question is whether he could avoid them. In his search for what Bernays described as "ideas in the flow of contemporary thought that could be dramatized and publicized" (*Biography* 280), could a publicity-conscious publisher come up with "stereotypes" in Bernays's sense that were not also "stereotypes" in *The New Negro* sense?

Black Writers as PR

The Boni and Liveright advertisement for *There Is Confusion* communicates a more complex set of meanings than simply that Jessie Fauset has

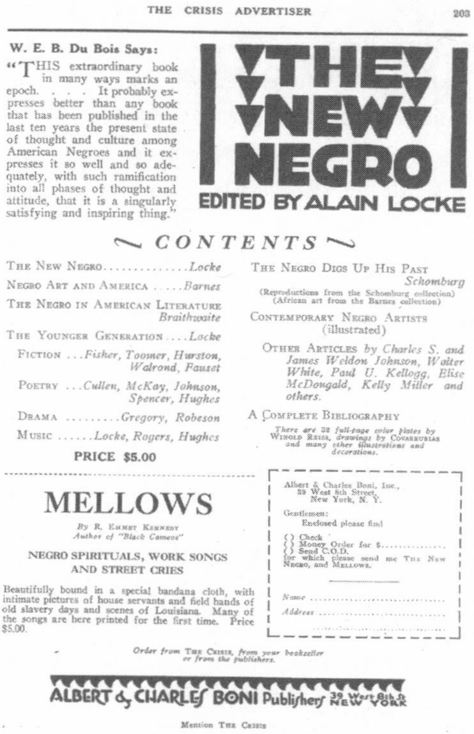

Fig. 6. Advertisement for books published by Albert and Charles Boni, from *The Crisis,* February 1926. (Courtesy of the New York Public Library; Astor, Lenox, and Tilden Foundations; General Research Division.)

a new book worth reading. It invites readers to think of themselves as discriminating in their literary tastes and thoughtful about race prejudice. It also promotes the publisher—explicitly in the border, implicitly in its self-congratulation for having recognized a worthy novel, and finally in its reference to the dinner honoring Fauset at the Civic Club. This event was itself a masterpiece of staged publicity. *Opportunity* magazine, the journal of the Urban League, had a new editor at the helm, the politically savvy Charles S. Johnson, and Johnson collaborated with Fauset's publisher to help make some news for the Writer's Guild, a loose collective of black artists whose work was little-known outside the readers of

African American journals.[15] Thus, at a dinner that historian David Levering Lewis calls "the dress rehearsal for what was soon to be known as
the 'Harlem Renaissance,'" Jessie Fauset, Countee Cullen, Eric Walrond,
Georgia Douglas Johnson, Langston Hughes, Gwendolyn Bennett,
Harold Jackman, and Regina Anderson were introduced to the white literary establishment, including Paul Kellogg of *Survey Magazine,* Frida
Kirchwey and Heywood Broun of *The Nation,* and Frederick Lewis Allen
of Harper and Brothers. Alain Locke, to whom *Opportunity* referred in its
coverage as the "virtual dean of the movement," acted as master of ceremonies for this "coming out party" ("The Debut" 143). On hand to
deliver endorsements of the writers and the movement they represented
were such authorities as Horace Liveright, Charles Johnson, W. E. B.
DuBois, and the eminent critic and *Century* magazine editor Carl Van
Doren. Words of encouragement were also offered by James Weldon
Johnson and his NAACP colleague Walter White, the assistant secretary
whose novel, *Fire in the Flint,* was in press at Knopf at the time (Lewis
93–94). Consider, then, this Civic Club dinner, the B&L ad in which it is
mentioned, and the *Pittsburgh Courier* column about the B&L ad. Taken
together, they exhibit a strange regress of self-referentiality. How is it
news in Pittsburgh that a New York publisher has taken out an ad report-
ing on its own publicity event? A kind of seamless telescoping is effected,
the ad certifying the newsworthiness of the Civic Club dinner, only to
become, itself, the news.

Today, of course, this is typical. The idea that publicity, once it is set
in motion, becomes self-generating is standard operating procedure in
late capitalism. But in the 1920s, the promise of this idea was only just
being recognized—and its practice just being formalized—in the field of
public relations, which emerged as a glimmer in the eye of the advertising industry. The notion that the news was not simply organic but could
be systematically manufactured had a long history prior to the 1920s,
from P. T. Barnum to Walter Lippmann. But the person who sought to
make a science of it, who professionalized the field of public relations
almost single-handedly, was Edward Bernays, B&L's chief public relations officer for a brief but critical stint just after Liveright became the
publisher. Bernays set down the principles of this science in such books
as *Crystallizing Public Opinion* (1923), *Propaganda* (1928), and *The Engineering of Consent* (1955). As is suggested by these titles—none of which

carried the sinister connotation for their author that they do today—
Bernays conceived of the public first and foremost as consumers, a mal-
leable mass of perceptions and desires that required expert direction,
whether the products were cars, books, or ideas about U.S. foreign policy. In addition to his private employment, he worked regularly for the
federal government, beginning his career with the U.S. Committee on
Public Information during World War I, burnishing Calvin Coolidge's
image for his 1924 presidential campaign, and working closely during
the Cold War with the Overseas Information Program of the Senate
Committee on Foreign Affairs.[16] Whereas advertisements cost money
and even the most respectable ads made overt, unseemly bids for public
attention, the cost and the explicitness of the appeal could be circum-
vented, Bernays argued, through the behind-the-scenes work of press
releases, ready-to-print reviews, promotional tie-ins, staged events, and
high-profile product placement. Although Bernays was no longer
officially employed by B&L after 1920, he and Liveright maintained very
close ties, for each man was instrumental in the other's professional success. Although the Civic Club event of 1924 was the brainchild of
Charles S. Johnson, it has all the contrived newsworthiness of a Bernays
event.[17]

For his own part, Bernays always cast public relations as a public service: in print and in interviews, he stressed the distinction between "propaganda" and "impropaganda," as well as the ethical responsibilities of
the public relations officer not to mislead his audience. Despite his Progressive rhetoric, however, the aims and implications of the field Bernays
pioneered are profoundly antidemocratic. Of his wartime work with the
U.S. Committee on Public Information, Bernays wrote chillingly, "We
opened the eyes of the intelligent few in all departments of life to the
possibilities of regimenting the public mind" (*Propaganda* 58). Above all,
public relations served the efforts of this "intelligent few," the self-
anointed experts of a culture of expertise; it provided great assistance as
the cultural elite battled the crisis of legitimation that consumer capitalism underwent in the 1920s and 1930s. "In Bernays," writes historian
William Leach, "the push, push promotional zeal of [advertising]
flowered into a carefully contrived system of manipulation" (320). As
advertising came under heavy fire in the 1920s for deception, with such
groups as Truth in Advertising provoking ritual exercises of self-disci-

pline within the ad industry, Bernays played a pivotal role in sanitizing the field, turning the nineteenth-century snake-oil salesman into the modern spin doctor. When Horace Liveright hired him in 1919, the title of "chief public relations officer" was a novelty at a publishing company, and "applying the new publicity direction to book publishing" was "a hitherto untried approach" (Bernays, *Biography* 277). Bernays's tenure with B&L proved brief but decisive.

Horace Liveright experienced the Bernays treatment firsthand when Bernays persuaded him in 1920 to publish the first American translation of a book by Bernays's uncle Sigmund Freud. The Viennese psychoanalyst's reputation in the United States had not yet reached beyond elite academic circles. Freud's *General Introduction to Psychoanalysis* marked B&L as an innovative firm early in its career, and by the end of the decade, it had sold twenty thousand copies and transformed Freud's stature in the United States (Dardis 118). But it only happened through Bernays's persistent endorsement in the face of skepticism among B&L's officers. Biographer Tom Dardis writes that, just as Liveright had trusted Ezra Pound's estimate of *The Waste Land,* he trusted Bernays on Freud's book, despite the skepticism of his editor in chief, Tommy Smith, his production manager, Manuel Komroff, and his sales manager, Julian Messner, who were "appalled at the notion of publishing what appeared to be a densely written German text about medical matters and predicted disaster for the undertaking" (117). As a public relations officer, Bernays adapted and distorted Freud's ideas, putting his analysis of the public unconscious in the service of whoever happened to employ him. William Leach writes:

Bernays conceived public relations as a nonjudgmental technique similar to psychoanalysis, to be applied to any institution, person, or commodity that needed its "image" (ego) refurbished in the public arena. He began studying his client, although, like many psychoanalysts, he refused to "treat" pathologically "antisocial" groups or people. Next he observed the "mental equipment" of his patron's targeted public, hoping to find their "stereotypes" that might be "tapped" and exploited. Then he interpreted his client's product, devising "associations" between the product and ideas, and drawing on his knowledge of the "stereotypes." Finally he "crystallized" these associations for the public through a coordinated mobilization of largely visual media. (321)

This goal to identify the selling associations and "crystallize" them into arresting—preferably visual—images is one worth considering in relation to the increase in production and circulation of African American literature in the 1920s.

Book publishers had been slower to embrace advertising than were the manufacturers and distributors of other commodities, because of the special status books have long held in Western culture as the quasi-sacred agents of enlightenment and repositories of civilization. Publishers were therefore reluctant to treat them simply as commodities—or, more precisely, to admit as much to the audiences of their advertisements. Perhaps for this reason, the stealthy "science" of public relations proved an attractive alternative and supplement to advertising. This was not simply a matter of money, of prosperity prompting the expansion of budgets and staff. It was a deliberate and strikingly rapid appropriation of public relations strategies, a commitment to the idea that books should compete for the public dollar not just with one another but with the manufacturers of other goods.

"It was not until recently," Bernays trumpeted in a *Publisher's Weekly* article in 1920, "that another method was introduced to supplement and reinforce advertising, namely propaganda and publicity, which proved such a powerful factor in the war." He continued: "Publishers advertise, of course, as heavily as they can afford to. But a publisher who puts out a number of books per year cannot possibly push any one of his books or authors as heavily as the manufacturer of tires, for example, can push his one product." Thus, Bernays submitted that "some other less expensive method must be found for the further sales promotion of books" ("Publishing Expert" 933). Resistance from the New England establishment was strong. "Book publishing was dominated by stuffy old firms who treated the business as if it were the practice of a sacred rite," Bernays recalled years later.

The Macmillan Company, Doubleday, Harper's, Scribner's, E. P. Dutton, Henry Holt & Company, and G. P. Putnam's were run like conservative banking houses. Books were handled in the same way they had been published—for a select audience and not for a larger public. Book publishing was static in the content of its books and in its promotion when it should have been, of course, vibrant with ideas . . . I was eager to try out our strategies and tactics on books. Books should respond more quickly to our techniques than almost any other commodity. The fact that our approach had not yet been applied to the book business was a further stimulus to my interest. Liveright and I agreed that a number of books should receive the dynamic treatment the entrepreneurs give a new drama, opera, or sporting event. (*Biography* 277–78)

Bernays held that demand could be manufactured for books, as it was for other commodities, but that they required a more subtly coordinated, multidimensional publicity program. The term B&L used in its advertising was "cooperation."[18]

Publishing routine up to then consisted of mailing the author's biography, photographs, and book notes to literary editors and distributing publishers' catalogs. We had made additional efforts. We sent circulars weekly to 300 bookstores in the United States (serving at that time a population of 105 million). We offered free to newspapers 100 newsworthy feature articles on our books, each described in 75 words. Skeptical newspaper editors wrote us asking whether they would have to pay for the features. One Midwest book editor, Julius Liebman of the Milwaukee *Sentinel,* said that he could not understand why this material should be offered free. Should there be any strings attached, he told us frankly to forget it. Editors today are more sophisticated about publicity . . . Presently feature stories about our books appeared in newspapers throughout the country. "As you know," wrote one editor, "all the papers are suffering terribly from the shortage of newsprint and it is only this which prevents us from using everything you send." (*Biography* 284)

With Liveright's collaboration, Bernays changed the premises of the publishing business, first at B&L, then at the firms who were compelled to take note of its success.

From its inception, B&L had been a curiously commercial firm. Liveright was not a "literary man," having first established himself as a bond trader on Wall Street and joining the Boni brothers only after a

Fig. 7. Advertisement featuring the coordinated marketing
strategy of Boni and Liveright, from *Publishers Weekly,*
January 27, 1923.

failed venture in manufacturing toilet tissue. B&L's fledgling publishing business was based on a provocative marketing gimmick. The Bonis had hired an executive from the prestigious J. Walter Thompson ad agency, Harry Scherman, and cut a deal with the Whitman candy corporation, packaging miniature, leather-bound volumes of Shakespeare plays inside boxes of chocolates. The demand far outstripped their expectations, the money to finance fifteen thousand copies was hastily gathered, and the Little Leather Library was born. Soon Woolworth's contracted for the distribution of the volumes, which expanded beyond Shakespeare to include many European classics and became the Modern Library. On the strength of its Modern Library backlist, B&L could soon take risks on experimental modernists on whom the publisher was likely to lose money. Harry Scherman moved on in 1926 to found what was arguably the most important U.S. literary institution of the twentieth century, the Book-of-the-Month Club, while B&L suffered from Liveright's profligate spending, sold the Modern Library to Bennett Cerf of Random House, and failed to survive the Depression. Before its demise, however, B&L published all of Eugene O'Neill's plays; the first edition of *The Waste Land* (1922); several volumes of poetry by Ezra Pound, E. E. Cummings, Hart Crane, and H.D.; the first novels by Ernest Hemingway and William Faulkner; and a great deal of work by Theodore

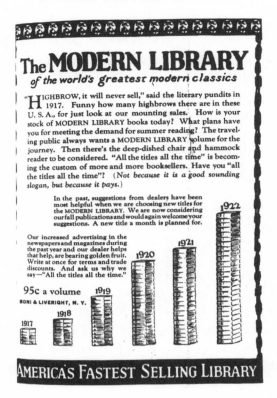

Fig. 8. Advertisement for the Modern Library,
from *Publishers Weekly,* April 28, 1923.

Dreiser, Waldo Frank, Sherwood Anderson, S. J. Perelman, Djuna
Barnes, and Nathanael West—in short, a fair share of the pantheon of
American modernism.[19] Once we add to these examples John Reed's
Ten Days That Shook the World (1919), Mike Gold's *Jews without Money,* and
the first U.S. translation of Trotsky's *The Bolsheviki and World Peace*
(1918), one can understand why Waldo Frank remarked, tongue in
cheek, that Liveright "sponsored half the advanced novelists who pollute
our homes, half the radical thinkers who defile our customs, half the free
verse poets who corrupt our English" and "has defiantly come out for
minorities in a land where the Majority is sacred" (111).

When it came to publishing "New Negro" writers, B&L was neither the
most prolific nor the most consistent (Knopf and Harcourt far outpaced

them), but it was involved early and often. B&L published the first books by Toomer (1923), Fauset (1924), and Eric Walrond, a West Indian émigré who was the business manager of *Opportunity* and wrote *Tropic Death* (1926), a stylized and widely praised collection of short stories. The thousand-dollar prize that the Boni brothers offered in 1926 for the best novel on "Negro life" by a black author was among the most lucrative of the many competitive literary awards of the era.[20] In 1925, B&L published several poems by Toomer and Claude McKay in *May Days,* a collection of verse culled from the left-wing journals *The Liberator* and *The Masses.* Perhaps its most enduring legacy, however, was the Civic Club event that occasioned a special issue of *Survey* magazine dedicated to Harlem in 1925, edited by Locke and republished by the Boni brothers as *The New Negro.* In *The Harlem Renaissance in Black and White,* George Hutchinson calls Liveright one of "the most important and fearless publishers of the Harlem Renaissance" (372).

The rhetoric of the publicity in B&L's catalogs suggests that the three most important qualities of the New Negro texts B&L published were their lack of "sentimentality," their rejection of stock "darky" figures, and their distance from "propaganda." The last two were common commitments among many publishing companies during the Harlem Renaissance, so I will not comment on them further. While a lack of "sentimentality" is related to the other two valorized qualities, it was expressed with unusual consistency and zeal at B&L. The spring 1924 catalog endorses *There Is Confusion* in terms that echo the previous generation's debates over "realism" and "romance." "In the place of sentimentality and darky humor," the novel is said to "give us the realities of [a] life utterly unknown to the great mass of educated readers," a black upperclass "milieu that, self-contained, parallels the life of the white American." Likewise, the entry for Walrond's book in the fall 1926 issue introduces it as "realistically done," going on to praise its "purely objective stories, devoid of prejudice, propaganda or excessive race consciousness." "With this book," it concludes, "the least sentimental of Negro prose writers arrives, and a region hitherto steeped in utter mist looms broodingly on the literary horizon."[21]

However, B&L's investment in New Negro writers arose from more complex circumstances than the "fearlessness" of its publisher or what Waldo Frank describes as a principled stand for minorities. Nor was it simply a question of exploiting for profit the "vogue in all things negro," as Langston Hughes famously put it. Contrary to the conventional wisdom that lumps B&L in with those David Levering Lewis has called the "dollars and cents salon Negrotarians," its interest in black writers was not simply exploitative, in the sense that no one really believed there was money to be made on black novelists and poets.[22] Hutchinson writes:

> Scholars have often intimated that white publishers would publish only works conforming to mainstream white audience expectations, but evidence for this is slim. The publishers that accepted Harlem Renaissance manuscripts do not seem to have been thinking mainly about the bottom line in doing so. (Of course, neither were they non-profits.) Many of the early volumes of the movement were collections of poetry, and such books were not expected to make money regardless of the poet's race. They were intended, instead, to give "tone" to a publishing house . . . Indeed, Liveright eventually went out of business largely because he did not pay enough attention to profitability and did not take care of his backlist . . . The "success publishers" of the 1920s . . . were not those that accepted the books of black authors. (346–47)

If, as Hutchinson contends, firms like B&L did not invest in black writers with an eye to profitability, perhaps it was simply to trend-set or to appear avant-garde. But Hutchinson suggests otherwise, arguing that the investment was part of a broad project (with which several of the newer firms were affiliated) to advance cultural pluralism in the face of the prevailing postwar current of "100 percent Americanism" and Anglo-Saxonism (346).

Indeed, the Jewishness of the founders of these newer firms was central to the sort of transformation they wrought in the industry, as was their recent (and, in some cases, ongoing) connection to Europe. Although their cultural pluralist challenge to the dominant Anglo-Saxonism was partly conscious and deliberate, it was as much a question of material conditions as one of religious beliefs or ideological commitments.[23] Jews were barred from many graduate programs and excluded from the Anglo-Saxon boys club that was the publishing establishment, so, as Jonathan Freedman argues in *The Temple of Culture*, many Jewish men with an interest in culture forged careers in business that conjoined the literary with the commercial, an arena in which Jews had established roots and a cultural identity. It was this very marginalization from the mainstream, Freedman argues, that ironically resulted in their flourishing as publishers and energizing the industry.

> Precisely because they were discouraged from pursuing careers in English departments, blackballed from genteel publishing firms, and excluded from meetings of the most prestigious publishers and advertisers, they had to create alternative mechanisms of cultural expression and dissemination. Fascinated by "culture" but excluded from its study as a profession, these Jews entered into the high culture industries with a subversive force—changing . . . the very nature of the literary field itself . . . Because of the traditional ways of most American houses, these new competitors were forced—or enabled—to seek out new kinds of writing. (167–68)

Prior to the establishment of these firms, "most American book publishers had certain editorial traits in common," writes Tom Dardis. "Politically speaking, their choices were on the conservative side; an exception to this would be Macmillan's publishing of Jack London. The basic conservatism was reflected in the kinds of literary books they published" (51). Because the established firms largely neglected the outpouring of experimental writing in Europe, many of the major works of twentieth-century modernism were published in the teens and twenties by Jewish publishers. This was true of all of Joyce's works in the United States, including *Dubliners* (Huebsch), *A Portrait of the Artist as a Young Man* (Huebsch), and *Ulysses* (Random House); D. H. Lawrence's *Women in Love* and *The Rainbow* (Seltzer); the work of Thomas Mann and Joseph Conrad (Knopf); and, as mentioned earlier, all of Ezra Pound's poetry (B&L) and Eliot's *The Waste Land* (B&L).[24] In this context, publishing New Negro writing may well have given "tone" to such publishing companies, but it also fulfilled ideological and ethnic commitments to "disaffiliate American from 'Anglo-Saxon' literature" (Hutchinson 344, 346). The new firms were far more alert than their established contemporaries to the significance of literary contributions of immigrants and others on the cultural margins (Hutchinson 382).

Not only were their booklists different from the publishing establishment, but also, as the origins of the Modern Library suggest, firms like B&L transformed the industry by developing entrepreneurial business practices that had characterized urban Jewish commercial development since the turn of the century. Historian Andrew Heinze has written brilliantly about the synergy between what he calls the Jewish commercial tradition and American mass consumption. "In commerce," Heinze writes, "Jews found an effective medium for realizing the powerful desire to contribute to the society that had accepted them" (182). This is perhaps too generous a characterization of a mainstream society that was still deeply anti-Semitic, but Heinze's overall argument—that a traditional eastern European Jewish belief in the virtue of material plenitude shaped Jewish immigrants' experience of American commercial abundance and encouraged their participation in the emerging culture of consumption—is instructive. Horace Liveright and Albert and Charles Boni may have been a generation removed from the pushcart peddlers of the Lower East Side, but they retained the street merchants' retail sensibility to provide high-quality merchandise at lower prices than were found in mainstream venues and to pursue innovative display, packaging, and marketing techniques.[25]

Appearing to "come out for minorities" and radicals also conferred a celebrity and symbolic capital that Liveright relished. When George Creel, U.S. director of public information, objected to Liveright's publication of Trotsky's book, a gesture that prompted many booksellers to remove it from their shelves, Liveright requested Creel's permission to use excerpts from his objection in B&L's publicity materials (Dardis 58). Liveright fashioned himself a champion of free speech, twice testifying in court in defense of books of his that were brought up on obscenity charges. Taking the stand on behalf of free speech furnished a good deal of free publicity. Moreover, a commitment to marginal voices and first amendment rights can also be seen as a pursuit of controversy for its own sake; Bernays writes of having solicited comments from Liveright on each author in order to decide which books to heavily promote.

Liveright's comments are interesting in light of subsequent literary history. Many of the authors and books Liveright was so enthusiastic about are forgotten; some remain among the American classics. A

number covered vital controversial areas—psychoanalysis, sex, alco-
holism, social unrest, the labor movement, strikes, and liberalism as it
affected college students and professors. (*Biography* 279)

For that matter, for every "polluter," "defiler," and "corrupter" among
B&L's authors were several mainstream writers being marketed for popular success, and the success B&L had with best sellers may go farther
toward explaining Liveright's willingness to take chances on Toomer,
Fauset, and Walrond than do altruistic principles or aesthetic vision. A
streak of best sellers—Hendrik Willem Van Loon's *Story of Mankind*
(1922), Gertrude Atherton's *Black Oxen* (1923), and Anita Loos's *Gentlemen Prefer Blondes* (1924)—allowed B&L to relocate in 1924 to a more
expensive and fashionable midtown office, and these sales also cush-
ioned the financial hit B&L took on authors who were "difficult" modernists or otherwise avant-garde. "Do you suppose I like to go on losing
money on you miserable highbrows?" Liveright needled Pound in an
April 1923 letter, conceding, "But no matter what you write, you know I
always want to publish your poetry and I know that I do and will do more
for it than anyone else" (quoted in Dardis 101). If Liveright proved willing to "come out for minorities in a land where the Majority is sacred,"
he also did so as a loss-leader strategy aimed at marketing a "good books"
image without sacrificing mainstream appeal. Popular success alone
would have compromised B&L's aggressive position in the market of
"advanced culture."[26] Michael Soto writes in an essay about *Cane*'s marketing, "The advertising campaigns of Jazz Age publishers might be
viewed as a early attempt to mediate between high and low, between an
avant-garde intellectual elite and an educable philistine mass market"
(163).

If Liveright was therefore not simply a "dollars and cents Negrotar-
ian," neither was he a civil rights crusader. The Civic Club publicity event
is illustrative, for it all but eclipsed the B&L novelist it was ostensibly
meant to honor. Although Jessie Fauset "received a place of distinction
on the program," she was discouraged from speaking at length and
yielded the floor to Locke, Liveright, Johnson, DuBois, and Van Doren
("The Debut" 143). Moreover, while B&L advertising trumpeted the
Civic Club event as a vehicle for their author and her book, in reality
Charles Johnson had intended from the start "to include as many of the

Fig. 9. Advertisement for two of Boni and Liveright's best sellers,
Black Oxen and *Flaming Youth*, March 10, 1923.

new school of writers as possible" (quoted in Hutchinson 390). "Miss
Fauset performed as her hosts expected," writes Cheryl Wall in *Women of
the Harlem Renaissance,* but she inwardly resented her treatment, particularly from Locke, the master of ceremonies and a notorious misogynist.[27]

> She thanked her friends for their assistance, and after singling out Dr.
> DuBois as her "best friend and severest critic," she sat down. Years
> later, in a private letter to Locke, she vented the rage her good man-
> ners compelled her at the time to conceal. Accusing him of going out
> of his way to tell even her own brother that the dinner had not been
> for her, she fumed that she "still remember[ed] the consummate clev-
> erness with which you that night as toastmaster strove to keep speech

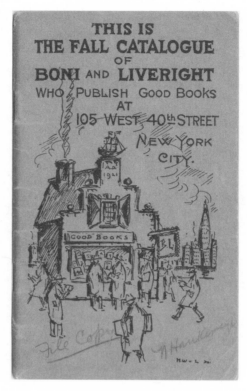

Fig. 10. Cover of Boni and Liveright's fall 1921 catalog,
featuring the new slogan "Good Books." (Courtesy of the
W. W. Norton Papers, Butler Library, Columbia University,
Rare Books and Manuscripts Division.)

and comment away from the person for whom the occasion was meant." (70)

For his part, Liveright's address made only cursory reference to Fauset. He insisted on the importance of publishing high-quality writing without regard to sales figures, citing his gamble on Toomer's *Cane,* which sold a mere 429 copies its first year (Soto 180). When Fauset presented Liveright with a follow-up novel the next year, however, he rejected it. He also passed on a volume of poems by Georgia Douglas Johnson, perhaps because she was, like Fauset, stylistically conventional.

As Gloria Hull points out, the lack of formal innovation and reliance on traditional themes that one finds in Fauset, Johnson, and the lyric poets Alice Dunbar-Nelson and Angelina Grimké had more to do with their socialization than with their imagination or skill. "Reared as proper, middle-class, almost Victorian black women who were trained to be proofs of black female morals and modesty, their restrained treatment of sex placed them outside of the sensational mainstream," observes Hull, and their formal and thematic conventionality "made their work relatively unexciting in a renaissance awakening that required some flash and newness" (24–25).[28] Moreover, although Liveright made something of a practice of hiring his authors as editors (even women), when Fauset left her editorship at *The Crisis* after a falling out with DuBois, Liveright made her no offer, thereby declining not only to support Fauset but also to make a forceful statement to the segregated publishing industry and to land one of the most highly accomplished editors and best-educated women in the northeast. Therefore, the advertisement that was said to mark "a new era in the treatment of colored writers" ("A few weeks ago a dinner was given . . . in honor of Jessie Redmon Fauset") may be better understood as a disingenuous distortion of the event's aims so as to redound principally to the credit of the publishing company. For publicity purposes, "Jessie Redmon Fauset" and *There Is Confusion* functioned less as an author and a text than as temporary signifiers of the "something new under the sun" that B&L was in the business of selling.

Toomer's Reluctant Authority: Blackness, Publicity, and the White Critique of Modernity

It is not surprising that Liveright cited *Cane* as evidence of his publishing savvy and commitment to the group of writers seated before him at B&L's Civic Club event. Despite its poor sales, *Cane* had immediately earned critical praise, particularly in the black press, as a promise of stylistic innovation among a new generation of black writers. In the September 1924 issue of *The Crisis*, William Stanley Braithwaite wrote:

> I believe that of all the writers I have mentioned, the one who is most surely touched with genius is Jean Toomer, the author of "Cane." I believe this, not only on account of what he has actually accomplished

in "Cane," but for something which is partly in the accomplishment and partly in the half articulate sense and impression of his powers. This young man is an artist; the very first artist in his Race who, with all an artist's passion and sympathy for life, its hurts, its sympathies, its desires, its joys, its defeats, and strange yearnings, can write about the Negro without the surrender or compromise of the artist's vision . . . Jean Toomer is a bright morning star on a new day of the Race in literature! (Quoted in Gates, *Figures in Black* 198–99)

Nevertheless, when many of this generation convened at the Civic Club, Toomer was conspicuously absent. He declined the invitation because of what he later described as a sudden disenchantment with all things "Negro." Among these was the "Negro" in himself. This disavowal of blackness caused a notorious spat with Liveright, one that underscores the complicated articulation of commercial publicity with racial thinking. It was of paramount importance to Toomer that he be identified, personally and professionally, as racially mixed, rather than reduced to any one racial identity, while for Liveright, Toomer's blackness was central to the publication and promotion of his work.

When Liveright agreed to publish *Cane* in 1923, he had not read the manuscript. He relied on the recommendations of Sherwood Anderson and Waldo Frank and agreed only on the condition that Frank write a preface. Above all else, Liveright seems to have acted on Toomer's growing association with an influential Greenwich Village literary set (though he lived in Washington, D.C.).[29] This circle revolved around Albert and Charles Boni's bookstore and the neighboring Provincetown Playhouse; consolidated itself through little magazines such as *The Seven Arts, Broom,* and *The Dial;* and included John Reed, Louise Bryant, Max Eastman, Frank, Anderson, Theodore Dreiser, and Eugene O'Neill.[30] Though their social and professional lives overlapped with H. L. Mencken and George Jean Nathan's "smart set" and the coterie at the Algonquin Hotel, the artwork and political causes by which they defined themselves tended to be more experimental and sensational than their midtown counterparts. Several were white writers writing about black people and publishing with B&L. From Waldo Frank's *Holiday* to Sherwood Anderson's *Dark Laughter* to E. E. Cummings's *The Enormous Room* to Eugene O'Neill's *The Emperor Jones* and *All God's*

Chillun Got Wings, B&L published a number of variations on a fantasy of idealized or atavistic blackness, a figure for the authenticity and proximity to nature that the authors felt had been drained out of white people by the industrial civilization and genteel morality that their own work was criticizing.

These writers did not change the qualities associated with African Americans in the white U.S. imaginary so much as they revalued them. Self-appointed white observers of "the Negro character," from statesmen like Thomas Jefferson to scientists like Louis Agassiz to novelists like Thomas Dixon, had long authorized the conventional wisdom that African Americans were less intelligent, more childlike, and more emotionally exuberant than whites and were less capable than whites of self-discipline and foresight. Marked with these overdetermined qualities, the figure of the Negro was a convenient vehicle for white modernists to use in expressing their disenchantment with Western civilization, though now African Americans found their "difference" valorized rather than vilified, their history of deprivations and exclusions romanticized rather than reviled.

Understandably, African American intellectuals were uncertain how to interpret this shift in treatment by white writers, and at least in their public statements, their enthusiasm was qualified by their perplexity. An *Opportunity* editorial in March 1924 sounded an optimistic note.

> There has been manifest recently a most amazing change in the public mind on the question of the Negro. There is a healthy hunger for more information—a demand for a new interpretation of characters long and admittedly misunderstood. The moderate success of books like "Black and White," "Birthright," "Nigger," followed by the even more daring departure, both in style and content, in books like "Holiday" and "Cane" is enormously significant. They point to a gentle awakening among a large mass of the reading public which until recently would take its pictures from virulent Negro baiters only, or remain indifferent. ("The New Generation" 68)

More circumspect, Rudolph Fisher wondered in the *American Mercury* in 1927 whether the white vogue for "Negro games" and dances was not predicated on erroneous assumptions about the ostensibly innate physical vitality and rhythm of African Americans.

It may be a season's whim, this sudden, contagious interest in everything Negro. If so, when I go into a familiar cabaret, or the place
where a familiar cabaret used to be, and find it transformed and relatively colorless, I may be observing just one form that the season's
whim has taken. But suppose it is a fad—to say that explains nothing.
How came the fad? What occasions the focusing of attention on this
particular thing—rounds up and gathers these seasonal whims, and
centers them about the Negro? . . . And what do we see? Why we see
them actually playing Negro games. I watch them in that epidemic
Negroism, the Charleston. I look on and envy them. They camel and
fish-tail and black-bottom and scronch, they skate and buzzard and
mess-around—and they do them all better than I! (216)

This primitivism was fueled in large part by the popularization of
Freudian ideas on the unconscious, but also by several of B&L's white
modernists. Toni Morrison notes in *Playing in the Dark* that U.S. writers
have long used race to explore far-reaching questions about modernity,
albeit in ways that reinscribed the binary opposition, deeply rooted in
European epistemology, linking whiteness to the mind and blackness to
the body. This "American Africanism," as Morrison calls it, furnished the
white literary imagination with "a way of contemplating chaos and civilization, desire and fear, and a mechanism for testing the problems and
blessings of freedom" (7).[31] In the work of B&L's white modernists, we
consistently see race put in the service of the literary ambitions that Morrison describes.

Perhaps the most literal expression of this revaluation of blackness
was Waldo Frank's effort in 1922 to pass as a "Negro" when he traveled
in the South gathering material for his novel *Holiday*. To facilitate this
performance, Frank, an olive-skinned Jew with dark, wavy hair, invited
his friend Jean Toomer to accompany him. The two were routinely mistaken for brothers on this trip, which also inspired Toomer's work in
Cane. In a review of *Cane* and *Holiday,* Bruno Lasker found the authors'
styles so similar that he suspected that Toomer was Frank: "Is not 'Jean
Toomer' a polite fiction?" (quoted in Gates, *Figures in Black* 214).

Sherwood Anderson's notebooks echo Frank's effort, as he expresses
a desperate desire, for the sake of his art, to move freely among the black
dockworkers whose strong bodies and lack of self-consciousness he

admires. *Dark Laughter*, which B&L published in 1925, laments the ener-
vation of urban, bourgeois whites and finds its antidote in a romanticized ideal of "the Negro." Anderson's protagonist, newspaper reporter
Bruce Dudley, observes:

> The men and women in the streets, such men and women as were
> now getting off and on the cars in the street before the apartment.
> Why did they all look so tired? What was the matter with them? What
> he had in his mind at the moment was not physical tiredness. In
> Chicago and in other cities he had visited the people were all inclined
> to have that tired, bored look on their faces when you caught them off
> guard, when they were walking along through the streets or standing
> at a street corner waiting for a car and Bruce had a fear he looked the
> same way. (22)

Likewise, Bruce's colleague asks whether he has noticed "that all of the
people you see are tired out, impotent." He attributes this impotence to
the influence of the newspaper, the theater, and the movies, concluding,
"[I]f this war isn't the sign of universal impotence, sweeping over the
world like a disease, then I don't know much" (23).

Nothing restores Bruce's potency more than watching "niggers,"
which he does more and more after leaving his wife and his job to drift
down the Mississippi River in the summer.

> People talked with a slow, drawling speech, niggers were hoeing cot-
> ton, other niggers fished for catfish in the river. The niggers were
> something for Bruce to look at, think about. So many black men
> slowly growing brown. Then would come the light brown, the velvet-
> browns, Caucasian features. The brown women tending up to the
> job—getting the race lighter and lighter. Soft Southern nights, warm
> dusky nights. Shadows flitting at the edge of cotton-fields, in dusky
> roads in sawmill towns. Soft voices laughing, laughing.
>
> O, ma banjo dog. / Oh, ho, ma banjo dog.
> An' I ain't go'na give you / None of ma jelly roll. (42)

Through euphemism ("brown women tending up to the job") and black
vernacular ("jelly roll"), Anderson figures the recovery of Bruce's sexual
potency with black women: "You're a nigger down South and you get

some white blood in you. A little more, and a little more. Northern travelers help, they say. Oh, Lord! Oh, my banjo dog!" (47). Bruce's thoughts are impressionistically rendered.

> Nigger girls in the streets, nigger women, nigger men. There is a brown cat lurking in the shadow of a building. "Come brown puss—come get your cream." The men who work on the docks in New Orleans have slender flanks like running horses, broad shoulders, loose heavy lips hanging down—faces like old monkeys sometimes—bodies like young gods—sometimes. On Sundays—when they go to church, or to a bayou baptizing, the brown girls do sure cut loose with the colors—gaudy nigger colors on nigger women making the streets flame—deep purples, reds, yellows, green like young corn-shoots coming up. They sweat. The skin colors brown, golden yellow, reddish brown, purple-brown. When the sweat runs down high brown backs the colors come out and dance before the eyes. Flash that up, you silly painters, catch it dancing. Song-tones in words, music in words—in colors too. Silly American painters! They chase a Gaugin shadow to the South Seas. Bruce wrote a few poems. (45)

A sort of prose Gaugin himself here, Anderson's colorful vision of sensuous, overembodied "niggers" plays a central role in the novel's extended rumination on bourgeois morality and "overcivilization."

Figures of idealized black masculinity figure prominently in the critiques of modernity in Eugene O'Neill's *The Emperor Jones* (1920) and E. E. Cummings's *The Enormous Room* (1922). "Jones enters from the right," O'Neill's stage directions read, "He is a tall, powerfully built, full-blooded negro of middle-age. His features are typically negroid, yet there is something decidedly distinctive about his face—an underlying strength of will, a hardy, self-reliant confidence in himself that inspires respect" (5). Cummings similarly describes Jean le Negre in *The Enormous Room,* an account of Cummings's confinement in a French prison, La Ferté Macé, during World War I: "Of all the fine people in La Ferté, Monsieur Jean ('le noir' as he was entitled by his enemies) swaggers in my memory as the finest" (219). Jean's stage entrance reads as follows:

> Even as the *plantons* fumbled with the locks I heard the inimitable unmistakable divine laugh of a negro. The door opened at last.

Entered a beautiful pillar of black strutting muscle topped with a tremendous display of the whitest teeth on earth. The muscle bowed lightly in our direction, the grin remarked musically, "*Bo'jour, tou'l-monde.*" (218–19)

Just as the feverish and embattled Emperor Jones drags himself through the jungle swamps at the end of O'Neill's play, Jean is struggling alone at the end of Cummings's story: "Jean alone occupied the stage. His lips were parted. His eyes were enormous." Jean is suffering the effects of having been beaten by prison guards: "He was panting as if his heart would break. He still kept his arms raised as if seeing everywhere before him fresh enemies. Blood spotted here and there the wonderful chocolate carpet of his skin, and his whole body glistened with sweat. His shirt was in ribbons over his beautiful muscles" (231). Unlike Jones, however, whose "eyes are alive with a keen, cunning intelligence," Jean's virtue resides in his simplicity and orality, his propensity for joking, in a word, his childishness (5): "His mind was like a child's" in that "he courted above all the sound of words, more or less disdaining their meaning" (220); and "like an inconsolable child who weeps his heart out when no human comfort avails and wakes the next day without an apparent trace of the recent grief—Jean le Negre, in the course of the next twenty four hours, had completely recovered the normal buoyancy of spirit" (221). This is just what Thomas Jefferson had told the French in his *Notes on the State of Virginia,* with the difference that Cummings transmutes the stereotype into an object of envy and desire.[32] Having seen Jean dragged away by the guards, Cummings closes the account with a plea.

Boy, Kid, Nigger, with the strutting muscles—take me up into your mind once or twice before I die (you know why: just because the eyes of me and you will be full of dirt some day). Quickly take me up into the bright child of your mind, before we both go suddenly all loose and silly (you know how it will feel). (238)

Not every white male B&L author shared this affective relationship with blackness. The philosopher Bertrand Russell was aghast at having been ushered by Liveright to a fancy Harlem nightclub to celebrate the publication of his first B&L book, *Education and the Good Life* (1927), in the company of Horace Kallen, Genevieve Taggard, and New York mayor Jimmy Walker: "I wanted to enjoy myself," he wrote in a letter to his wife, "but when we got there they invited black ladies to our table & one was expected to dance & flirt with them. To my surprise, the mere idea was unspeakably revolting to me, & I left the place and went home. I couldn't bear the jazz music or the futurist walls of the negro ladies got up like Americans or anything about the place. I just felt jungle poison invading all our souls" (quoted in Dardis 147). Nevertheless, the desire Cummings articulates, a wish to be taken up into the black man's mind, even if only "once or twice before I die," recurs throughout a great deal of B&L's white modernism, an atavistic fantasy of recuperated sexual potency and relief from a debilitating self-consciousness.

Thus, the brooding lyricism of *Cane*'s verse and the lilting cadences of its prose were of relatively little moment to Liveright; though *Cane* was far from a simple primitivist text, it complemented an aesthetic and a critique of modernity that were becoming B&L signatures, and Toomer's blackness was his authorizing difference. Here was a certifying element that B&L had been missing. Like his B&L contemporaries, Toomer's sense of the spiritual ravages of industrial modernity led him to romanticize "niggers"; he, too, was taken by what he called "the rich sweet taste of dark-skinned life" (quoted in Gates, *Figures in Black* 205). In a 1922 letter to Frank, Toomer writes of having had the stories "Fern" and "Karintha" rejected by Gilbert Seldes at *The Dial,* then he invites Frank to make a "fresh start" with him on a trip to Kentucky.

> The name itself has a special charm and beauty for me. Men I have met and asked about the place . . . tell me that nowhere in the country can such a riot of life be had as in Lexington and Louisville, and that in many of the outlying districts things have changed but little since the Civil War. The actual Kentuckians whom I have seen seem to carry the vividity and color, the dash and love and waywardness conjured to the art mind by "nigger." I'd love to go there. At worst, it can serve as a convenient door into regions farther south. (*Toomer Reader* 14)

Because it is the fullest articulation of Toomer's figurative placement of "the Negro" as at once marginal and oppositional to modernization, the following undated letter to Frank is worth quoting at length.

There is one thing about the Negro in America which most thoughtful persons seem to ignore: the Negro is in solution, in the process of
solution. As an entity, the race is losing its body, and its soul is
approaching a common soul. If one holds his eyes to individuals and
sections, race is starkly evident, and racial continuity seems assured.
One is even led to believe that the thing we call Negro beauty will
always be attributable to a clearly defined physical source. But the fact
is, that if anything comes up now, pure Negro, it will be a swan-song.
Don't let us fool ourselves, brother: the Negro of the folk-song has all
but passed away: the Negro of the emotional church is fading. A hundred years from now these Negroes, if they exist at all, will live in art.
And I believe that a vague sense of this fact is the driving force behind
the art movements directed toward them today. (Likewise the
Indian.) America needs these elements. They are passing. Let us grab
and hold them while there is still time. Segregation and laws may
retard this solution. But in the end, segregation will either give way, or
it will kill. Natural preservations do not come from unnatural laws.
The supreme fact of mechanical civilization is that you become a part
of it, or get sloughed off (under). Negroes have no culture to resist it
with (and if they had, their position would be identical to that of the
Indians), hence industrialism the more readily transforms them. A
few generations from now, the Negro will still be dark, and a portion
of his psychology will spring from this fact, but in all else he will be a
conformist to the general outlines of American civilization, or of
American chaos. (*Toomer Reader* 24)

There is a great deal one might say about this passage, but most
significant in the context of the present discussion is Toomer's insistence on memorializing through art (in "a swan-song") an authentic folk
culture threatened by the integrative force of modernity. The purity of
the "pure Negro" has little to do with skin color itself, Toomer suggests,
and everything to do with the material conditions to which the dominant
culture has used skin color to relegate him. In the absence of those material conditions, skin color and race lose their meaning to Toomer.

When B&L sought to advertise *Cane* as the work of a "Negro" writer,
Toomer surprised and angered Liveright by telling him that he was not
a "Negro." He stopped identifying himself as one as soon as he finished

writing *Cane.* His maternal grandfather was indeed the black Reconstruction senator P. B. S. Pinchback of Louisiana, making Toomer a
"Negro" by law and convention. But by his own account, he had "seven
blood mixtures," "French, Dutch, Welsh, Negro, German, Jewish, and
Indian," which he wished to "function as complements" (*Toomer Reader*
15). In a 1922 letter to *The Liberator,* which had printed a few of *Cane's*
stories, Toomer wrote, "My growing need for artistic expression . . .
pulled me deeper and deeper into the Negro group" while writing *Cane.*
"And as my powers of receptivity increased, I found myself loving it in a
way that I could never love the other. It has stimulated and fertilized
whatever creative talent I may contain within me" (*Toomer Reader* 15).
Locating his creativity in his blackness and his blackness in his creativity,
Toomer had put a temporary fix on his racial indeterminacy. Thus,
Liveright felt authorized to publicize *Cane* as the work of a Negro writer,
and one can hear the influence of B&L's former chief of public relations, Edward Bernays, in Liveright's entreaty to Toomer: "I feel that
right at the very start there should be a note sounded about your colored
blood. To my mind this is the real human interest value of your story and
I don't see why you should dodge it" (quoted in Soto 167). This made
Toomer bristle. "As I was not a Negro, I could not feature myself as one,"
he recalls having written. To the publisher, the writer was denying his
race; to the writer, the publisher's search for "the real human interest
value" falsely advertised him as a Negro. "I must insist that you never use
such a word, such a thought, again," he wrote. "As a B and L author, I
make the distinction between my fundamental position and the position
which your publicity department may wish to establish for me in order
that *Cane* reach as large an audience as possible. In this connection I
have told you, . . . make use of whatever racial factors you wish. Feature
Negro if you wish, but do not expect me to feature it in advertisements
for you." Submitting grudgingly to the publicity that would make him a
Negro, Toomer posited a prior, private, and authentic Jean Toomer
apart from what he calls "specific advertising purposes." But in this very
insistence is inscribed the collapse of such distinctions under the pressures of commercial publicity as well as its injunction to embody racial
identity rather than indeterminacy. Toomer wanted his race to not matter, or to matter in any event as neither Negro nor white but, rather, irreducible to the conventional taxonomy of race. "All of this may seem over-

subtle and over-refined to you," he told Liveright, "but I assure you that it isn't" (*Toomer Reader* 94).

Subtlety was emphatically not what emerged in the publicity for *Cane*. Michael Soto has shown that there was a good deal of oscillation between campaigns to market Toomer as "a Negro author" and to market him as an avant-garde modernist, as though B&L was uncertain about the audience *Cane* could be made to reach. But what is finally most striking is how readily Toomer's publicized blackness inscribed itself across a palimpsest of paratexts.[33] B&L's *New York Times Book Review* advertisement that accompanied *Cane*'s publication in September 1923 read: "Cane . . . presents emotional, dramatic, genre pictures (in Washington and Georgia) of negro life whose rhythmic beat, like the primitive tom-toms of the African jungle, you can feel because it is written by a man who has felt it historically, poetically, and with deepest understanding." When B&L publicity called *Cane* "a vaudeville out of the South" in which "one feels the primitive rhythm of the Negro soul," reviewers from Boston to Kansas City reproduced this characterization verbatim. By parroting the vaudeville reference, these reviewers adopted the path of least resistance for themselves and their readers, analogizing *Cane* to a familiar genre and mapping a reading practice that was codified and comfortable—vaudeville spectatorship—onto a text that was actually challenging and formally elusive.[34]

Moreover, even as John Armstrong's review in the October 1923 *New York Tribune* disputed the vaudeville characterization ("there is nothing of the theatrical, coon-strutting high-brown, none of the conventional dice-throwing, chicken-stealing nigger of musical comedy and burlesque"), he keys the authenticity of the text's performance to the authenticity of its author's black experience. Toomer's "voice is synchronized with the aspirations, the hopes and the fears of the genuine darky," writes Armstrong, a "heavy, languorous" voice that "stuns the intelligence entirely, lulls it into torpor and compels it to recognize the authenticity of the racy negroes delineated" (quoted in Soto 173). Finally, one anonymous reviewer for the *Boston Transcript*—who must not have read Thomas Dixon, Lothrop Stoddard, or T. S. Stribling—maintained that *Cane* "presents the black race as we seldom dare represent it, mournful, loving beauty, ignorant, and full of passion untutored and entirely unconnected with the brain" (quoted in Gates, *Figures in Black*

Fig. 11. Advertisement for *Cane*, by Jean Toomer,
from the *New York Times Book Review*, September 16, 1923.
(Courtesy of the New York Public Library; Astor, Lenox,
and Tilden Foundations; General Research Division.)

214). If, as Henry Louis Gates asserts, *Cane* "elicited from critics an attention to literary language unprecedented . . . in the Afro-American tradition before 1923" (Gates, *Figures in Black* 211), it also seems to have
elicited from critics an unprecedented fidelity to the very different language of its publicity campaign. Set thus at odds, commercial discourse
and literary discourse contended mightily with one another to determine what readers would make of *Cane*, its author, and his publisher.

"Mere Notoriety and Publicity": Claude McKay's Color Scheme

Scholars have long alleged, with varying degrees of condemnation, that
the African American writers of the Harlem Renaissance encountered
interference (whether direct or indirect) from patrons, publishers, and
promoters. Seldom noted but arguably more significant was the
influence exerted by a relatively new group of professionals who were
otherwise uninterested in African American literature: the marketing
experts. Upon reading Walter White's manuscript for *Fire in the Flint*, for

example, publisher George Doran decided to submit it to the informal market research of a friend, Kentucky humorist Irwin Cobb. Cobb persuaded Doran to reject the manuscript on the grounds that the forthrightness of White's critique of southern lynching rendered the book virtually unsalable to the white mainstream. Ultimately, H. L. Mencken, who had urged both Fauset and White to write novels as rejoinders to T. S. Stribling's *Birthright* (1922), helped White's novel find a home at Alfred A. Knopf. Likewise, much has been made of Alain Locke's influence on the transformation of *Survey Graphic*'s special Harlem issue into *The New Negro*, but less noted are the marketing considerations informing the *Survey* project from the start, including the cover itself. The month before the Harlem issue came out, *Survey* editor Paul Kellogg wired Locke that he had consulted "Sales and Advertising experts" who believed that they could double the sales of the Harlem issue if the cover bore the likeness of Roland Hayes, the popular black performer of Negro spirituals. Locke immediately wired Hayes for permission, which was granted (Long 16).

Less compliant in the *Survey–New Negro* project were Toomer and Claude McKay, for they sought to forge a measure of self-determination within the web of publicity. According to Toomer, his stories "Fern" and "Carma" appeared in *The New Negro* despite his expressed objection, for he claims to have forbid Locke to "dismember" *Cane*. He goes as far as to accuse Locke of having "tricked and deceived" him into sitting for a portrait by Winold Reiss (*Wayward* 133). Darwin Turner notes that two years later, "Toomer gave Locke permission to use the drama 'Balo' in Locke's *Plays of Negro Life* (1927), even though it is reported that Toomer insisted that the title should not suggest that all the authors were Negro" (*Wayward* 132).

McKay harbored deep reservations about Locke's project as well. When Locke decided McKay's poem "Mulatto" was too caustic and radical, McKay called him a "dyed-in-the-wool pussy-footing professor" and accused him of a "playing safe attitude—the ultimate reward of which are dry husks and ashes." McKay proclaimed: "There are many white people who are longing and hoping for Negroes to show they have guts. I will show you by getting a white journal to take Mulatto." McKay met Locke's rejection by rescinding his work tout court: "Send me back *all* the things—and I do not care to be mentioned at all—don't want to—in

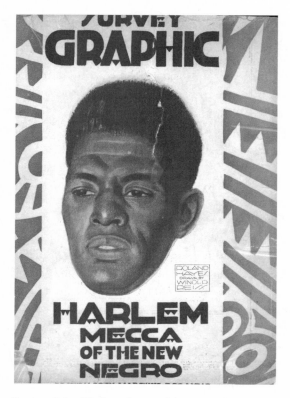

Fig. 12. Cover of the Harlem issue of *Survey Graphic,* March 1925,
featuring Winold Reiss's portrait of tenor Roland Hayes.
(Courtesy of the New York Public Library; Schomburg
Center for Research in Black Culture; Manuscripts,
Archives, and Rare Books Division.)

the special Negro number of the Survey. I am not seeking mere notoriety and publicity. Principles mean something in my life" (quoted in
Cooper 225). Locke proceeded not only to defy McKay's request, publishing several of his poems in *Survey*'s Harlem issue, but also to change
the title of McKay's poem "The White House" to the less inflammatory
"White Houses." McKay's reference to "mere notoriety and publicity"
was a characteristically strident denunciation. But by 1929, when Harper
Brothers published his novel *Banjo,* he seems to have made his peace
with commercial publicity. Book historian John Tebbel calls the cam-

Fig. 13. Boni and Liveright advertisement in the Harlem issue
of *Survey Graphic,* March 1925. (Courtesy of the New York
Public Library; Schomburg Center for Research in Black Culture;
Manuscripts, Archives, and Rare Books Division.)

paign for *Banjo* among the "bizarre lengths" to which "even the old
houses were going" by the late twenties to compete for visibility. They
put a black Frenchman on the back of a wagon that roamed the New
York streets; he strummed a banjo, the placard beside him announcing
that McKay's book was "On Sale Everywhere" (Tebbel 335).

Perhaps McKay had softened his hard line between "principles" and
"mere notoriety and publicity" because of the rejection he had sustained
in the intervening years. His poetry collection *Harlem Shadows* (1922)
was, along with *Cane,* a principal catalyst for the New Negro movement.

But McKay's attempt to then publish a novel met only with resistance. Working from France, at a great distance from New York and with few resources, and having burned many bridges with his dogmatic tirades, McKay implored his friend Arthur Schomburg (the bibliophile whose name the Harlem branch of the New York Public Library now bears) to help him find a publisher for his manuscript *Color Scheme*. He specified B&L as a likely publisher of his work, naming them among the "best firm[s] to try at first."35 But he expected reluctance: "I don't make virgins of my colored girls. No sir!" he wrote, so it "will shock some of our ultra-respectable hypocritical Negroes." "For it is *not* a 'moral' book. I make my Negro characters yarn and backbite and fuck like people the world over." "But I think I'm nearer the truth and tragedy and gaiety of Negro life than Miss Jessie Fauset."36

Evidently, Miss Fauset's publisher did not agree; B&L passed on *Color Scheme*. For that matter, so did all of the other publishers McKay pursued, and *Color Scheme* never made it into print.37 If McKay's characters were not sufficiently respectable, however, the ultrarespectability of Fauset's characters was no golden formula either, as she, too, failed to win B&L's acceptance for her follow-up effort to *There Is Confusion*. Like McKay, Fauset also suspected skittishness over her characters, but for opposite reasons than McKay's. She felt publishers were uninterested in the genteel class of African Americans, those not "pressed too hard by the Furies of Prejudice, Ignorance, and Economic Justice" (quoted in Sylvander 72). Sour grapes, perhaps, but the two authors' grievances suggest the degree to which publishers' marketing considerations generated cynicism among writers that their work would be evaluated "objectively" according to literary merit. Writers came to fully understand the situatedness of such a standard.

The publicity campaign for McKay's *Banjo* may say more about his publisher and about the industry more generally than it says about McKay's own accommodation to commercial publicity. Such firms as Harper Brothers followed B&L's lead, changing the appearance, typeface, and layout of ads and manufacturing news through press releases, ready-to-print reviews, and promotional tie-ins and spectacles. Former B&L employees founded some of the commercial titans of the industry in the twenties, such as the Book-of-the-Month Club, Simon and Schuster, and Random House. Even Alfred A. Knopf, who far outpaced B&L in publishing black writers and whose reputation for quality Liveright always envied and sought to approximate, in turn envied and sought to approximate the publicity Liveright generated.

It is instructive to return, at this point, to Floyd Calvin of the *Pittsburgh Courier,* who had bemoaned the poor publicity for, among others, *The Autobiography of an Ex-Colored Man.* This novel sold poorly when it was published anonymously by Sherman, French, and Company in 1912 with little publicity, but when Knopf reissued it as a novel by James Weldon Johnson in 1927, it was accompanied by a major promotional campaign.

> Knopf agents set up appearances for Johnson to read selections from his novel on three New York radio stations, arranged for an autograph session at Gimbels department store, synchronized publicity and appearances in Chicago bookstores to take advantage of a Johnson lecture tour there, and solicited from Johnson a portrait photograph by Carl Van Vechten and a quote from a congratulatory note from Clarence Darrow to use in their promotion. (Wintz, *Black Culture* 162–63)

The fact that the novel sold better in 1927 than in 1912 cannot be attributed to Knopf's publicity campaign alone. After all, "the negro was in vogue," and the market for all black writers had expanded considerably. But as I have suggested here, this market was itself a product of a systematic, industry-wide shift toward commercial publicity, a shift that Knopf's campaign exemplifies and that B&L pioneered.

When a group of the more radical artists led by Wallace Thurman and Zora Neale Hurtson solicited "aid from interested friends" on the first page of their ill-fated journal *Fire!!* they explicitly stated that such aid "is necessary" because the journal was "a non-commercial product only interested in the arts." They never truly had the chance to test the viability of such an undertaking—their office was irretrievably damaged, in a stroke of tragic irony, by a fire after the printing of only one issue (November 1926). But the distinction on which they pinned their hopes at the outset is significant. A study of one black culture industry, such as the one discussed in this chapter, can only be suggestive; but it suggests a couple of important things. It suggests how vital was the consolidation of consumer capitalism to reproducing racism and racial thinking more broadly. It also suggests that this role is easily mystified if we look only to individual historical actors and ignore the economic transitions in which they participated.

For all practical purposes, when the economic boom of the 1920s ended with the stock market crash of 1929, the Harlem Renaissance ended with it. The funding for contests and cultural programs dried up, and philanthropists and patrons grew increasingly tightfisted. But the emergent field of public relations and its elder cousins, advertising and marketing, did not end. In fact, the fallout from the Great Depression compelled these industries to substantially retool and refine their practices for leaner times. Far from receding from view, advertising, marketing, and public relations became savvier and more aggressive as the competition for consumer dollars and market share grew tougher and as cynicism spread toward the capitalist ethos of material abundance as progress. The ubiquity of the discourses of advertising, marketing, and publicity in the Depression era became a frequent subject of this period's cultural productions, from John Dos Passos's media fragments in the *U.S.A.* trilogy to the ironic juxtapositions of Margaret Bourke-White's photographs for the Works Progress Administration.[38] The next chapter focuses on two such works by authors who, despite their differences, shared a critical perspective on this transition and its implications for American culture and whose work suggests a shift in the articulation between consumer culture and race by the 1930s.

6 Confessions of the Flesh

THE MASS PUBLIC IN
EPIDERMAL TROUBLE IN
NATHANAEL WEST'S *MISS
LONELYHEARTS* AND GEORGE
SCHUYLER'S *BLACK NO MORE*

> But while the language may have been refined, the scope of the
> confession—the confession of the flesh—continually increased.
> —Michel Foucault, *The History of Sexuality*, vol. 1

> This is an application for naturalization. The applicant . . . writes his
> name in Arabic, cannot read or write English, and speaks and under-
> stands English very imperfectly, and does not understand any questions
> relating to the manner and method of government in America, or of the
> responsibilities of a citizen . . . In color, he is about that of walnut,
> or somewhat darker than is the usual mulatto of one-half mixed
> blood between the white and negro races . . . The applicant is
> not one the admission of whom to citizenship is likely to be
> for the benefit of the country.
> —South Carolina Federal District Judge Smith, *Ex Parte Shahid* (1913)

BY 1930, THE QUANTITY OF goods manufactured in the United
States had grown at nearly three times the rate at which the population
had increased since the turn of the century, according to a federally
commissioned study by *Middletown* author Robert Lynd ("People" 857).
This discrepancy had been a fundamental crisis in the early years of
postindustrial capitalism: demand had to be manufactured. By the turn
of the century, advertising had begun to shake off its nineteenth-century
association with snake-oil salesmen, P. T. Barnum, and peddlers of

patent medicines and had become a respectable business practice. But it was not until the next three decades that, as Raymond Williams writes, "we first hear, with any emphasis, of advertising as a profession, a public service, and a necessary part of the economy." Bolstered by the prosperity of the twenties, observes Williams, advertising "began staking its claims to be not only a profession, but an art and a science" (329). The advertising trade journal *Printer's Ink* boasted in 1926 that ads were "beginning to occupy the place in inspiration that religion did several hundred years ago" (quoted in Marchand 265). No longer a discrete set of amusing distractions, advertising had become an ambient social force.

The authors on which this chapter focuses, Nathanael West and George Schuyler, were both concerned with the way advertising and the consumer economy that depended on it was seizing on existing social inequalities and exploiting the genuine anxieties and desires that these inequalities generated. For Schuyler, these had to do with racial segregation and white-supremacist thinking; for West, they had to do primarily with class and the vulnerability of ordinary people to the false promises of the culture industry. But I suggest that the overt concerns of one author turn out to be the implicit concerns of the other. In Schuyler's novel, *Black No More* (1931), it is not possible to think about race without also thinking about consumer culture. Likewise, for West in *Miss Lonelyhearts* (1933), it seems that writing about consumer culture also involves making recourse to a peculiar rhetoric of race.

West and Schuyler were very different as writers and as people, but both were gifted, gimlet-eyed satirists whose best work appeared in the 1930s. Schuyler may be best known for writing a 1926 essay in *The Nation*, "The Negro-Art Hokum," to which Langston Hughes's "The Negro Artist and the Racial Mountain" responded in an important polemical exchange during the Harlem Renaissance.[1] Schuyler spent his long career writing primarily for journals and newspapers that were owned and read by African Americans, a project that in equal measures sustained and enraged him. He wrote a take-no-prisoners column called "Shafts and Darts" for the socialist journal *The Messenger,* whose involvement in the literary Harlem Renaissance is traceable to Schuyler's arrival in 1922;[2] and he contributed pieces to the house organs of the Urban League and the NAACP, for which he also served as business manager for several years. His combination of wit, irreverence, and erudition endeared him to H. L. Mencken, who featured Schuyler's work in the *American Mercury,* but it also alienated him from the Harlem establishment and, along with his increasingly conservative political views, eventually landed him at a less radical but widely read black weekly, the *Pittsburgh Courier.* By the time he died in 1977, Schuyler had written extensively on the African diaspora, Liberia, and the African slave trade and had become notorious for publicly denouncing Martin Luther King and endorsing Richard Nixon. His picaresque novel *Black No More* is an extended riff on his most controversial claim in "The Negro-Art Hokum," that "the Aframerican is merely a lampblacked Anglo-Saxon."

Nathanael West, born Nathan Weinstein, ran mainly with a Greenwich Village crowd that included Sinclair Lewis, Mike Gold, Edmund Wilson, S. J. Perelman, and William Carlos Williams. With Williams, he revived the dormant *Contact,* a little magazine that managed to publish some of the most impressive experimental U.S. writers in its brief three-issue run.[3] He is perhaps best known for *The Day of the Locust,* often called the first Hollywood novel. The interest West shows in that novel in challenging the dominant, sentimental myths of American identity is also evident in his earlier work, which includes the anti–Horatio Alger story *A Cool Million* and *Miss Lonelyhearts,* his bleak treatment of the spiritual crisis facing a newspaper advice columnist. Like his hunting partner William Faulkner, West became a Hollywood screenwriter in the late thirties, before a fatal car crash cut his life short in 1940. Harold Bloom has approvingly called West a "rhetorician of the abyss," and while West scholarship has traditionally concerned itself with the existential issues raised by his fiction, recent studies bring a new theoretical sophistication to bear on his work at the same time that the Library of America has lent him its imprimatur of canonicity by bringing out a volume of West's collected works.[4]

The experience of reading these two authors is very different. Schuyler's work is laugh-out-loud funny in a way that West's rarely is. Schuyler's parodic sensibility has earned him comparisons to Twain and Shaw, while West's satire has a violent desperation that seems to me to anticipate Joseph Heller in *Catch-22.* Whereas Schuyler's protagonist in *Black No More* is a trickster in the African American folk tradition (a characterization that he would likely have dismissed), Miss Lonelyhearts evokes the pathos of Chekhov or Isaac Babel. However, both writers were ironists of the first order, and more interesting for our purposes, both of their novels from the early 1930s were originally conceived in 1929 as responses to advertisements.

Racial Energy and the Unhinging of Race from Color

There is a moment in *Miss Lonelyhearts* when the title character—who, despite the name, is actually a man—looks up at the Manhattan sky, "searching for clues to his own exhaustion." What he decides is that "Americans have dissipated their racial energy in an orgy of stone-breaking" (27). West does not allow Miss Lonelyhearts to elaborate, but it seems clear from the context that the "orgy of stone-breaking" is a figure for an American rush to modernize, to throw up the skyscrapers that surround the park in which he is seated.[5] But what are we to make of the reference to the dissipation of Americans' racial energy? What did it mean in the early 1930s to write of Americans as having a racial energy in the first place, much less one whose dissipation is traceable to "an orgy of stone-breaking"? What, in other words, is the relationship between this story's primary concern with urban-industrial modernity, on one hand, or "city troubles," as one character calls them, and race on the other? One of West's most astute commentators, Jonathan Veitch, expresses the critical consensus when he writes that "West had almost nothing to say about the vexed question of race" (134). But my analysis will suggest, by contrast, that West had almost nothing to say—at least in *Miss Lonelyhearts*—that did not also involve that vexed question of race.

Racial thinking was shifting by the 1930s such that the dominant biological account of race began to give way, however fitfully and unevenly, to an ethnicity-based approach, a transformation that was hastened by the need among Americans to distance themselves from the vicious expression of racial essentialism gathering in Nazi Germany. However, as we have seen in previous chapters, scientific, popular, and legal discourses on race are never perfectly aligned. Nowhere are the convolutions and contradictions that accompanied the ascendance of an ethnicity-based definition of race better illustrated than in the petitions for citizenship naturalization that crowded the dockets of the court system in the early twentieth century, ultimately requiring the intervention of the U.S. Supreme Court in the 1920s. The wildly inconsistent rulings in these cases demonstrate that the national origin, religion, and somatic features of immigrants seeking U.S. citizenship continually vexed the binary logic of race that underwrote the naturalization statute, which had stipulated since 1790 that only "free white persons" were eligible.[6]

This crisis of racial definition reflected in the Supreme Court's intervention in the naturalization cases coincided (though not by chance) with a struggle in Congress to craft more restrictive immigration legislation. Fueled by post–World War I nationalism and by the popularization of white-supremacist pseudoscience in Madison Grant's *The Passing of the Great Race* (1916) and Lothrop Stoddard's *The Rising Tide of Color against White World Supremacy* (1921), both of which were passionately invoked in legislative sessions, this struggle resulted in the Johnson-Reed Immigration Act of 1924.[7] Johnson-Reed not only reduced the number of newcomers in absolute terms but also imposed quotas by national origin to heavily favor immigration from "Nordic" (i.e., northern and western European) countries over all others. The results were extraordinary: of the 35.9 million Europeans who immigrated to the United States between 1820 and 1975, 32 million came before 1924. "Nordic Victory Is Seen in Drastic Restrictions," read a *Los Angeles Times* headline.[8] Taken together, the nativism that gave rise to Johnson-Reed and the high court's tortuous defenses of the whiteness of America's naturalized citizenry indicate the prevalence of an anxiety about the fitness of nonwhites for self-government, even as they reveal the contradictory construction of the very racial categories they presupposed. In very different forms, the works of fiction at the center of this chapter dramatize the ways in which skin color, which was in the process of disarticulation from race and nation, was rearticulated as an index of fitness for citizenship.

Although this process is illustrated most vividly in the naturalization decisions I discuss later in this chapter, it arguably began as early as 1898, with the U.S. Supreme Court decision in *Williams v. Mississippi*, which was not a naturalization petition but a challenge to racial discrimination in the selection of jurors. The decision, written by Justice McKenna, upheld the lower court's ruling that while discrimination on the basis of race was forbidden by the Fourteenth Amendment to the U.S. Constitution, nothing prevented electoral officials (one had to be a registered voter to be eligible to serve on a jury) from discriminating on the basis of a race's "characteristics," or acquired traits. McKenna quoted the lower court's decision.

By reason of its previous condition of servitude and dependencies, this [negro] race had acquired or accentuated certain peculiarities of habit, of temperament, and of character, which clearly distinguish it as a race from the whites; a patient, docile people, but careless, land-less, migratory, within narrow limits, without forethought, and its criminal members given to furtive offenses, rather than the robust crimes of the whites. Restrained by the federal constitution from dis-criminating against the negro race, the convention discriminates against its characteristics, and the offenses to which its criminal mem-bers are prone.[9]

Clearly, the U.S. Supreme Court was engaged, in its affirmation of the Mississippi court's decision, in a racist sleight of judicial hand in which race was disavowed as a criterion only to then be reinvoked with a vengeance. But it is the strategic splitting of race into inherent and acquired qualities that interests me here. In order to discriminate against African Americans in a post-Fourteenth-Amendment era, the courts were compelled to redescribe race in terms of experiential, acquired behaviors rather than essential, biological determinants. What defined "the negro," in other words, was not skin color or other somatic traits but the experiences of the race to which these qualities referred and the "characteristics" to which these experiences ostensibly gave rise. Of course, somatic traits like skin color remained, tautologically, as the visible signifier of "the negro" experience and its attending qualities.

It was precisely this tension between color and race that later enabled a federal district court to claim, in 1921, that because of their skin color, Asians could not be naturalized citizens of the United States—not because of their race, mind you (though race is still the tacit referent), but because of the qualities of mind and habit for which skin color serves as evidence. In his decision, District Judge Cushman insisted that skin color itself did not determine one's fitness for the republican form of government of the United States but was an expression of those imma-nent qualities that did.

It is obvious that the objection on the part of Congress is not due to color, as color, but only to color as an evidence of a type of civilization which it characterizes. The yellow or bronze color is the hallmark of Oriental despotisms. It was deemed that the subjects of these despo-

tisms, with their fixed and ingrained pride in the type of their civilization, which works for its welfare by subordinating the individual to the
personal authority of the sovereign, as the embodiment of the state,
were not fitted and suited to make for the success of republican form
of Government. Hence they were denied citizenship. (Quoted in
Lopez 55–56)

If the prerequisite law were interpreted as having biologized fitness for
republican self-government as inherently white, color could logically be
objected to not "as color" but, as Judge Cushman put it, as evidence of an
undesirable type of civilization.[10] In *Williams v. Mississippi*, the very color
that was disavowed on one hand was tacitly reinvoked on the other, in
order to anchor a prior "blackness" to which racial "peculiarities" were
supposed to correspond. Judge Cushman's decision in *Terrace v. Thompson* liberated this logic from the black-white axis of segregation law and
deployed it toward more broadly nativist ends in naturalization law.[11]

Beyond its obvious racism, Judge Cushman's dual gesture to reduce
color to the "type of civilization which it characterizes" yet simultaneously to invoke its biological authority seems to have interesting implications for the referentiality of what it pretended to repress. The cultural
logic of race on which Judge Cushman relied (following *Williams v. Mississippi*) makes skin color a more available signifier for different "types of
civilization" and "characteristics." I now turn, then, to discuss what might
be called the freighting of skin with referentiality in the U.S. Supreme
Court naturalization cases, in order to examine a corresponding compulsion to produce legible skins in Nathanael West's *Miss Lonelyhearts*
and a deft deconstruction of skin's referentiality in George Schuyler's
Black No More.

Chromatic Emancipation, Chromatic Repatriation:
Black No More, Ozawa, *and* Thind

Black No More is about the hijinks that ensue when one Dr. Junius Crookman invents a treatment that turns Negroes into white folks. Soon, everyone in Harlem—the site of Crookman's sanitarium—is saving up the
fifty dollars for what Schuyler refers to as "chromatic emancipation," and
the rest of the country quickly lines up behind them. "It looked as

though science was to succeed where the Civil War had failed," writes
Schuyler (10). As the plot unfolds, the characters who are most convinced of their whiteness turn out to have the least basis for that conviction, and those who have the most African ancestry turn out to make
excellent white supremacists. When the protagonist, Max Disher, first
emerges from his Black-No-More treatment, he finds that he is white in
every visible respect. "At last," Schuyler writes, "he felt like an American
citizen" (26). On one hand, this is a common observation about the privileges of whiteness, the freedom to move through social space and enjoy
a sense of universal personhood and to be rid of Jim Crow laws and customs. On the other hand, the scene that Schuyler stages—a nonwhite
person having the privileges and sensations of American citizenship conferred on him by being manufactured as a white person—has a more literal antecedent that I want to pause to consider.

Because of the way Congress wrote the law about naturalizing immigrants as U.S. citizens in 1790, U.S. courts had the power until 1952 to
manufacture white people. I do not mean manufacture literally, since it
was not human bodies themselves that the courts produced, but they did
manufacture the race to which those bodies referred. Specifically, I want
to look at two Supreme Court cases that preceded the work of West and
Schuyler by less than a decade. Because the law of the land until 1952
was that citizenship naturalization was restricted to "free white persons"
and because not every immigrant was obviously white or not white, the
court system was occasionally confronted with the hard cases whose skin
color, ancestry, or national origin defied easy classification in the existing racial taxonomy. By maintaining the "free white persons" clause of
the citizenship law, lawmakers ensured that immigrants would vigorously
seek out the privileges of whiteness if they were within reach, and that
sometimes meant bringing a lawsuit. By the end of World War I, the
influx of immigrants from southern and eastern Europe, Asia, and the
Middle East had provoked an extension of white-supremacist thinking
beyond the so-called Negro problem of the Progressive Era into a virulent nativism. Calls for "100% Americanism" rattled in Congress, and in
May 1924, after years of debate and expert testimony from ethnologists,
Congress passed the aforementioned Johnson-Reed Act, the most
restrictive immigration law since the 1882 Chinese Exclusion Act.[12]

This was the only period in U.S. history when a petition for naturalization for citizenship reached the Supreme Court, and it happened twice. As Ian Haney Lopez explains in *White by Law,* the Court ruled against a Japanese man named Takao Ozawa in 1922 because, although he had light skin, had been educated in American schools, and was in other respects thought to resemble a white person, it was common knowledge that the Japanese were not of the Caucasian race, and therefore Ozawa was not white in the sense that Congress intended in 1790. Three months later, in 1923, the second petitioner to reach the Supreme Court, Bhagat Singh Thind, a high-caste Indian man from the province of Punjab, had his claim to whiteness denied as well, but for precisely the opposite reason. In its decision, the Court opened up a space between the terms *Caucasian* and *white* that it had collapsed in order to find against Ozawa in the previous case. "Mere ability on the part of [the] applicant to establish a line of descent from a Caucasian ancestor will not *ipso facto* and necessarily conclude the inquiry," wrote Justice Sutherland, who explained: "'Caucasian' is a conventional word of much flexibility, as a study of the literature dealing with racial questions will disclose, and while it and the words 'white persons' are treated as synonymous for the purposes of that case, they are not of identical meaning—*idem per idem*" (quoted in Lopez 222). As far as the Court was concerned, too many obviously nonwhite people had been designated Caucasian by "scientific manipulation," when mere "familiar observation and knowledge [showed] that the physical group characteristics of the Hindus render them readily distinguishable from the various groups of persons in this country commonly recognized as white" (quoted in Lopez 225). Thus, the Court invoked the authority of science to declare the visibly light-skinned Ozawa not Caucasian, thus not white, and thus unfit for citizenship, only to then reject science's definition of a white person in favor of "the understanding of the common man" in denying whiteness and citizenship to Thind.[13]

Of course, the reason that these two decisions are wildly inconsistent and that the entire history of the racial prerequisite cases is rife with contradiction is that the discrete races they presupposed do not exist as such but are the products of the very acts of legal construction the courts were performing. This was the Pandora's box that the naturalization petitions threatened to open if the courts failed to reaffirm the basis of discrete races in biology. The contradictions may look to us like evidence of the arbitrariness of racial distinctions and even of the fictive quality of race itself, but from the Supreme Court's vantage, precisely this appearance of arbitrariness needed to be dispelled to maintain the biological account of race that underwrote Jim Crow and differential access to national citizenship.

I am not suggesting that Schuyler was writing about the naturalization cases when he had the newly white Max Disher feel for the first time like an American citizen, nor am I suggesting that West was writing about them either. It is quite possible that neither one ever heard of these cases. But I think the arguments advanced by the Supreme Court tell us important things about racial discourse at the time, about the heights of absurdity and contradiction that were required to avert the prospect that race might self-deconstruct right there on the witness stand, and in particular about the cultural anxiety over the status of skin color as an index of fitness for citizenship. Schuyler's satire grew where this soil of bad faith, contradiction, and willfully flawed reasoning lay the rankest. His novel poses the same questions the Supreme Court justices faced, but in a different register, with irony and parody supplying the critical difference.

The first of these is the question of fraudulent whiteness. The specter of racial imposture haunts the Supreme Court's arguments, the fear that overbroad definitions of whiteness not only confer a fraudulent racial status on those who do not truly deserve its privileges but also deprive authentically white people of their freedom from association with nonwhites. Of course, the real specter behind the specter of racial imposture is miscegenation, as Schuyler was never slow to note. Just when Dr. Junius Crookman's company, Black-No-More, Incorporated, appears poised to turn the entire population of American blacks white, a newspaper headline appears: "Wealthy White Girl Has Negro Baby." It sounds the alarm to the guardians of white racial integrity that by allowing unsuspecting white women to partner with men whose whiteness is fraudulent, Black-No-More is facilitating miscegenation. "The real white people were panic-stricken," Schuyler continues, "There was no way, apparently, of telling a real Caucasian from an imitation one. Every stranger was viewed with suspicion" (88). Thus, Schuyler takes this notion of racial imposture, which of course the Supreme Court was compelled to take quite seriously, and suggests through exaggeration the impracticality of taking it at all seriously. If the Court was able to claim, in sanguine moments, that it could continue to adjudicate claims to whiteness in the face of mounting evidence of its arbitrariness, Schuyler's white folks certainly cannot similarly cope with the intractable problem Dr. Crookman's treatment presents. The only nonwhite citizens will be newborn babies, and even they, Schuyler writes, will be quickly converted by any dutiful parent, in Crookman's newly devised lying-in hospitals.

The second question Schuyler satirizes is whether nonwhites have the stuff that American citizens are made of. His novel is populated by various strains of white supremacists, each of which has a particular class inflection. Working-class white supremacy is embodied by the Knights of Nordica, particularly in its Imperial Grand Wizard, Reverend Givens. Schuyler punctures their pretensions by staging the ascendancy of Max Disher, now renamed Matthew Fisher, through its ranks to a leadership post. Though we readers know Matthew to have been a Negro client of Dr. Crookman's, he ingratiates himself to the Knights of Nordica by denouncing Black-No-More as a dire threat to the integrity of the white race. His speech echoes the naturalization arguments: "For an hour Matthew told them at the top of his voice what they already believed: i.e., that a white skin was a sure indication of the possession of superior intellectual and moral qualities; that all Negroes were inferior to them; that God had intended for the United States to be a white man's country and that with His help they could keep it so; that their sons and brothers might inadvertently marry Negresses or, worse, their sisters and daughters might marry Negroes, if Black-No-More, Incorporated, was permitted to continue its dangerous activities" (55). Matthew Fisher is soon named Imperial Grand Giraw of the Knights of Nordica. Likewise, Schuyler represents ruling-class white supremacy through characters he refers to as "professional Anglo-Saxons." The descendants of the First Families of Virginia, they reproduce the logic of racial purity that the Supreme Court had legitimated eight years earlier. "He had been the genius that thought up the numerous racial integrity laws in Virginia and many other Southern states," Schuyler writes of Arthur Snobbcraft, president of the Virginia Anglo-Saxon Association, "He was strong for the sterilization of the unfit: meaning Negroes, aliens, Jews and other riff raff, and he had an abiding hatred of democracy. Snobbcraft's pet scheme now was to get a genealogical law passed disfranchising all people of Negro or unknown ancestry. He argued that good citizens could not be made out of such material" (120). Finally, the pseudoscientific white supremacy on which the ruling class relied for legitimation is represented by the unfortunately named Dr. Buggerie, who "held that the only way to tell the pure whites from the imitation whites was to study their family trees. He claimed that such a nationwide investigation would disclose the various non-Nordic strains in the population. Laws, he said, should then be passed forbidding these strains from mixing or marrying with the pure strains that had produced such fine specimens of mankind as Mr. Snobbcraft and himself . . . [T]he results of some of his preliminary researches . . . tended to show . . . that there must be as many as twenty million people in the United States who possessed some slightly non-Nordic strain and were thus unfit for both citizenship and procreation" (122).

To capitalize on the mounting anxiety about the millions of fraudulent whites in their midst, the ruling-class and working-class white supremacists join forces on an old-fashioned Southern Democratic party ticket featuring Snobbcraft and Givens. Their campaign strategy? To prove through genealogical investigation that a previously unimagined number of Americans are not white, among them their adversaries on the Republican ticket. Schuyler has Dr. Buggerie deliver the following account to Democratic party operatives:

> "I am now prepared to prove," gloated the obese statistician, "that fully one quarter of the people of one Virginia county possess non-white ancestry, Indian or Negro; and we can further prove that all of the Indians on the Atlantic Coast are part Negro. In several counties in widely separated parts of the country, we have found that the ancestry of a considerable percentage of the people is in doubt. There is reason to believe that there are countless numbers of people who ought not to be classed with whites and should not mix with Anglo-Saxons." (131)

There is a tradition of critique in African American letters of the so-called one-drop rule and of the law of matrilineal descent, and while Schuyler retains the conventions of this tradition, *Black No More* is also alert to the affinity between traditional white supremacy and rising xenophobia.

Schuyler's parodic treatment culminates with the champions of white integrity hoisted by their own petard. Genealogical investigation reveals that Snobbcraft and Buggerie have black ancestors, the public disclosure of which discredits their effort to smear the Republican candidates and the Black-No-More corporation that bankrolled their campaign. Forced on the lam, Snobbcraft and Buggerie are ultimately caught, in another of Schuyler's ironic flourishes, by a parish of Mississippi Christian fundamentalists, who punish them with death by lynching for their imposture as white men.

What does any of this have to do with consumer culture? Schuyler suggests that in the modern era, white supremacy—whether it is white folks' jealously guarded light-skin privilege or the desire among African Americans to buy themselves "pork-colored" skin—is everywhere invigorated by commercial publicity, advertisements, and spectacles. Radio stations, magazines, news articles, editorials, press releases, photo supplements, lurid headlines—the novel depicts a media-saturated public sphere and crowd after crowd of readers, listeners, audiences, and spectators.[14]

Indeed, Schuyler notes in his preface that his inspiration for writing *Black No More* came from a very concrete instance of the reciprocity between American-style white supremacy and American-style commercialism. A newspaper report he read in October 1929 told of a Japanese physician claiming that he could change a Negro into a white man through a series of treatments in "glandular control and electrical nutrition" (xx). This struck Schuyler as a logical, if despicable, extension of the trend he had begun to note twenty years earlier, in ads for a hair straightener called Kink-No-More and all manner of skin bleaches and toners.

> Many chemists, professional and amateur, have been seeking the means of making the downtrodden Aframerican resemble as closely as possible his white fellow citizen. The temporarily effective preparations placed on the market have so far proved exceedingly profitable to manufacturers, advertising agencies, Negro newspapers, and beauty culturists, while millions of users have registered their great satisfaction at the opportunity to rid themselves of kinky hair and grow several shades lighter in color, if only for a brief time. (xix)

Schuyler goes on to note that a New York electrical engineer offered his services to the NAACP in 1930 to develop and patent a procedure for removing "a surplus of pigment" (xx). If one of the satirist's tools is the reductio ad absurdum, the actual state of affairs did not require that Schuyler's reductio travel too far. The schemes of Dr. Crookman may be fanciful, but they were not merely science fiction.

Schuyler could have cast Dr. Crookman as some mad scientist who cooks up a laboratory concoction that exceeds his control or falls into the wrong hands—this is a familiar story arc. Instead, he makes Crookman a corporate CEO, the shrewd, profiteering chair of Black-No-More, Incorporated. *Incorporated* is a tag that Schuyler never omits, for Black-No-More is not just Dr. Crookman; it is funded by a Harlem numbers boss and an unscrupulous realtor.[15] Together, they "grow" the company from one sanitarium in Harlem to hundreds nationwide, which they visit in a private jet with the logo "BNM" emblazoned on the side. Moreover, Max Disher first learns of the treatment through newspaper headlines on New Year's Day in 1934, and the mass media become a constant presence in the narrative thereafter, at once the least reliable and most relied-on source of public misinformation, the chief instruments in the ruling class's exercise of ideological control. When Max first seeks out Dr. Crookman to inquire about a race-change, he finds Crookman's room (at the Phyllis Wheatley Hotel) overrun by "white reporters from the daily newspapers and black reporters from the Negro weeklies" (10). The next day appeared interviews and photographs of Crookman, who immediately became "the talk of the town and soon the talk of the country" (13). A similar celebrity is thrust upon Max when he first emerges from Black-No-More's outpatient ward, "bathed, fed, clean-shaven, spry, blonde and jubilant" (19). Readers of Nathanael West will recognize an affinity in the fact that two mobs then confront Schuyler's protagonist— "the milling crowd of colored folk [who] spread over the sidewalk, into the street and around the corners," on one hand, and "a mob of newspaper photographers and reporters," on the other, "journalistic gnats," fifteen of whom "begged him almost with tears in their eyes for a statement" (20). In a short time, with "100 sanitariums going full blast from Coast to Coast," Black-No-More "announced in full page advertisements in the daily press that it was establishing lying-in hospitals in the principal cities where all prospective mothers could come to have their babies, and that whenever a baby was born black or mulatto, it would immediately be given the 24-hour treatment that permanently turned black infants white" (89).

Thus, Schuyler represents the commercial media as the condition of possibility for this effort to capitalize on what he never lets us forget is a very real desire among African Americans for social equality with whites, which has been mystified as a fetishization of whiteness itself. But this turns out to be only half of the equation, for if the profitability of Black-No-More, Incorporated, is one expression of white-supremacist thinking, it provokes another: the frenzy among the original white people in the novel to protect the integrity of their race against the impostors. The commercial media are also enlisted in this project. "Just look at this bunch of clippings we got in this morning," Crookman tells his cronies, exclaiming, "Listen to these: 'The Viper in Our Midst,' from the Richmond *Blade;* 'The Menace of Science' from the Memphis *Bugle;* 'A Challenge to Every White Man' from the Dallas *Sun;* 'Police Battle Black Mob Seeking White Skins,' from the Atlanta *Topic;* 'Negro Doctor Admits Being Taught by Germans' from the St. Louis *North American.*" The editorial pages of southern newspapers crackle with anti-Crookman sentiment, and the protagonist, Matthew Fisher, is "able to see . . . from the vantage point of having formerly been a Negro . . . how the newspapers were fanning the color prejudice of the white people." Fisher finds that "[b]usiness men . . . were also bitterly opposed to Dr. Crookman and his efforts to bring about chromatic democracy in the nation" (44). At first he is puzzled: "Was not Black-No-More getting rid of the Negroes upon whom all of the blame was placed for the backwardness of the South?" But he soon recalls a Harlem street speaker warning "that so long as the ignorant white masses could be kept thinking of the menace of the Negro to Caucasian race purity and political control, they would give little thought to labor organization" (44). In short, the mass media are in collusion with the ruling class in the interest of higher profits, and the ruling class is in collusion with the white supremacists for the same reason.[16] Whiteness turns out always to be an idea whose currency depends on how much money can be made off of it. Whether it appears in the form of the ruling class using race to divide workers and thereby keep labor costs down or in the form of entrepreneurs selling relief from the stigma of dark skin, race seems to be bound up inextricably with consumer capitalism everywhere in Schuyler's novel.[17]

At the same time that Schuyler was using satire in *Black No More* to lampoon consumer capitalism's reliance on racial thinking and to criticize his fellow African Americans' desire for "pork-colored" skin, he was also channeling his critique into a social program that demonstrated a contrasting political earnestness and a racial pride. In the same post–Depression era moment in which many other consumer-oriented movements were initiated to educate, organize, and protect ordinary citizens against corporations, Schuyler established the Young Negroes' Cooperative League in 1930.[18] It "was directed to the common man—the consumer—instead of the businessman," Schuyler said, "to educate people to establish buying clubs and later to transform them into organizing societies" (quoted in Peplow 117). The Young Negroes' Cooperative League foundered under hostile pressure from Harlem's business community and the religious leaders whom Schuyler's lack of tact and diplomacy had managed to alienate. But its objectives reflect the confluence of concerns we also find—now refracted through the prism of irony and cynicism for a different, literary audience—in his concurrent project *Black No More*.

Legible Skin: Corporate Personalization and the Miscegenated Mass Public

Like Schuyler, West was moved to write *Miss Lonelyhearts* by a 1929 encounter with a particular newspaper ad. It was the ad's insidious exploitation of the mass public's credulity and vulnerability that struck West, as it had Schuyler. He was introduced by S. J. Perelman to the writer of an advice column for the *Brooklyn Eagle*, who wrote under the pseudonym *Susan Chester*. Susan Chester shared several of his readers' letters with West, one of which began:

> Dear Susan: I have always enjoyed reading your column, and have benefited from your expert advice. Now I must ask you for advice for myself. I have been married for twenty years. I have a girl 19 and a boy of 17. From the very beginning I realized that I had made a mistake in marrying my husband. But the children came soon after, and I was obliged for their dear sakes to stand through thick and thin, bitter and sweet. And also for decency sake. (Quoted in Martin 110)

This letter was signed "Broad Shoulders," though the writer added: "Susan, don't think I am broad shouldered. But that is just the way I feel about life and me." Another letter tells of a woman finding the face of the Devil under her bed when she went to sweep there. West reproduces both letters almost verbatim in *Miss Lonelyhearts*. According to his biographer, the letters appealed to West as "a key to the real character of the time." Though they were "romantic and shot through with fantasy thinking, . . . there was no pretension in them, only unbearable pathos" (Martin 109–10). In the novel, readers sign their letters to Miss Lonelyhearts with such names as "Desperate," "Sick of It All," and "Disillusioned with Tubercular Husband."

The genre of the advice column was not an advertisement in the same sense as the promotion for Kink-No-More hair straightener to which Schuyler objected, but it was very much an advertisement for the newspaper itself. Forums for exchanges with figures like "the Miss Lonelyhearts of the New York *Post-Dispatch*" were first devised by publishers William Randolph Hearst and Joseph Pulitzer to mitigate the impersonal quality of urban life, to perform the services of advice giving and expertise that had previously fallen to family members, clergy, or a more organic network of social relations.[19] Of course, their purpose was to broaden the readership, to sell more newspapers, and in turn to bring more customers to their advertisers, goals that were belied by the appearance of intimacy and community that these columns cultivated.[20] That readers failed to demystify these economic motives and continued to put their faith in Susan Chester seems to have struck West as evidence of their willful desperation, their ignorance, or both. Thus, *Miss Lonelyhearts* initiates a critique that West would develop later (in *The Day of the Locust*) of what Adorno and Horkheimer soon called "the culture industry" and what West referred to as "the business of dreams." "Men have always fought their misery with dreams," Miss Lonelyhearts sighs, lamenting: "Although dreams were once powerful, they have been made puerile by the movies, radio, and newspapers. Among many betrayals this one is the worst" (39).[21]

His recognition that his column amounts to a tremendous exercise in bad-faith public relations leads to the undoing of Miss Lonelyhearts. "Let's start from the beginning," he tells his girlfriend, Betty:

A man is hired to give advice to the readers of a newspaper. The job is a circulation stunt and the whole staff considers it a joke. He welcomes the job, for it might lead to a gossip column, and anyway he's tired of being a leg man. He too considers the job a joke, but after sev-

eral months at it, the joke begins to escape him. He sees that the
majority of the letters are profoundly humble pleas for moral and
spiritual advice, that they are inarticulate expressions of genuine suffering. He also discovers that his correspondents take him seriously.
For the first time in his life he is forced to examine the values by which
he lives. This examination shows him that he is the victim of the joke
and not its perpetrator. (32)

Laughter fills the spaces of *Miss Lonelyhearts,* from the speakeasies to the
restaurants to the movie theaters. As Shrike's wife, Mary, tells Miss Lonelyhearts, "Everyone wants to be gay—unless they're sick" (23). Those like
Mary laugh along with the culture industry, while others laugh at it, at its
efficacy at creating a docile public of consumers. The first group is
duped, sometimes willfully; the second is depraved. The staff of the *Post-
Dispatch,* for example, laugh at a story about the gang rape of a woman
writer. They laugh at the loyalty Miss Lonelyhearts shows to his readers.
They laugh at his anachronism: "He wants to cultivate his inner garden.
But you can't escape, and where is he going to find a market for the
fruits of his personality?" (14–15). They are jeering, standardized
automatons: "Like Shrike, the man they imitated, they were machines
for making jokes. A button machine makes buttons, no matter what the
power used, foot, steam, electricity. They, no matter what the motivating
force, death, love, or God, make jokes" (15). The laughter of the
depraved and the laughter of the duped are the flip sides of the culture
industry's single laugh track. "Fun is a medicinal bath," Adorno and
Horkheimer would soon write, "The pleasure industry never fails to pre-
scribe it. It makes laughter the instrument of the fraud practiced on happiness" (140).[22]

Having felt the indeterminacy of the victim/perpetrator binary opposition, Miss Lonelyhearts can no longer laugh at the culture industry's
exploitation of the credulous mass public's desires and grievances. West
would soon write in *The Day of the Locust:* "It is hard to laugh at the need
for beauty and romance, no matter how tasteless, even horrible, the
results of that are. But it is easy to sigh. Few things are sadder than the
truly monstrous" (61). During dinner at the trendy El Gaucho restau-
rant, West has Miss Lonelyhearts similarly observe:

Guitars, bright shawls, exotic foods, outlandish costumes—all these
things were part of the business of dreams. He had learned not to

laugh at the advertisements offering to teach writing, cartooning, engineering, to add inches to the biceps and to develop the bust. He should therefore realize that the people who came to El Gaucho were the same as those who wanted to write and live the life of an artist, wanted to be an engineer and wear leather puttees, wanted to develop a grip that would impress the boss, wanted to cushion Raoul's head on their swollen breasts. They were the same people as those who wrote to Miss Lonelyhearts for help. (22)

Thus, Miss Lonelyhearts is a counselor for whom it is impossible to be in earnest—or, more precisely, whose earnestness is simply a tool that his cynical editor, Shrike, can use to legitimate a circulation stunt. When Miss Lonelyhearts had once tried to get himself fired by recommending suicide to a reader, "[a]ll that Shrike had said was: 'Remember, please, that your job is to increase the circulation of our paper. Suicide, it is only reasonable to think, must defeat this purpose'"(18).

So Miss Lonelyhearts suffers through his days with an affliction of the spirit that his colleagues refer to sardonically as his "Christ complex," until he is provoked by a reader's letter into stepping out from behind the safety of his trademark and into the lives of his beloved mass public. "Dear Miss Lonlyhearts," begins the letter from Fay Doyle,

I am not very good at writing so I wonder if I could have a talk with you. I am 32 years old but have had a lot of trouble and am unhappily married to a cripple. I need some good advice bad but cant state my case in a letter as I am not good at letters and it would take an expert to state my case. I know your a man and am glad as I dont trust women. You were pointed out to me in Delehantys as the man who does the advice in the paper and the minute I saw you I said you can help me. You had on a blue suit and gray hat when I came in with my husband who is a cripple. I don't feel so bad about asking to see you personal because I feel almost like I knew you. So please call me up at Burgess 7–7323 which is my number as I need your advice bad about my married life. (25)

When they meet, Fay tells Miss Lonelyhearts about an occasion on which her husband hit her, but as she enumerates her grievances, West makes her out to be the more abusive partner in the couple, and her interest in Miss Lonelyhearts turns out to have an ulterior, amorous motive. Still imagining himself as a priest of the commercial public sphere, Miss Lonelyhearts becomes deeply invested in mending the Doyles' wounded souls and broken marriage. The story reaches its crisis when Fay's husband, Peter, who initially finds comfort in the company of Miss Lonelyhearts, begins to resent him for becoming the object of his wife's affection, and willy-nilly ends up putting a bullet into Miss Lonelyhearts to end the story.

In *The Cultural Front,* Michael Denning refers to West as a "poet laureate of the culture industry's 'extras'" and calls his stories "bleak allegories of the great American amusement park, the world of capitalist pleasure" (255–56). Indeed, many allegorical readings of *Miss Lonelyhearts* exist, but the one I wish to advance seeks not only to understand the novel's engagement with "the business of dreams," its explicit subject, but also to reconcile this aspect of the text with its implicit concern with race and the color of American identity. I see West's story as a revision of one of the most significant corporate promotional strategies to emerge from the 1920s, which was "personalization"—that is, devising a trademark persona, a character with a face that could bring the scale and abstraction of the corporation down to size and whose trustworthiness and congeniality encouraged consumers to feel an intimate relationship with the corporation's products. The second half of the novel, in which Miss Lonelyhearts becomes entangled with the Doyles and is ultimately shot by Peter Doyle, takes this fantasy of corporate intimacy and turns it on its head.

Historian Roland Marchand writes that by the 1920s, "advertising leaders perceived a limitless public demand to be addressed personally, to obtain intimate confidences and advice" (353). For example, within a year of Betty Crocker's incarnation in 1925, the thirteen women General Mills employed to play her on regional radio networks were deluged with over four thousand letters a day, to which Betty responded with "friendly advice and reassurance."

> Advertising leaders were impressed and a bit astonished by the number and intimacy of the letters that poured in whenever a media personality like Betty Crocker, real or invented, invited personal communications. When Postum introduced the friendly advisor "Carrie Blanchard" in search of a "personal note," it soon reported that this

fictitious public confidante was receiving "more letters than a movie star." *True Story* [magazine] found its readers eager to submit first-person stories of their "real life experience." Personalized cooking correspondents, like "Mary Hale Martin for Libby Products," found that nearly half of the flood of incoming letters required personal replies. The General Electric Company, in evaluating its entrance into radio, noted that many of the 136,000 letters that greeted its first series of broadcasts "were of so confidential a character—so intimate revelations of personal trials and aspirations—as to testify to the widening acceptance of G-E as, in truth, 'The Initials of a Friend.'" (Marchand 354)

In short, consumers were more than willing to collaborate with advertisers in this illusion of intimacy, conflating the impersonal, disembodied corporation with the person of its trademark.

The profitability of these simulations of corporate corporeality had been recognized by mass magazine editors as early as the 1890s, when Edward Bok of the *Ladies' Home Journal* and George Lorimer of the *Saturday Evening Post* pushed to turn magazines from "an inanimate printed thing," as Bok put it, into "a vital need in the personal lives of its readers" (quoted in C. Wilson 51). "I want you to look upon us," he wrote in 1890, "as if we actually came in person to your home." "Just as you would talk to us if we were in your home," he continued, "tell us where we fail to meet some want in your daily life" (quoted in C. Wilson 59). By thus positing a seamless identity between the disembodied corporation and the embodied editor, this strategy of "personalization" fostered an illusion of intimacy and reciprocity that concealed its profit motive. By 1924, the circulation numbers of the *Saturday Evening Post* and the *Ladies' Home Journal* were roughly sixty times those of such older magazines as *Harper's* and *The Century* (C. Wilson 51).

What I think West's story dramatizes, then, is the mass public's demand that the corporation make good on this promise of identity, which of course it cannot do. Fay Doyle's request of Miss Lonelyhearts "to see you personal" treats his public and private selves as identical: "Please call me up at Burgess 7–7323, which is my number," she continues, "as I need your advice bad about my married life" (25). The bad faith of such "personalization" campaigns constitutes for West an elabo-

rate betrayal of the mass public, of its credulity and its genuine grievances. This is the betrayal for which the shooting of Miss Lonelyhearts by
Peter Doyle serves as symbolic revenge. Peter Doyle is represented as a
"mass man," a "cripple," yet also an everyman. We are even told that he
looks like a composite photograph (45). "You can know nothing about
humanity," Shrike yells at him, exclaiming, "You are humanity" (45). In
Doyle's shooting of Miss Lonelyhearts, the violence perpetrated against
the mass public is visited on the corporation, but since the corporation is
a disembodied abstraction, the corporation's surrogate body, Miss Lonelyhearts, takes the bullet. In effect, the mass public has produced this surrogate body as a site on which to enact a kind of revenge for the ungrievable pain of their exploitation. As always in West, the unleashing of the
accumulated resentment of the mass public misses its real target.[23]

What, then, are we to make of West's reference to the "dissipation of
America's racial energy"? To be sure, it was not unusual to speak of
Americans as a distinct race at this time. When West attributes to Americans a "racial energy," he seems to be referring to something that does
not reduce to skin color or "phenotype." His usage seems to confirm an
argument advanced by Walter Benn Michaels, who sees this period's
American fiction as rewriting race as culture rather than biology.[24] The
only way that Teddy Roosevelt could speak in 1907 of the importance of
securing loyalty to "the American race," Michaels writes, was by conceiving of race as something that "transcended color while at the same time
invoking its biological authority" (Our America 191). Thus, for Michaels,
the fiction of this period was vital to a broad cultural project to redefine
race as culture rather than biology, character rather than skin.[25] What
therefore strikes me as strange in West is precisely his attention to skins:
far from disappearing behind questions of culture and character, references to skin abound and get elaborated in striking detail.

West makes of skins a peculiar spectacle. Hallucinating, Miss Lonelyhearts sits at his desk imagining a kind of urban-industrial desert made
"not of sand, but of rust and body dirt" (25). He envisions his readers
fashioning his name first out of seashells, then out of "faded photographs, soiled fans, time-tables, playing cards, broken toys, imitation
jewelry" (25–26). Despondent, he retrieves from the wastebasket a plain-
tive letter from Fay Doyle. The letter undergoes a strange transubstanti-
ation: "Like a pink tent, he set it over the desert. Against the dark

mahogany desk top, the cheap paper took on rich flesh tones. He thought of Mrs. Doyle as a tent, hair-covered and veined, and of himself as the skeleton in a water closet, the skull and cross-bones on a scholar's bookplate" (26). Describing the color and quality of fleshy membranes becomes a regular, somewhat anxious task for Miss Lonelyhearts. While waiting in the park to meet Fay Doyle and "still thinking of tents," "he examined the sky and saw that it was canvas-colored and ill-stretched." "He examined it," explains West, "like a stupid detective who is searching for a clue to his own exhaustion" (27). Miss Lonelyhearts sees the sky as a membrane covering the city, specifically one with measurable qualities, color, and tautness. This one lacks the hair and veins of Mrs. Doyle's letter, and its canvas color suggests an indistinct tone, much as an earlier "gray sky" had looked to him like "it had been rubbed with a soiled eraser" (5). In addition to its unsatisfying color, among the other possible "clues to his own exhaustion" is the membrane's sagging quality, for it is "ill-stretched."

The sagging, gray membrane covering the city and the pink tent of a letter would be less remarkable if Miss Lonelyhearts were not similarly preoccupied, in this same idiom, with his girlfriend, Betty, as she hangs the laundry, naked, during their pastoral weekend. He sees her as another membrane, this one in exuberant contrast with the skin over the city: "She looked a little fat, but when she lifted something to the line, all the fat disappeared. Her raised arms pulled her breasts up until they were like pink-tipped thumbs" (39). Unlike the city sky, Betty is well-stretched. A more satisfying membrane, her color is revealed and accentuated where she is most taut. Made freshly potent by this erotic fantasy of pink skin, Miss Lonelyhearts "vaulted the porch rail and ran to kiss her." He and Betty make love in a "mixture of sweat, soap and crushed grass" (38).

Whether it is the "flesh"-colored letter thrown into relief by the rust and body dirt of his readers' detritus, the inadequately white and sagging sky, or the eroticized pink tautness of Betty's flesh, Miss Lonelyhearts finds skins everywhere. Having found them, he reads them like texts, identifying their qualities and placing them in a kind of epidermal economy in which the most purely pink is the most satisfying. Fay Doyle even casts her troubles as the result of racial miscegenation and a misreading of skin. "It all came through my trusting a dirty dago" named Tony

Benelli, she tells Miss Lonelyhearts. "I thought he was a gent, but when I asked him to marry me, why he spurned me from the door and wouldn't even give me money for an abortion" (29). The consequence of Fay's mistaking "a dirty dago" for "a gent" is a daughter whose refusal to accept Peter Doyle as her father causes domestic strife (30). In *The Day of the Locust,* a similar miscegenation anxiety becomes explicit. The trauma that precipitates the novel's cataclysmic resolution is that a "dark" Mexican named Miguel has sex with Faye Greener, the fallen white girl who is also West's figure for the wanton Hollywood culture industry. This miscegenation between the dark, incompletely Americanized American and the vessel of tarnished white virtue is anxiously forecast throughout the novel, and their discovery in bed is framed as its traumatic moment. Likewise, in *Miss Lonelyhearts,* the source of Fay Doyle's troubles is a compromised Americanness. While this Americanness may not be reducible to skin color, her references to Tony Benelli as a "dirty dago," a "dirty wop," and a "skunk" cast him as insufficiently Americanized and equate this deficiency with incompletely white skin.

We may be able to get our bearings among these references to skin by revising Michaels's claim—that this period's fiction rewrites race as culture—in light of the account Ian Haney Lopez offers of the citizenship naturalization cases. Lopez argues that the 1920s saw a retrenchment of the commonsense idea that people's fitness for citizenship can—indeed must—be read off of their skin. The operative word is *read,* for what is interesting is how the courts' practice of keying their determinations of fitness for citizenship to skin required them to produce discourse—that is, to produce a discourse of legibility for skins. They offered jarringly detailed accounts of their readings of skins in the texts of their decisions. "In color, he is about that of a walnut," one district judge writes of a Syrian whom he denied citizenship, "or somewhat darker than is the usual mulatto of one-half mixed blood between the white and the negro races." This judge calls his next petitioner "darker than the usual person of white European descent, and of that tinged or sallow appearance which usually accompanies persons of descent other than purely European" (quoted in Lopez 69).

In *Miss Lonelyhearts,* the story's critique of modernization, or "city troubles," depends similarly on the production of legible skins. Freighting skin with such referentiality, West participates in the discursive production of legible skins that the naturalization decisions instantiate. Like the Supreme Court's decisions, West's novel seems to have it both ways—to imply that although Americanness is not reducible to skin, skin is nevertheless a reliable index of the fitness of its citizens. Even Miss Lonelyhearts himself, on whose physical attributes West seldom remarks, has a place within this epidermal economy, in that he seems to transcend it, to occupy its constitutive exterior. "A beard would become him, would accent his Old Testament look," West writes. "But even without a beard no one could fail to recognize the New England puritan. His forehead was high and narrow. His nose was long and fleshless. His bony chin was shaped and cleft like a hoof" (3). Rhetorically eliminating skin altogether ("fleshless," "bony," and "hoof"-like), this passage effectively removes Miss Lonelyhearts, descendent of "the New England puritan," from the story's epidermal economy.

Indeed, the mass public's unfitness and its inscription on the surfaces of its bodies is nowhere better illustrated than at the moment when Miss Lonelyhearts and Betty drive through "the Bronx slums" on their return from a recuperative weekend in the country. At this point, he

> knew that Betty had failed to cure him and that he had been right when he had said that he could never forget the letters . . . Crowds of people moved through the street with a dream-like violence. As he looked at their broken hands and torn mouths he was overwhelmed by the desire to help them . . . He saw a man who appeared to be on the verge of death stagger into a movie theater that was showing a picture called "Blonde Beauty." He saw a ragged woman with an enormous goiter pick a love story magazine out of a garbage can and seem very excited by her find. (38–39)

The damaged bodies—the broken hands, torn mouths, and enormous goiters—are the outward signs of the city dwellers' wounded inner condition. Injured and duped, they seek salvation in advice columns and consolation in movies about someone else's "blonde beauty" or in someone else's love story in a magazine that someone else already discarded. The novel frames consumption as categorically unpromising, yet it situates its characters in a publicity-saturated consumer culture whose effects they are condemned either to misrecognize or ignore.

Why has West—who, as the child of Russian Jewish immigrants, was alert to the ethnic geography of New York—located this pivotal moment in "the Bronx slums" (38)? Why is it here that Miss Lonelyhearts feels especially threatened, overwhelmed by the uncountable number of apparently interchangeable people, all of whose limbs and surfaces look damaged? Why is the movie named *Blonde Beauty,* or named at all for that matter? Taken alone, these choices seem fairly arbitrary; *Blonde Beauty,* for example, could be just a throwaway reference to the popular 1929 film *Blonde Venus.* But they seem to me symptomatic of the story's recourse to race, however figuratively, in its characterization of mass culture.

The terms in which West casts the dangerously incompetent mass public with whom "the New England puritan" struggles resonate uncannily with prevalent assumptions about the consequences of race mixing on the minds and bodies of the citizenry. It was widely held that race mixing—not just between blacks and whites, but also between ostensibly distinct European "types"—resulted in mental and physical degeneracy. "At the present time the contact of racial stocks is incomparably greater than at any previous time in world history," E. B. Reuter wrote in *Scientific Monthly* in 1930, "This wholesale and indiscriminate intermixture of biological strains is, in extent at least, unlike anything before known in the contact of peoples." Reuter added:

> The general public as well as many social students impute great significance to the amalgamation of races. The prevailing note in the sociopolitical discussion is one of pessimism: there is fear of racial degeneracy, moral decadence and cultural decline; an uneasy and unanalyzed sense of impending racial and cultural disaster. (442)

Reuter goes on to insist that such pessimism is unfounded. But the appearance of this and other efforts to bring scientific authority to bear on the popular wisdom about race mixing leave no question of the popularity of the wisdom that needed dispelling. In his presidential address to the American Association for the Advancement of Science in June 1931, Franz Boas called his audience's "attention to the scientific aspects of a problem that has been for a long time agitating our country and which, on account of its social and economic implications, has given rise to strong emotional reactions and has led to varied types of legislation."

"I refer," he said, "to the problems due to the intermingling of racial types" (1). Boas maintained, "We have not had any opportunity to observe any degeneracy in man as clearly due to this cause." But it is instructive that, like Reuter, Boas was compelled in the first place to dispel the idea that "matings between individuals of different descent and different type result in a progeny less vigorous than that of their ancestors" (3).

Of particular interest in relation to West's representation of the "mass man," Peter Doyle, is Boas's challenge to the notion that race mixing produces physically distorted offspring. "It is sometimes claimed," writes Boas, that "the progeny of individuals of decidedly distinct proportions of the body would be what has been called disharmonic in character" (3). A year earlier, Harvard University's W. E. Castle had also found this misconception either sufficiently widespread or pernicious to warrant a rebuttal. In "Race Mixture and Physical Disharmonies," Castle sought to discredit the notion—recently given the imprimatur of science in H. S. Jennings's book *The Biological Basis of Human Nature*—that one "disadvantage" of "wide racial crosses" is a "possible disharmony in details of structure" (603). He quotes Jennings's contention:

> Certain human races differ in such ways that union of their characteristics may yield combinations that are in details inharmonious. In the mixture of races found in the United States, . . . some of the stocks differ greatly in physique from others . . . Judging from what occurs in other organisms, when such diverse races are crossed, the offspring, receiving genes from both sides, may well develop combinations of parts that lack complete harmony . . . [T]he occurrence of inharmonious combinations of certain bodily parts as a result of race crossing has been observed both in man and in other organisms . . . A great St. Bernard dog was crossed with a dachshund. Some of the progeny had the large, heavy body of the St. Bernard, resting on the short crooked legs of the dachshund. The result was neither beautiful nor efficient. (603)

The murderer of Miss Lonelyhearts is by no means represented as mixed-race and certainly not as a product of the white-black miscegenation that H. S. Jennings sought to discourage, but his most striking fea-

tures are his mental degeneracy, the lack of harmony in his physical proportions, and his consequent inefficiency. As a representative "mass
man" ("You can know nothing about humanity, you *are* humanity"),
Doyle has figuratively distilled in his individual body those "crowds of
people who moved through the streets with a dream-like violence" in the
Bronx. To Miss Lonelyhearts, his face looks distorted, as though many
faces were combined unnaturally into one.

> The cripple had a very strange face. His eyes failed to balance; his
> mouth was not under his nose; his forehead was square and bony; and
> his round head was like a forehead in miniature. He looked like one
> of those composite photographs used by screen magazines in guess-
> ing contests. (45)

Physically as well as symbolically, then, Doyle embodies a collectivity. On
his face, the failure of natural balance bears the traces of the technique
that massifies and miscegenates it. The pieces fail to coalesce harmo-
niously. Doyle is described as a "little cripple" who "used a cane and
dragged one of his feet behind him in a box-shaped shoe with a four-
inch sole," and his body furnishes irrepressible testimony to his
inefficiency at the business of daily life (44). He "made many waste
motions" as he hobbled along and "made vague, needless adjustments to
his clothing" as he talked.[26]

On one hand, Doyle is a casualty of economic exploitation and
bureaucratic rationality. "What I want to know," he writes Miss Lonelyhearts, "is why I go around pulling my leg up and down stairs reading
meters for the gas company for a stinking $22.50 per while the bosses
ride around in swell cars" (46). The dignity of his frustration derives
from his having been so victimized. On the other hand, West's depiction
of his chaotic inefficiency make Doyle repugnant and somewhat dangerous. Inherently disorderly and unpredictable, this "mass man"—the
mass public mapped onto a single body—constitutes a danger to Miss
Lonelyhearts, who has cast off the prophylaxis of his surrogate public
body.

Had Doyle been more articulate, West suggests, or had Miss Lonelyhearts understood that Doyle was not seeking his counsel but looking to
shoot him, disaster might have been averted.

[Doyle] shouted some kind of warning, but Miss Lonelyhearts continued his charge. He did not understand the cripple's shout and heard
it as a cry for help from Desperate, Harold S. Catholic-mother, Bro-
ken-hearted, Broad-shoulders, Sick-of-it-all, Disillusioned-with-tuber-
cular-husband. He was running to succor them with love. (57–58)

I have suggested that the shooting performs a kind of retribution in its
effect, but in its execution, it fails to dignify the avenger. It is an ending
that, as West himself put it, leaves readers with "nothing to root for."[27] It
is a botched encounter from start to finish, the "shooting" actually an
accidental explosion that occurs as Doyle tries to remove his hand from
the gun: "The cripple saw [Betty] cutting off his escape and tried to get
rid of the package. He pulled his hand out. The gun inside the package
exploded and Miss Lonelyhearts fell, dragging the cripple with him.
They both rolled part of the way down the stairs" (58). The sacrificed
body is the protagonist's, not the corporation's or even Shrike's—the latter being the one body to which we might reduce the *Post-Dispatch* if it
were reducible to one. We are a long way, in other words, from the
revenge narrative of corporate self-destruction in Frank Norris's 1901
The Octopus, for example, where poetic justice is served as the financier
meets his death in the hull of a ship under tons of cascading wheat.[28]

West's novel is not simply a story about the exploitation of the masses
by the public sphere of consumption. It is also about a middle-class man
of good intentions, descended (with a visible evidence that would have
gratified Henry James) from Puritan New England stock, who is
destroyed by the inevitably frenzied miscalculations of the mass public.
The narrative's production of legible skins and the terms in which it
characterizes the mass subject register contemporaneous discourses and
suggest that, however tacitly, the telling of these stories was bound up
with the articulation of race. By pretending to refer to color not "as
color" but only as the outward expression of racialized "types of civilization," the cultural logic of the citizenship naturalization cases served dramatically to expand the significance—the signifying capacity—of skin
color, even and especially as it pretended to ignore it. In effect, it made
it problematic to refer to skin color simply "as color" and made color
available as a means of expressing and, by implication, racializing "types
of civilization."

Coda: On Biographical and Genealogical Criticism

I want to return, in closing, to this chapter's first epigraph, which appears in *The History of Sexuality:* "But while the language may have been refined," Foucault writes, "the scope of the confession—the confession of the flesh—continually increased." I have been pursuing a similar claim in a different context, and I have taken as a premise an idea for which Foucault performed the heavy historiographic lifting: that our culture "speaks" us as much as we "speak" our culture. The notion that the novels by West and Schuyler share some of the same discursive space, even oppositionally, with the judicial decisions, popular eugenics, and commercial publicity practices that immediately preceded their publication—that they illuminate and are illuminated by these extraliterary discourses—rests largely on this Foucauldian insight. Surely, however, this is not the whole story. Schuyler and West were not inert prisms through which the dominant discourses of 1929 were refracted. Their texts' preoccupation with skin color is also attributable in part to their own experiences of racialization.

"A sort of black Horatio Alger," as biographer Michael Peplow calls him, Schuyler grew up in a white community in Syracuse, New York; internalized and made good on the traditional Protestant virtues of "self-discipline, independence, thrift, and industry"; and served in the U.S. Twenty-fifth Infantry Division in World War I (19). Although he was steeped in the rich history of African Americans as a boy (his mother had him read widely about such luminaries as Alexander Crummel, Booker T. Washington, Frederick Douglass, and Harriet Tubman), Schuyler consistently took the position, rare among his generation, that there was no real difference between whites and blacks in America. Time and again, he insisted on the absence of any basis in biology or experience between Americans of African descent and Americans of any other ancestral background: in his view, the shared American experience was paramount. Battling the myths of white supremacy, Schuyler was fond of reminding readers of the scandalous facts that African Americans came in every shade in the spectrum, including the light shades associated with whiteness, and that most American blacks had some white ancestry.

While every African American ought to take pride, he felt, in African Americans' accomplishments and contributions to their nation's history, it did not follow in his view that a distinctive "black culture" should be promoted or even recognized as a coherent idea. George Hutchinson writes:

> The notion of the "peculiarity" of African American culture seems always to have connoted "racial" inferiority for Schuyler, despite the fact that his own fiction suggested a preference for the "warmth" and "spontaneity" of black folks . . . Clearly this point of view distinguished Schuyler from most of the canonical Harlem Renaissance writers, whose efforts to develop a black aesthetic he regarded as submission to the racialist absurdities of the other authors of his generation. (299)

Because Schuyler believed all racial distinctions were inherently invidious (a position that is understandable as a response to segregation's "separate but equal" fallacy) and scientifically unsupportable, he came under continual fire from the progressive-minded "champions of the race," for whom the distinctiveness of an African American experience, if not an African American biological essence, was the basis of claims for social advancement and political equality. If he was therefore an irritant in the side of most advocates of "the Negro," he was no friend of the Anglo-Saxon purists (whose popularity flourished during the early years of Schuyler's career), for he believed that interracial marriage was "the only genuine, far-reaching solution to America's 'race problem'" (Peplow 40). Indeed, in 1928, he married a white ex-model from Texas, confirming for many a sense that Schuyler held his own race in low regard. A generation later, Schuyler was still scandalizing the African American establishment by criticizing the leadership of the black civil rights movement, from Martin Luther King to Malcolm X, and by accepting the New York State Conservative Party's nomination to run against Adam Clayton Powell. The contempt that he elicited (even solicited) may often have been deserved, but it also obscured the brilliance of his literary career. *Black No More,* "surely the most iconoclastic (not to mention hilarious) product of the Harlem Renaissance," according to one contemporary critic, is neglected in the recent efflorescence of scholarship on whiteness and the literature of racial "passing."[29]

For his part, Nathanael West came of age during a period in which American Jews found themselves invited, however unevenly, into the more capacious definition of whiteness that emerged after the "new immigration." Although the World War I years saw a recrudescence of anti-Semitism and a popular conflation of "the International Jew" and "the Negro" as threats to American civilization, the whitening of eastern European Jews in America was greatly facilitated, as my previous chapter noted, by the commercial success of Jewish entrepreneurs in the early 1900s and the relative ease with which immigrant Jewish families integrated the ethic of consumerism into their existing value systems. Of course, many eastern European Jews preserved an ethnic identity in the United States that distinguished them from "native" Americans, even as they also struggled to cast off the stigma of that ethnicity to enjoy the privileges of whiteness that were denied African Americans and other people of color. However, Nathan von Wallenstein Weinstein's parents, who arrived from Lithuania in 1887, had never identified with the Russian Jewry, who, in their view (as in the view of many bourgeois families), represented a vulgar peasantry.[30] Instead, West's parents thought of themselves as Germans while they lived in Lithuania, because their ancestral roots were German, because German home rule prevailed in Lithuania until the early 1880s, and because their wealth and social standing permitted them to live outside the pale to which most Jews were relegated. When they moved to New York, they kept the ethnic ghetto at a distance, residing on Manhattan's Upper (rather than Lower) East Side. They observed religious services only twice a year, when they attended the German Temple Israel, where a British rabbi "preach[ed] the learned message of Judaism in an impeccably correct and rhetorically distinguished English accent" (Martin 26).

Like many immigrant families with the means to do so, the Weinsteins actively pursued Americanization by rejecting aspects of their experience and ethnicity that would particularize or minoritize them. "No doubt their rapid assimilation to American ways was facilitated by the way they had earlier regarded themselves as aliens," writes Jay Martin, "as Russians but not Russians, as Jews but not Jews. Essentially, the Weinsteins gave up their Judaism with their emigration. The two families had refused to become Russian, but now they would be Americans. They no doubt agreed with the voice of the German intelligentsia, the *Hebrew Standard,* when it declared that 'the thoroughly acclimated American Jew . . . has no religious, social, or intellectual sympathies with [Russian

Jews]. He is closer to the Christian sentiment around him than to the Judaism of these miserable darkened Hebrews'" (25). This is not to say that West uncritically internalized and reproduced the white-supremacist ideology espoused in the *Hebrew Standard*. But it underscores how present were issues of race, class, nation, and color to West's generation of Americanizing immigrant Jews.

If it was not possible for West to think of himself as white in an unqualified way, his Jewishness did not compel him to identify with "darkened Hebrews," "Negroes," or other racially marked Americans. In fact, much like F. Scott Fitzgerald's James Ganz, that canny midwestern Jew who crafted a spectacularly convincing, mythic WASP persona as Jay Gatsby, the young Nathan Weinstein spun a web of stories around his signature Brooks Brothers suit to generate a new social identity. Having altered his high school academic record to gain admittance to Tufts, where he flunked out after one year, West managed to conflate his transcript with another Nathaniel Weinstein enrolled at Tufts, in order to transfer to Brown, which he entered in 1922 as a fraudulent upper sophomore. There, one of his friends recalls, he let it be known "that he had burst on the Brown campus full-blown out of the United States Navy" (quoted in Martin 52). Although it is simplistic and dogmatic to call West a self-hating Jew, as some commentators have, he extended the largely class-based disavowal of Jewish ethnicity that his parents had initiated, even as the tensions attending this process registered in the audacity with which he pursued this alternative identity: a secular intellectual whose refined tastes and demonstrably WASP-inflected behavior unmarked him in the racial economy of his time.

These biographical observations about Schuyler and West help orient us to their novels' preoccupation with skin. As I have argued, however, I think both authors were participating in a broader transition in the discourse of race. I have sought here to develop the seemingly paradoxical notion that even when race was not being directly discussed as such—indeed, precisely because race was being legally barred from discussion as such—the ways in which race could be referenced proliferated. Here, we might recall Foucault's thesis in *The History of Sexuality*, his rebuttal to the "repressive hypothesis" that saw the official aversion to sexual matters as having rendered discourse about sexuality increasingly scarce in Europe beginning in the eighteenth century. Foucault argues, to the contrary, that despite official efforts to repress sexuality by suppressing sexual discourse, what is most striking is the accompanying (and, in his view, causally linked) proliferation of the discussion of sexuality, or what he calls "the incitement to discourse."

> It is quite possible that there was an expurgation—and a very rigorous one—of the authorized vocabulary. It may indeed be true that the whole rhetoric of allusion and metaphor was codified. Without question, new rules of propriety screened out some words: there was a policing of statements. A control over enunciations as well: where and when it was not possible to talk about such things became much more strictly defined; in which circumstances, among which speakers, and within which social relationships. Areas were thus established, if not of utter silence, then at least of tact and discretion . . . This almost certainly constituted a whole restrictive economy . . . At the level of discourses and their domains, however, practically the opposite phenomenon occurred. There was a steady proliferation of discourses concerned with sex—specific discourses, different from one another both by their form and by their object: a discursive ferment that gathered momentum from the eighteenth century onward . . . [Most] important was the multiplication of discourses concerning sex in the field of exercise of power itself: an institutional incitement to speak about it and to do so more and more; a determination on the part of the agencies of power to hear it spoken about, and to cause *it* to speak through explicit articulation and endlessly accumulated detail. (17–18)

The "discursive ferment" that Foucault is concerned here to elucidate—the compulsion that sex speak itself "through explicit articulation and endlessly accumulated detail"—finds an analogy in the proliferation of racial discourses in the twentieth-century United States, even and especially as the biological basis of race came under attack and as the somatic traits thought to anchor, express, and lend coherence to the concept threatened to reveal themselves as floating signifiers.

We may certainly hear, in Foucault's discussion of the "incitement to discourse," the dual logic of repression and production that similarly obtained in racial discourse in the early twentieth-century United States, a period in which official racial segregation prevailed despite the equal protection clause of the Fourteenth Amendment. As the various "confessions of the flesh" in this chapter have illustrated, it was critical that, as Foucault maintained, race "must not be named imprudently, but its aspects, its correlations, and its effects must be pursued down to their slenderest ramifications" (19). The important difference between the period with which Foucault is concerned and the early twentieth-century United States is that the "agencies of power," as he calls them, were no longer simply (or even principally) the institutions of religion and the state, though Supreme Court naturalization cases demonstrate the continued significance of the latter. Additionally, the institutions of consumer culture—particularly the emergence of advertising as the ambient social force that Schuyler and West characterize them to be—served to bolster the currency of race. As my analysis of *Black No More* and *Miss Lonelyhearts* suggests, race not only survived its strategic decoupling from skin color but was in fact retained like an irrepressible trace as skin was freighted with legibility and meaning.

Thus, in the years leading to and including the Great Depression, I would locate an early, pivotal moment in the transition in racial thinking, whose legacy for contemporary American culture has been, as Toni Morrison describes it, a redefinition of race as metaphor rather than biology. Far from having diminished race's effects, Morrison claims that this metaphorization of race—its "way of referring to and disguising forces, events, classes, and expressions of social decay and economic division"—is "far more threatening to the body politic than biological 'race' ever was" (63). In my conclusion, I consider that present-tense deployment of race in America to which Morrison alerts us by returning to the questions about consumer culture scholarship with which I began this book.

Conclusion

LEAVING MUNCIE

In 1923, ROBERT S. LYND hit a methodological snag while in the final planning stages for the research that would become *Middletown*—a text that, along with Veblen's *Theory of the Leisure Class,* helped found a "native" critical tradition on consumer culture. He realized that questions of race were going to intrude onto his project. He felt that studying the population in South Bend, the city he had originally selected, in its full racial complexity would be far too problematic and decided instead to restrict his study "to the white American stock" of the city. "The reason for this," he explained in a memo to the executive director of the Institute of Social and Religious Research, "is obvious. Since we are attempting a difficult new technique in a highly complicated field, it is desirable to simplify our situation as far as possible. The interaction of the material and cultural trends in the city with our native psychology is problem enough without introducing into this initial study the complicating factor of a psychology molded by a foreign environment" (quoted in Fox 118). The ISRR found his argument sound and in fact suggested that, rather than finesse the problem in South Bend, he find a smaller "white American" city that could be studied as a whole. On this suggestion, Lynd visited Decatur, Illinois, and Kokomo and Muncie, Indiana, in 1924, ultimately choosing Muncie for his study. A town of thirty-eight thousand, Muncie simplified the methodological problems raised by South Bend: 92 percent of its residents were native-born whites; of that group, another 92 percent were the children of native-born whites (Fox 119). Lynd would not have to reckon with what he had called the "complicating factor of a psychology molded by a foreign environment."

In effect, Lynd and the ISRR put an artificial fix on things, segregating in their method what was not fully segregated in the society they studied. However enabling for Lynd, this decision symbolizes the artificial segregation that obtains more broadly in consumer culture's critical tradition. The presupposition is that consumer culture can be studied in isolation from other social phenomena, even race. What I hope to have shown by attending to several cultural productions from the period of consumer culture's emergence, however, is precisely the opposite: that in the United States at this time, questions of consumer culture were often already caught up in questions of race. Lynd's determination to study Muncie does not prove that consumer culture can be studied in isolation; it shows at best the expediency and at worst the artificiality of having to go to Muncie to make such autonomy seem possible. If such scholars as Lynd have previously suspended race or simply made race peripheral to their inquiry, this seems to me neither possible nor advisable any longer. In fact, as I have been suggesting, the alternately deliberate and inadvertent bracketing of race from the critical discourse on consumer culture has tended to confirm the normativity of the white public citizen, tacitly but no less surely than the consumer culture it seeks to critique.

This book has sought to stage a kind of disloyalty to the very critical tradition to which it is most indebted. At the back of this effort is a desire to understand the reciprocity between two of the most persistent anti-democratic forces that have animated (and vitiated) contemporary American culture: white supremacy and commercialism. Their force has been invigorated to the extent that their reciprocity has remained mystified. Another way to put this is to say that resistance to either force is disabled as long as the other is understood as peripheral or irrelevant to its reproduction. To the contrary, the culture of consumption thrives off of the normativity of whiteness, from the most overt exploitation of racist caricatures to the most insidious consolidation of the privileges of white racial identity. White supremacy survives and transforms itself for many material reasons, but also in part because of the contexts that consumer culture proliferates for its tacit, powerful expression and reinforcement. As commercial media have come to dominate public discourse and the circulation of racialized imagery over the course of the twentieth century, the discourses and institutions of consumer culture have come increasingly to constitute the terrain on which projects of racial formation take place.

For illustration, one need look no further than the television, by far the most influential medium in the contemporary public sphere and, in its national scope and commercial foundation, an exemplary one as well. Television has become formally inclusive, mediating to viewers a culturally and racially diverse, if not always harmonious, American public. Of course, what is mystified is the relationship between television's representations and the conditions of their production, which is that programs must deliver consumers to advertisers, television's sine qua non. But what is also mystified by television's appearance of democratic inclusiveness, its menu of formally equivalent choices among programs, is how racially segregated are its practices of reception. Though it could not have been news to many African Americans, who have seldom had the luxury of overlooking the persistence of racial segregation or of imagining themselves as national-normative, a front-page article in the *New York Times* in 1998 revealed television viewing patterns sharply divided by race. According to the Nielsen ratings, the most popular show among blacks ranked number 118 among whites. Conversely, although the top-rated show among whites ranked number 15 among blacks, none of the next four most popular shows among whites ranked higher than number 84 among blacks.[1] It may seem like the height of self-evidence to note such a survey when a mere glance around America's neighborhoods and schools reveals similar patterns of segregation. It may also seem naively culturalist to attribute to television a determining, rather than merely reflective, role in relation to the racial contours of the public sphere. Nevertheless, just as George Lipsitz has argued that a postwar liberal-humanist political program effectively created the racial segregation in housing and access to life opportunities that it was credited with redressing, these viewing patterns seem to me to represent precisely the fact of a racial segregation that resists being experienced as such because of the atomizing conditions of participation in the commercial public sphere of television and because of the powerful liberal-humanist rhetoric accompanying it.[2] The problem is not that everyone does not watch the same television shows but that the source of discrepant viewing patterns is obscured by the commercial public sphere's disavowal of a role in naturalizing the very racial identities and patterns of segregation that these statistics highlight in the first place.

For this reason, I am skeptical of the claim, advanced most recently and popularly by Leon Wynter in *American Skin* (2002), that contemporary consumer culture serves to challenge the normativity of whiteness and in turn to condition the possibility for a more equitable society. Wynter, who for ten years wrote the column "Business and Race" for the *Wall Street Journal,* maintains that the "browning," as he calls it, of commercial popular culture should not be mistaken for full social and political equality for nonwhites but does act as a leading edge. It encourages nonwhites to press for more in social and political spheres, he claims, and provokes a corresponding questioning among whites of their whiteness. Wynter's argument, a classically Keynesian one, is that because it is no longer in the financial interest of corporations to maintain white-supremacist ideology, whiteness itself is bound to crumble—hence the bravado of *American Skin*'s subtitle, *Pop Culture, Big Business, and the End of White America.* But it seems to me, to the contrary, that while commercial popular culture has indeed proliferated representations of nonwhites, their effects are far from unambivalent; that, in fact, the "browning" of which Wynter writes functions less often as a spur to individual or collective investment in political or social change and more often as a smoke screen or a safety valve.

Wynter's argument also fundamentally ignores the uses to which differences coded as racial get put in commercial popular culture, which thrives off a ceaseless pursuit of "cool" and "style." Naomi Klein points out in *No Logo* (1999): "The truth is that the 'got to be cool' rhetoric of the global brands is, more often than not, an indirect way of saying 'got to be black.' Just as the history of cool in America is really (as many have argued) a history of African-American culture—from jazz and blues to rock and roll to rap—for many of the superbrands, cool hunting simply means black-culture hunting" (74). She quotes designer Christian Lacroix, who candidly told *Vogue* magazine, "It's terrible to say, very often the most exciting outfits are from the poorest people" (quoted in Klein 73). While Wynter's *American Skin* might identify a destabilization of race and an augury of the end of racism in the mass consumption of black-coded commodities and images via, for example, Nike and Tommy

Hilfiger, Klein identifies the "harnessing of ghetto cool into a mass-marketing science" (75). Nonwhite children in America's inner cities are not leveraging pop culture's endorsement of brown skin toward political and social change so much as they are being targeted as focus groups by manufacturers who seek to "brand" them and conduct informal market research. As Klein explains, Nike marketers and designers even have a name for this practice, "bro-ing," which constitutes bringing prototypes of their products to inner-city parks and saying, "Hey, bro, check out the shoes," in order to gauge interest, cultivate brand loyalty, and generate hype (75). She goes on to describe the dynamic of desire—between black images of white wealth and white images of black style—that produced a windfall for Hilfiger in the 1990s. Hilfiger ads present nationalist tableaux of "Cape Cod multiculturalism," Klein writes, "scrubbed black faces lounging with their wind-swept white brothers and sisters in that great country club in the sky, and always against the backdrop of a billowing American flag." But the company's transformation from $53 million in sales in 1991, when it was still primarily making "Young Republican clothing," to a mass market yielding $847 million in 1998 relied entirely on the mythology of style produced by racialized structures of inequality. Klein writes:

> Tommy Hilfiger started off squarely as white-preppy wear in the tradition of Ralph Lauren and Lacoste. But the designer soon realized that his clothes also had a peculiar cachet in the inner cities, where the hip-hop philosophy of "living large" saw poor and working-class kids acquiring status in the ghetto by adopting the gear and accoutrements of prohibitively costly leisure activities, such as skiing, golfing, even boating. Perhaps to better position his brand within this urban fantasy, Hilfiger began to associate his clothes more conspicuously with these sports, shooting ads at yacht clubs, beaches and other nautical locales. At the same time, the clothes themselves were designed to appeal more directly to the hip-hop aesthetic . . . Once Tommy was firmly established as a ghetto thing, the real selling could begin—not just to the comparatively small market of poor inner-city youth but to the much larger market of middle-class white and Asian kids who mimic black style in everything from lingo to sports to music . . . Like so much of cool hunting, Hilfiger's marketing journey feeds

off the alienation at the heart of America's race relations: selling white youth on their fetishization of black style, and black youth on their fetishization of white wealth. (78)

Far from challenging racial thinking, as Wynter's *American Skin* contends, contemporary consumer culture exploits the profits that structures of racialized inequality make possible and, in the process, reinscribes them with a vengeance. I say "with a vengeance" because the visual rhetoric of commercial popular culture is so effective at mystifying the systemic inequalities that race props up. It is difficult to experience social and political alienation as such when one is so thoroughly "represented" in the commercial public sphere. These are complexities that cannot be engaged through a critical discourse and genealogy stuck in a methodological Muncie.[3]

For an alternative, we might look to Toni Cade Bambara's 1972 story "The Lesson," in which a provincialism of its own kind is being challenged—that of a group of raggedy and rebellious kids from a black ghetto that they rarely leave. The schoolmarmish Miss Moore looks to engender in them—particularly in Sylvia, the story's narrator—an experience of alienation as such, one that leads, however painfully and incrementally, to a critical consciousness of the mutually sustaining forces of consumer capitalism and race in the United States. Putting the children in taxi cabs, Miss Moore brings them to the FAO Schwarz toy store in midtown Manhattan. When they spill out of the cabs onto Fifth Avenue and see fancy-looking women in stockings and fur coats, Sylvia says simply, "white folks crazy." Miss Moore does not bring the children to FAO Schwarz to shop, of course—she is well aware that they cannot afford the twelve-hundred-dollar sailboat featured in the shop window. Nor, I would argue, does she bring them there to see how the "other half" lives, to whet their appetites for what they could have one day if they strive and make it out of the ghetto (though my students have often disagreed with me about this reading). Rather (to return to the terms of chapter 2), she brings them there to transform a critical distance from consumer culture that has been thrust on them to one that is elected. She looks to move them from the initial, dismissive "white folks crazy" to something more difficult to think but also more politically engaged. "I'm thinkin about this tricky toy I saw in the store," Sylvia reflects on the subway ride home,

A clown that somersaults on a bar then does chin-ups just cause you yank lightly at his leg. Cost $35. I could see me askin my mother for a $35 birthday clown. "You wanna who that costs what?" she'd say, cocking her head to the side to get a better view of the hole in my head. Thirty-five dollars could buy new bunk beds for Junior and Gretchen's boy. Thirty-five dollars and the whole household could go visit Granddaddy Nelson in the country. Thirty-five dollars would pay for the rent and the piano bill too. Who are these people that spend that much for performing clowns and $1,000 for toy sailboats? (94)

Thus, the compulsory critical distance that expresses itself in the wholly alienated rejoinder "white folks crazy" gradually gives way, through a painful process of reflection, to a gnawing sense in Sylvia that her whole world is being transformed in a way she cannot yet name, much less intellectualize: "somethin weird is goin on," she says, adding, "I can feel it in my chest" (95). We ought to be mindful, as the demise of white America at the "invisible hand" of consumer capitalism is trumpeted, of something Sylvia and her pals learn in Bambara's story: just because it is summer does not mean "school supposed to let up" (88).

Notes

Introduction

1. Though the rumor was technically inaccurate, it took on the ring of truth in 1895, when Alfred Nussbaum and Julius Rosenwald bought Alva Roebuck's half of the company. Of course, the accuracy of the rumor is less significant than the fact that it was used in the first place to intimidate rural consumers from mail-order shopping with remote merchants whose race they could not verify.

2. "Reconfigured genealogy" is a term Jennifer Devere Brody uses in her reassessment of "the usually aporetic relationship between [British] Victorian studies and African American studies . . . so that the putative 'objects and subjects' of these disciplines, which are thought to be distinct and mutually exclusive, are read together" (*Impossible Purities: Blackness, Femininity, and Victorian Culture* [Durham: Duke UP, 1998], 6). The term *genealogy* itself is tremendously useful in thinking about the sort of intersection I am describing. Michel Foucault has contrasted genealogy with conventional history in terms of a distinction between *entstehung* and *ursprung* in the work of Friederich Nietzsche. Conventional history's obsession with fixing origins and tracing linear causal chains that arrive unerringly at a predictable present (*ursprung*) requires the sacrifice of the rich texture of history itself, Foucault argues, including its radical difference from the present, while genealogy (*entstehung*) "is gray, meticulous, and patiently documentary" in its effort to "identify the accidents, the minute deviations—or conversely the complete reversals—the errors, the false appraisals, and the faulty calculations that gave birth to those things that continue to exist and have value for us" ("Nietzsche, Genealogy, History" [1971], reprinted in *The Foucault Reader* [New York: Pantheon, 1984], 76, 81).

3. On "articulation," see Stuart Hall, "Race, Articulation, and Societies Structured in Dominance," *Sociological Theories: Race and Colonialism* (Paris: UNESCO, 1980), 305–45; Ernesto Laclau and Chantal Mouffe, *Hegemony and Socialist Strategy: Towards a Radical Democratic Politics* (London: Verso,

1985), 105–14. This concept emerged out of post-structuralism's intervention in a Marxist tradition of thinking about the historical contingency versus the historical necessity of relations among elements in a society. If, for
classical liberalism, the social field consisted of autonomous elements whose
relation to the economic system was arbitrary, for Marx and even for such
Marxist structuralists as Althusser, the social field was unified, every element
in necessary relation with each other as expressions of a prior totality (for
Marx, the relation between economic base and social superstructure; for
Althusser, the relation between the state and the ideological state appara-
tus). Drawing on Foucault on the operation of discourse and on Gramsci on
hegemony, the post-structuralist concept of articulation retains the Marxist
insistence that the reproduction of the relations of production requires collaboration among elements in a society without therefore conferring a
sutured totality upon the social field and an a priori identity upon its elements.

4. Recent works that emphasize the transgressions and subversions
occasioned by race's articulation with consumer culture during this period
include Grace E. Hale's *Making Whiteness: The Culture of Segregation in the
South, 1890–1940* (New York: Vintage Books, 1998), Christopher Reed's *All
the World Is Here! The Black Presence at White City* (Bloomington: Indiana UP,
2000), Paul R. Mullins's *Race and Affluence: An Archaeology of African America
and Consumer Culture* (New York: Kluwer Academic/Plenum Publishers,
1999), and Andrew Heinze's *Adapting to Abundance: Jewish Immigrants, Mass
Consumption, and the Search for American Identity* (New York: Columbia UP,
1990). I count Heinze's brilliant study among works about race because Jews
were in fact widely considered a distinct racial type during some of the
period under discussion—rather than an ethnicity, as we would typically say
today. Nevertheless, the version of "difference" embodied by Jews and others
whose whiteness was "on probation" at this time should not be considered
equivalent to that of African Americans. I develop this point in the present
chapter, but it should be stressed that this has to do not with the spurious
questions of comparative oppression that discussions of blacks and Jews in
history tend to raise but with the black/white binary within which all negotiations of racial naming took place during this period.

5. "Commodity racism" is Anne McClintock's term for the proliferation
in Victorian England of advertisements, expositions, and exhibits that "converted the imperial progress narrative into mass produced consumer spectacles" (*Imperial Leather: Race, Gender, and Sexuality in the Colonial Conquest* [Lon-
don: Routledge, 1995], 133). McClintock is one of the few scholars whose
work casts emerging commercialism as central to managing this era's crisis
in scientific accounts of race. Another exception in this regard is Susan
Willis, who identifies the early twentieth-century roots of a shift from understanding race as a biological category to an aesthetic or cultural one, a shift
in which commodity consumption was pivotal. See Willis, *A Primer for Daily
Life* (London: Routledge, 1991). The passage excerpted in text from DuBois

appears in a 1920 essay (DuBois, "The Souls of White Folk," *W. E. B. DuBois: A Reader* [New York: Henry Holt, 1995], 461).

6. In their defense, Blackwell Publishers is an English company, and the volume's editor teaches at an English university. But the contributors come from many different countries, including several from the United States, and their book is marketed and widely available in the United States. Thus, despite its many virtues, I would maintain that it typifies the scholarly tendency I am identifying.

7. Cohen's study was published in 1990, yet the analogy between immigrants and African Americans is still commonplace. For example, Gary Cross writes that consumer culture was not simply a white phenomenon, but he conflates the experiences of European immigrants and African Americans: "A strategy for substituting consumer aspirations for producerist dreams extended beyond the ranks of the native Caucasian blue-collar worker. It appealed also to the immigrant or uprooted American, for whom new consumer goods offered a relatively quick way of assimilating in a city or suburb . . . The Italian peasant or country black could avoid some humiliation and establish an identity with a new suit of fashionable clothes and new products as easy to find as canned soups or the movies" (*An All-Consuming Century: Why Commercialism Won in Modern America* [New York: Columbia UP, 2000], 19). If commodity consumption helped the Italian peasant assimilate in a city or suburb (and this was a big "if" in certain years and certain places), Cross's parallel claim about the "country black" is absurd on the face of it. Through markers of genteel consumption, European immigrants could exchange ethnicity for whiteness while African Americans could exchange "vulgarity" for "respectability." Further, consumer culture's abjection of blackness figured crucially in the rhetoric of assimilation through which white America addressed immigrants.

8. "Not-yet-white ethnics" is Matthew Jacobson's term in *Whiteness of a Different Color: European Immigrants and the Alchemy of Race* (Cambridge: Harvard UP, 1998).

9. Chip Rhodes argues that representations of African Americans in popular novels by T. S. Stribling and Dubose Heyward, for example, helped naturalize consumer desire by locating its source in an inherent human propensity to desire, a human nature and essence figured by blackness. See Rhodes, "Writing Up the New Negro: The Construction of Consumer Desire in the Twenties," *Journal of American Studies* 28.2 (1994): 198–99.

10. Lauren Berlant uses this phrase to refer to a spectacularized airing of subaltern grievances that, though it does not immediately change the world, does transform a scene of abjection into "a scene of teaching and an act of heroic pedagogy," compelling the more privileged audience—through what Berlant portrays as an alchemy of courage, suasion, and faith in reason—to "change the social and institutional practices of citizenship to which they currently consent" (*The Queen of America Goes to Washington City: Essays on Sex and Citizenship* [Durham: Duke UP, 1997], 222–23). Most compelling to me

about Berlant's formulation is her emphasis not only on individual conviction and enormous inequities of social power as conditions of possibility for acts of diva citizenship but also on the commercial public sphere as the vehicle for visual spectacle.

11. Noteworthy exceptions to this tendency, which is embodied in the otherwise magisterial work of David Levering Lewis and Ann Douglas, are Cary Wintz's *Black Culture and the Harlem Renaissance* (College Station: Texas A&M UP, 1996) and George Hutchinson's *The Harlem Renaissance in Black and White* (Cambridge: Harvard UP, 1995).

12. See Rita Barnard, *The Great Depression and the Culture of Abundance: Kenneth Fearing, Nathanael West, and Mass Culture in the 1930s* (Cambridge: Cambridge UP, 1995); Lawrence Levine, "The Folklore of Industrial Society: Popular Culture and Its Audiences," *American Historical Review* 97 (Dec. 1992), 1369–99.

13. This discussion is inspired by the analysis of naturalization cases that Ian Haney Lopez develops in *White by Law: The Legal Construction of Race* (New York: New York UP, 1996).

14. Foucault, "Nietzsche," 81–82.

Chapter 1

1. Gramsci, *Selections from the Prison Notebooks* (New York: International Publishers, 1971), 262–63. See also Laclau and Mouffe 67–68.

2. See Douglas and Isherwood, *The World of Goods* (New York: Basic Books, 1979), 56–70; Fiske, *Understanding Popular Culture* (London: Unwin Hyman, 1989), 23–24.

3. See Michael Denning, "'The Special American Conditions': Marxism and American Studies," *American Quarterly* 38.3 (1986): 356–80; George Lipsitz, "Listening to Learn and Learning to Listen: Popular Culture, Cultural Theory, and American Studies," *American Quarterly* 42.4 (1990), 615–36.

4. Influential studies include Kathy Peiss's *Cheap Amusements: Working Women and Leisure in Turn-of-the-Century New York* (Philadelphia: Temple UP, 1986), Roy Rosenzweig's *Eight Hours for What We Will: Workers and Leisure in an Industrial City, 1870–1920* (Cambridge: Cambridge UP, 1983), John Kasson's *Amusing the Million: Coney Island at the Turn of the Century* (New York: Hill and Wang, 1978), Lary May's *Screening Out the Past: The Birth of Mass Culture and the Motion Picture Industry* (New York: Oxford UP, 1980), Lizabeth Cohen's *Making a New Deal: Industrial Workers in Chicago, 1919–1939* (Cambridge: Cambridge UP, 1990), Elizabeth Ewen's *Immigrant Women in the Land of Dollars: Life and Culture on the Lower East Side, 1890–1925* (New York: Monthly Review Press, 1985), and Lawrence Levine's *Highbrow/Lowbrow: The Emergence of Cultural Hierarchy in America* (Cambridge: Harvard UP, 1988).

5. See T. J. Jackson Lears, "The Concept of Cultural Hegemony: Problems and Possibilities," *American Historical Review* 90.3 (1985): 567–93. This exchange was made more explicit in work by Roland Marchand in *Advertising the American Dream: Making Way for Modernity, 1920–1940* (Berkeley: U

California P, 1985), by William Leach in *Land of Desire: Merchants, Power, and the Rise of a New American Culture* (New York: Vintage Books, 1993), by Lears in *Fables of Abundance: A Cultural History of Advertising in America* (New York: Basic Books, 1994), and by Richard Ohmann in *Selling Culture: Magazines, Markets, and Class at the Turn of the Century* (London: Verso, 1996).

6. Of course, periodizing claims about the inception of consumer culture are notoriously arguable, depending as they do on which symptoms and indicators one looks for: the moment at which the rate of manufactured goods began to outpace domestic production, the birth of the department store and the credit system, or the "post-Fordist" economy of finance capital and flexible accumulation. Nevertheless, as I hope to demonstrate, my choice of the period from the 1890s through the 1930s is far from arbitrary.

7. In making this distinction, I do not mean to suggest that race is a separate analytic from class and gender, since race has always been discursively constructed in relation to the dynamics of class and gender. Moreover, while ethnicity has also been a significant category of analysis in consumer culture scholarship and though race and ethnicity are intimately related conceptually and in their historical deployment, it seems important to distinguish between the two. The redefinition of race as ethnicity since the 1930s has succeeded at challenging pernicious biological assumptions about race, but it has also discouraged attention to the specificity of race per se by falsely analogizing the historical experiences of European immigrants with those whose physical features or national origins prevented their ascent to whiteness. On one hand, historians of immigration have diminished the importance of race, Matthew Jacobson argues, by mapping a late twentieth-century notion of ethnicity onto nineteenth-century uses of the term *race* so as to suggest that the use of that term is simply a mistake (6–7). On the other hand, as Michael Omi and Howard Winant argue, the ethnicity paradigm has served to falsely universalize the "common circumstances" each "ethnic group" has had to face. They point out: "'[B]lacks' in ethnic terms are as diverse as 'whites.' They resist comparison to the Jews and Irish, and even to Mexican Americans or Japanese Americans. The notion of 'uniqueness' doesn't go far enough because it is still posed within the ethnic group framework, while 'black,' like 'white,' is a palpably racial category" (*Racial Formation in the United States from the 1960s to the 1990s* [London: Routledge, 1994], 22).

8. I raise the distinction between intellectual and vernacular not to impugn the thinking ability of nonspecialists but to emphasize that our understanding of African American perspectives on the relationship between race and consumer culture is limited when we confine ourselves, as I do here, to the pages of published scholarly texts. For noteworthy efforts to challenge this distinction, see Davarian L. Baldwin, "Chicago's New Negroes: Consumer Culture and Intellectual Life Reconsidered," *American Studies* 44.1,2 (2003): 121–52; Grant Farred, *What's My Name? Black Vernacular Intellectuals* (Minneapolis: U Minnesota P, 2003).

9. See Barthes, *Mythologies* (New York: Noonday, 1972); Williamson, *Decoding Advertisements: Ideology and Meaning in Advertising* (London: Marion Boyars, 1978). The importance of national brands in the history of African American consumption is underscored in the recent ethnographic work of Paul Mullins in *Race and Affluence* and in the cultural studies work of Lauren Berlant in "National Brands/National Body: *Imitation of Life*," *The Phantom Public Sphere* (Minneapolis: U Minnesota P, 1993), 173–208.

10. For an extraordinary overview of the significance of race in British cultural studies in particular, see Celia Lury, *Consumer Culture* (New Brunswick: Rutgers UP, 1996), chapter 6.

11. See Mercer, "Black Hair/Style Politics," *New Formations* 3 (1987): 33–54; Gilroy, *There Ain't No Black in the Union Jack* (London: Unwin Hyman, 1987), 164.

12. The visual iconography of print advertisements and material culture has been skillfully examined in such studies as Marilyn Kern-Foxworth's *Aunt Jemima, Uncle Ben, and Rastus* (Westport: Greenword Publishing, 1994) and Patricia Turner's *Ceramic Uncles and Celluloid Mammies: Black Images and Their Influence on Culture* (New York: Anchor Books, 1994), both of which demonstrate how reliant U.S. popular culture has been on racist imagery and caricature and how limited and denigrating, as Marchand also suggests, were the roles for nonwhites in print advertisements. "Blacks never appeared as consumers," Marchand notes, "or as fellow workers with whites, or as skilled workers." "Primarily," he argues, "they functioned as symbols of the capacity of the leading lady and leading man to command a variety of personal services" (193).

13. See, for example, Craig Calhoun, ed., *Habermas and the Public Sphere* (Cambridge: MIT Press, 1992); Bruce Robbins, ed., *The Phantom Public Sphere* (Minneapolis: U Minnesota P, 1993); Michael Warner, ed., *Fear of a Queer Planet: Queer Politics and Social Theory* (Minneapolis: U Minnesota P, 1993); Black Public Sphere Collective, eds., *The Black Public Sphere* (Chicago: U Chicago P, 1995); Oscar Negt and Alexander Kluge, *Public Sphere and Experience: Toward an Organizational Analysis of Proletarian and Middle-Class Public Opinion* (Minneapolis: U Minnesota P, 1993). Such exchanges were also conducted throughout the 1990s in the pages of the journals *New German Critique, Social Text*, and *Public Culture*.

14. See Michael Warner, "The Mass Public and the Mass Subject," *Habermas and the Public Sphere* (Cambridge: MIT Press, 1992), 377–401; Berlant, "National Brands."

15. Nancy Fraser, "Rethinking the Public Sphere: A Contribution to the Critique of Actually Existing Democracy," *Habermas and the Public Sphere* (Cambridge: MIT Press, 1992), 109–41; Nancy Fraser, *Unruly Practices: Power, Discourse, and Gender in Contemporary Social Theory* (Minneapolis: U Minnesota P, 1989); Joan Landes, *Women and the Public Sphere in the Age of the French Revolution* (Ithaca: Cornell UP, 1988); Peiss, *Cheap Amusements;* Berlant, "National Brands" and *Queen;* Warner, "Mass Public" and introduc-

tion to *Fear;* Robyn Wiegman, *American Anatomies: Theorizing Race and Gender* (Durham: Duke UP, 1995); Negt and Kluge, *Public Sphere.*

16. On the institutionalization of this principle of self-abstraction, see Jurgen Habermas, *The Structural Transformation of the Public Sphere: An Inquiry into a Category of Bourgeois Society* (Cambridge: MIT Press, 1989), section II, "Social Structures of the Public Sphere." On the ways this principle served not only as a utopian promise but also as an instrument of domination, see Warner, "Mass Public"; Fraser, "Rethinking the Public Sphere."

17. Elsa Barkley Brown, "Negotiating and Transforming the Public Sphere: African American Political Life in the Transition from Slavery to Freedom," *The Black Public Sphere* (Chicago: U Chicago P, 1995), 112–15.

Chapter 2

1. For critical perspectives on Aunt Jemima's commercial deployment, see M. M. Manring, *Slave in a Box: The Strange Career of Aunt Jemima* (Charlottesville: U Virginia P, 1998); Kern-Foxworth, *Aunt Jemima;* Turner, *Ceramic Uncles.*

2. May Wright Sewell, ed., *The World's Congress of Representative Women* (Chicago and New York: Rand McNally, 1894), 433, 696–729.

3. See Berlant, "National Brands" 177–78 and *Queen* 227.

4. George Knox, "Douglass' Wasted Zeal," *Indianapolis Freeman* Aug. 5, 1893: 1.

5. Ida B. Wells, letter, *Cleveland Gazette* July 22, 1893: 1.

6. One African American man—Hale Parker, a St. Louis high school principal and attorney—was appointed as an alternate member of the national board. See Reed 23.

7. Even Hallie Quinn Brown's April 1892 letter of inquiry to each member of the Board of Lady Managers, in which she proposed that the board appoint "some colored person" who would oversee African American contributions to the exposition, met with indifference at best. "If the object of the Woman's Department of the Columbian Exposition is to present to the world the industrial and educational progress of the breadwinners—the wage women," wrote Brown, "how immeasurably incomplete will that work be without the exhibit of the thousands of colored women of this country" (Ida B. Wells, *The Reason Why the Colored American Is Not in the World's Columbian Exposition: The Afro-American's Contribution to Columbian Literature, Selected Works of Ida B. Wells-Barnett* [New York: Oxford UP, 1991], 124). Fewer than half of the board members responded to Brown, and while a few gave lukewarm endorsements of her proposal, some "were frank enough to speak their pronounced opposition to any plan that would bring them in contact with a colored representative," emphasizing their opposition by declaring that they would resign if such an appointment were made (Wells, *The Reason Why* 126). For a fully elaborated discussion of these negotiations, see Ann Massa, "Black Women in the 'White City,'" *Journal of American Studies* 8 (Dec. 1974): 319–37.

8. The intended "Negro Annex" would have been a "Statistical Exhibit which would show the moral, educational, and financial growth of the American Negro since his emancipation" (Wells, *The Reason Why* 135). Exceptions to the policy of exclusion can be found, some of which Barnett notes, but the instances of participation that he misses hardly compromise the pamphlet's broad claim that "the whole history of the exposition is a record of discrimination against the colored people" (Well, *The Reason Why* 128). Even taken together, the exceptions tend to prove the rule: that these few cases can be counted testifies to their more general absence from the fair. See Wells, *The Reason Why* 128–29; Dreck Spurlock Wilson, "Black Involvement in Chicago's Previous World's Fairs" (unpublished manuscript, Library of the Chicago Historical Society, 1984), 6–11.

9. Horace Cayton and St. Clair Drake, *Black Metropolis: A Study of Negro Life in a Northern City* (Chicago: U Chicago P, 1993), 9.

10. Christopher Reed's *All the World Is Here!* contends that African American exclusion was not nearly as successful as suggested by *The Reason Why* and the many historical accounts it has informed. Reed's scholarship is tremendous, but his conclusions are not wholly persuasive. As he points out, *The Reason Why* fails to note several instances of African American participation in the fair. I mention some in this chapter, but the others Reed notes are the participation of poet Paul Laurence Dunbar, Hampton Institute's Robert S. Abbott, and Tuskegee's Booker T. Washington in the ceremonies of "Colored American Day"; the participation of Frederick Douglass and many African American soldiers in the fair's Opening Day Parade; and the speeches such African Americans as Henry Ossawa Tanner and Ferdinand Barnett delivered at the "African Congress." However, a good deal of Reed's argument rests on the participation of Africans rather than African Americans, two very different constituencies that Reed collapses into the somewhat misleading umbrella category "continental and diasporan Africans." Reed's project seeks to rescue the "positive human agency" of African Americans from what he calls the "protest" school of historiography that has dominated scholarship on the 1893 fair. This approach, he argues, focuses too narrowly on "externally imposed limits" at the expense of attention to "the transcendence of black human agency in the face of external constraints" (ix). Although my own examination of Wells's effort to exploit the fairgrounds against their intended purposes is clearly akin in spirit with Reed's injunction to recover actual historical agency, his analysis strikes me as willfully optimistic. It belies the evidence I have seen (including the evidence gathered in Reed's own impressive archive) to claim, as Reed does, that the fair amounted to a "race's dream realized—not a recognition of its humanity and advancement on terms it desired, but participation gained to a degree significant enough to lay a firm foundation for a brighter future" (xxi). It is difficult to square this thesis with the readings Reed himself offers of the impact of "Colored American Day," of the media coverage of the Midway's exhibition of Africans, and of the racism within the fair administration, to

name a few sites of inquiry. Moreover, Reed's commitment to emphasizing black agency as a rebuttal to the many existing "ideological" interpretations of the fair threatens, at several points, to excuse or downplay the significance of racist practices in evidence at the fair, such as the Quaker Oats exhibition of Nancy Green and the Midway display of Fon people from Dahomey by impresario Sol Bloom and anthropologist Frederick Putnam, whom he ingenuously characterizes as having "assembled the world's humanity to allow them to perform their daily routines as they did in indigenous settings" (xxvii).

11. It is worth noting, on this point, the "surrogate" public body Wells attained in print and the presumption about its gender that surfaced when she anonymously published her antilynching editorial in the Memphis *Free Speech* in 1892. Responses indicate that readers thought the author was a man. They threatened "him" with castration and death before destroying the offices of the newspaper. See Mildred Thompson, *Ida B. Wells-Barnett: An Exploratory Study of an American Black Woman, 1893–1930* (Brooklyn: Carlson, 1990), 29–30.

12. On the institutionalization of this principle of self-abstraction, see Habermas, section II. On the ways this principle served not only as a utopian promise but also as an instrument of domination, see Warner, "Mass Public." My understanding of counterpublics is indebted to Nancy Fraser's "Rethinking the Public Sphere." Borrowing terms from Gayatri Spivak and Rita Felski, Fraser describes "subaltern counterpublics" that are "parallel discursive arenas where members of subordinated social groups invent and circulate counterdiscourses to formulate oppositional interpretations of their identities, interests, and needs" (123). The contradictory relation to one's body that I attribute here to Wells operated in the bourgeois public sphere not only among minoritized subjects but even as the precondition for participation for its privileged subjects, propertied white males. The utopian promise of bourgeois publicity was that particular people could stand in for people in general. Minoritized subjects were prevented from experiencing themselves as universal; privileged subjects were encouraged to perform the ideological gesture of mistaking their own particular attributes for universals.

13. George Knox, "No 'Nigger Day,' No 'Nigger Pamphlet,'" *Indianapolis Freeman* Aug. 12, 1893: 4.

14. Wells, letter.

15. Wells, letter.

16. "The Women and the World's Fair," *New York Age* Oct. 24, 1891.

17. See James Gilbert, *Perfect Cities: Chicago's Utopias of 1893* (Chicago: U Chicago P, 1991).

18. Burnham hoped to render visible the levels of value among the fair's exhibits, as he explained in Rand-McNally's *Handbook:* "Three distinct motives are apparent in the grouping of the buildings. Those about the Great Basin—the Administration, Manufactures, Agriculture, Machinery, Electricity, Mines, and also the Art Building—are essentially dignified in

style; those lying farther to the north—the Horticultural, Transportation, and Fisheries—being less formal, blend readily with the more or less home-like headquarters buildings of the States and foreign governments, which are grouped among the trees of the extreme northern portion of the grounds. Upon the Midway Plaisance, no distinct order is followed, it being instead a most unusual collection of almost every type of architecture known to man—oriental villages, Chinese bazaars, tropical settlements, ice railways, the ponderous Ferris wheel, and reproductions of ancient cities. All these are combined to form the lighter and more fantastic side of the Fair" (quoted in Alan Trachtenberg, *The Incorporation of America: Culture and Society in the Gilded Age* [New York: Hill and Wang, 1982], 213).

19. See Wells, *The Reason Why* 58; Massa, "Black Women"; Meier and Rudwick, "Black Man"; Robert Rydell, *All the World's a Fair: Visions of Empire at American International Expositions, 1876–1916* (Chicago: U Chicago P, 1987), chapter 2; Gilbert, *Perfect Cities;* Trachtenberg, *Incorporation* chapter 7. Gilbert and Rydell make this argument based on their interpretations of the Midway in particular.

20. See Robert Rydell, "The World's Columbian Exposition of 1893: Racist Underpinning of a Utopian Artifact," *Journal of American Culture* 1 (1978): 271, 256.

21. See Mary Oldham Eagle, *The Congress of Women, Held in the Women's Building* (New York: Wilson, 1894). Further illustrations of the ambivalence of the fair's endorsement of politicized women abound. The Midway's parodic "World's Congress of Beauty" was an ensemble of belly dancers and "Forty Ladies from Forty Countries," mimicking the internationalism of the Women's Congress yet reinscribing the pleasure of the male gaze that the politicized version of women's publicness subordinated. Moreover, discussions at the Women's Congress were "widely known, influential, and provocative," as one contemporary put it, but studies also note tellingly that its best-attended session was "Women's Place in Drama." See Rossiter Johnson, ed., *A History of the World's Columbian Exposition* (New York: D. Appleton, 1898), 6; Stanley Appelbaum, *The Chicago World's Fair of 1893: A Photographic Record* (New York: Dover, 1980), 106.

Chapter 3

1. An index of James's distance from these writers is Bourne's elegant repudiation of the melting-pot model in his essay "Trans-National America," which first appeared in *Atlantic Monthly* in 1916. See Bourne, *War and the Intellectuals: Collected Essays, 1915–1919* (Indianapolis: Hackett Publishing, 1999), 107–23. See also Boas, "What Is a Race?" *The Nation* 120 (1925): 91; Kallen, *Culture and Democracy in the United States* (New York: Boni and Liveright, 1924).

2. The U.S. Bureau of the Census (*Historical Statistics of the United States, Colonial Times to 1970, Bicentennial Edition* [Washington, DC: U.S. Bureau of

the Census]) reports that in 1907, Italian immigration peaked at 285,731, and Russian immigration, which was largely Jewish, peaked at 258,943.

3. Commerce and race in *The American Scene* have separately been the subjects of a great deal of critical debate. But little of the existing work seems to me adequately to examine their coarticulation. While there is a consensus among readers of *The American Scene* that it shows James at the height of his bourgeois elitism, there is considerable disagreement over how to understand the particularly vexed relationship James has to these two rhetorical targets. At one end of a spectrum of readings of his relationship to the commercial ethos he indicts, for example, are Kevin McNamara, who attributes to James the creation of "an original, nonreproducible artifact by means of the critical consciousness he brings to bear on what are without this additional element merely the alienating products of alienated labor in industrialized America" ("Building Culture: The Two New York's of Henry James's *The American Scene,*" *Prospects: An Annual of American Cultural Studies* 18 [1993]: 121), and Richard Salmon, who "attempt[s] to preserve the critical character of James's response to the formation of mass culture" (*Henry James and the Culture of Publicity* [Cambridge: Cambridge UP, 1997], 5); at the other end of this spectrum, such critics as Mark Seltzer and Jean-Christophe Agnew argue that James's challenges to the market are implicated in the very discourses they denounce. On James's relationship to racial otherness, likewise, the spectrum reaches from Ross Posnock, Beverly Haviland, and Alan Trachtenberg, who "take James seriously as a social critic" in order "to overturn the remarkably durable image of him as a genteel formalist" in flight from heterogeneity (Posnock, "Henry James, Veblen, and Adorno: The Crisis of the Modern Self," *Journal of American Studies* 21 [1987]: 32), to the efforts that Kenneth Warren, Jonathan Freedman, and Sara Blair have made to demonstrate the ways in which James either voices or makes a tacit peace with white-supremacist and xenophobic thinking.

4. The recent scholarship of Sara Blair and Patricia McKee is exceptional in this respect, and my argument is indebted to them. Both writers forge frameworks for understanding commercialization and race as mutually constitutive instead of coincidental. Blair argues that *The American Scene* is less "an autobiographical record of repatriation or literary ascendancy" than "a fluidly responsive, contextually alert study of emerging idioms and technologies for constructing national and racial subjects" (*Henry James and the Writing of Race and Nation* [Cambridge: Cambridge UP, 1996], 13), while McKee sees James pursuing "a critical modernist consciousness, with its power of choice as a mark of American character and an American 'non-race'" (*Producing American Races: James, Faulkner, and Morrison* [Durham: Duke UP, 1999], 98). Although Dana Nelson's *National Manhood: Capitalist Citizenship and the Imagined Fraternity of White Men* (Durham: Duke UP, 1998) does not address Henry James, I draw on her observations about the structuring importance (and democratically vitiating effects) of an imagined fra-

ternity among white men in the United States. Nelson provides a compelling model for understanding the relationship between the desire for civic fraternity and the consequences of that desire's affective reroutings under the market's competitive, individualist demands.

5. See James Baldwin, "On Being 'White' . . . and Other Lies," *Essence* 14 (Apr. 1984): 90–92.

6. Perhaps it is not a question of James confining these terms to an aesthetic register but of his construing aesthetics so broadly as to encompass all social questions, race included. After all, terms do not need to be confined to a lexicon that they already inhabit. When aesthetics is construed so broadly that race is always an aesthetic matter, this only means (as Walter Benn Michaels writes in *Our America: Nativism, Modernism, and Pluralism* [Durham and London: Duke UP, 1995]) that the discourse of aesthetics becomes a racial discourse: race does not cease to function as the referent; instead, the possibilities for signifying race proliferate. For a consequential juridical illustration of this principle, see *Williams v. Mississippi* (1898).

7. This seems to me Kenneth Warren's tendency in his otherwise persuasive treatment of race in *The American Scene, The Souls of Black Folk,* and *Iola Leroy.* See *Black and White Strangers: Race and American Literary Realism* (Chicago: U Chicago P, 1993), chapter 4.

8. Among the most important agents in the legitimation of a specifically racial nationalism, Higham writes, were the American translation of European heredity studies into eugenics; the widely publicized anthropological demonstration of European "types" performed by William Z. Ripley; and, in a body of work contemporaneous with the later stage of James's own writing, Madison Grant's contention that different races do not really blend but that mixing two races causes a "reversion to the lower type" (Higham, *Strangers in the Land: Patterns of American Nativism, 1860–1925* [New Brunswick: Rutgers UP, 1996], 149–56).

9. On the formation of "mass culture" in the context of the historical process in which "high culture" was generated as its mutually defining other, see, for example, Frederic Jameson, *The Political Unconscious: Narrative as a Socially Symbolic Act* (Ithaca: Cornell UP, 1981), chapter 5; Andreas Huyssen, *After the Great Divide: Modernism, Mass Culture, Postmodernism* (Bloomington: Indiana UP, 1986); Levine, *Highbrow/Lowbrow.* On the investment of James's texts in the capitalist structures of power and value that they explicitly oppose, see, for example, Mark Seltzer, *Henry James and The Art of Power* (Ithaca: Cornell UP, 1984); Jean-Christophe Agnew, "The Consuming Vision of Henry James," *The Culture of Consumption: Critical Essays in American History, 1880–1980* (New York: Pantheon, 1983).

10. For James, "science" is like instrumental reason. It is intelligence and knowledge when it moves from being disinterested to being applied, particularly being "applied to gain" (*American Scene* 60).

11. On the proximate relation between the iconography of industrial

machinery and black men in postbellum American fiction, see Bill Brown, "The Prosthetics of Empire," *Cultures of U.S. Imperialism* (Durham: Duke UP, 1993), 130–33.

12. "In the public spaces of whiteness, which whites identify as open space, with much room for distinction and also with much room for circulation" McKee writes, "whiteness has been experienced in extraordinary variety." She continues: "White persons, therefore, can experience their identity not merely as self-same but as diverse. They thus enter into exchanges of identity that seem open and inclusive of difference even as they are exclusive" (13). Trachtenberg writes: "Perhaps the most pervasive means of forgetting national origins came in the form of racial definition: we are if nothing else a *white* nation . . . Save for the exclusion of Native Americans and enslaved blacks, and the denial of suffrage to women, membership in the new nation might indeed seem a legal or political rather than a cultural (linguistic, religious) matter. The notion of an original universalist ground for national identity took hold as America's exception. Not by conquest or coercion but by free political choice do the many become one" ("Conceivable Aliens," *Yale Review* 82.4 [Oct. 1994]: 51).

13. Also worth noting here are the terms in which James characterizes the market as voraciously, insatiably sexual.

14. The construction of whiteness as property figured centrally in the argument for the plaintiff in the landmark U.S. Supreme Court case of the segregation era, *Plessy v. Ferguson* (1896), a decade before *The American Scene* appeared. However, it was summarily dismissed in the opinion of the Court written by Justice Brown and not directly addressed in the dissenting opinion of Justice Harlan.

Chapter 4

1. The so-called Great Migration, spurred by World War I, meant that between 1910 and 1920, New York's black population grew by over 66 percent, Chicago's by 148 percent, Cleveland's by 307 percent, and Detroit's by over 611 percent. In each of these cities, the black population would at least double again between 1920 and 1930. See Charles E. Hall, *Negroes in the United States, 1920–1932* (Washington, DC: U.S. Bureau of the Census, 1935), 55.

2. On this imperative, see Cheryl Harris, "Whiteness as Property," *Black on White* (New York: Schocken Books, 1998), 117. Of course, neither the phenomenon of racial "passing" nor its treatment in literary texts was unique to the segregation era. Slavery created a tremendous incentive for enslaved African Americans to use "passing" as a subterfuge in their pursuit of freedom. Elaine Ginsberg refers to one of many such examples in *Passing and the Fictions of Identity* (Durham: Duke UP, 1996), in which she quotes from a slaveholder's 1836 announcement in the Richmond *Whig* offering a hundred-dollar reward for the return of one Edmund Kenney: "He has

straight hair, and complexion so nearly white that it is believed a stranger would suppose there was no African blood in him. He . . . escaped under the pretence of being a white man" (1).

3. See, for example, Cable's *Old Creole Days* (1879) and *The Grandissimes* (1880), Tourgee's *A Royal Gentleman* (1881) and *Pactolus Prime* (1890), Twain's *Pudd'nhead Wilson* (1894), Harper's *Iola Leroy* (1892), Hopkins's *Contending Forces* (1900) and *Of One Blood* (1903), and Chesnutt's *The House behind the Cedars* (1900).

4. Notably, Walter White's *Flight* (1926), Jessie Fauset's *Plum Bun* (1928), and Nella Larsen's *Quicksand* (1928) and *Passing* (1929). For a discussion of other pre-1920 African American writers who "treat the color line as nonexistent of unimportant," see Robert Bone, *The Negro Novel in America* (New Haven: Yale UP, 1958), 49.

5. Two scholars who have recently advanced performative readings of race in this novel are Samira Kawash and Walter Benn Michaels. For Kawash, however, exposing the "fiction" of race does not require her to treat racial thinking merely as false consciousness, as is Michaels's tendency, nor does she follow Michaels's tendency to treat "black" and "white" as equivalent kinds of fictions. See Kawash, "*The Autobiography of an Ex-Coloured Man:* (Passing for) Black Passing for White," *Passing and the Fictions of Identity* (Durham: Duke UP, 1996), 59–74; Michaels, "Autobiography of an Ex-White Man," *Transition* 73 (1996): 122–43.

6. For this account of racial performativity, I am drawing on Judith Butler's introduction to *Bodies That Matter: On the Discursive Limits of Sex* (New York: Routledge, 1993), Diana Fuss's chapter "Poststructuralist Afro-American Literary Theory" in *Essentially Speaking: Feminism, Nature, and Difference* (New York: Routledge, 1989), and Colette Guillamin's *Racism, Sexism, Power, and Ideology* (New York: Routledge, 1995), 133–52.

7. For a more elaborated version of the argument Lipsitz makes in *American Quarterly,* see his *The Possessive Investment in Whiteness: How White People Profit from Identity Politics* (Philadelphia: Temple UP, 1998), 1–23.

8. Theodore Allen locates "the invention of the white race" in the United States in the earliest European colonists' efforts to induce their compatriots of a lower class to participate in the plantation agricultural economy in Virginia and Maryland. Despite the fact that "European Americans who did not own bond-laborers" were denied social mobility, writes Allen, they could feel "satisfied with the presumption of liberty, the birthright of [even] the poorest person in England" (*The Invention of the White Race* [London: Verso, 1997], 248–49).

9. I here cite Eric Lott's title phrase from *Love and Theft: Blackface Minstrelsy and the American Working Class* (New York: Oxford UP, 1993) because his observation about minstrelsy—and about commercial performances of blackness more broadly—seems pertinent to the project the ex-colored man undertakes. Lott observes that such performances are not well comprehended as efforts strictly to denigrate or strictly to celebrate black folk cul-

ture but, rather, retain each impulse ambivalently and inextricably.

10. See Michael P. Rogin, *Blackface, White Noise: Jewish Immigrants in the Hollywood Melting Pot* (Berkeley: U California P, 1998).

Chapter 5

1. Though the Boni brothers, Albert and Charles, began publishing in 1917, Horace Liveright did not take over as publisher until two years later. By 1933, Liveright had bankrupted the company through lavish personal expenditures and losing investments in Broadway productions.

2. On the role that "New Negro" writing played in this deliberate effort among several U.S. publishers to transcend the genteel tradition, see Nathan Huggins, *The Harlem Renaissance* (New York: Oxford UP, 1971), chapter 3; Hutchinson, chapter 12.

3. This asymmetry in the scholarship is striking. Not only is Tebbel silent on this score, so are Walker Gilmer and Tom Dardis in their biographies of Horace Liveright. But their omissions are characteristic of traditional publishing histories, which treat the publication of African American writers (or the lack thereof) as a footnote at best. For example, James L. W. West's *American Authors and the Literary Marketplace since 1900* (Philadelphia: U Pennsylvania P, 1988) contains no mention of African American authors or publishers, much less of any white publishers' relationship with African American authors in the Harlem Renaissance. That this would be so despite extensive discussion of Boni and Liveright, Alfred A. Knopf, and Viking is very conspicuous. More recently, Jason Epstein's *Book Business: Publishing Past, Present, and Future* (New York: Norton, 2001) dwells on Horace Liveright for several pages but relies almost exclusively on Dardis's *Firebrand: The Life of Horace Liveright* (New York: Random House, 1995) for its information and thus omits any reference to the publication of African American authors.

4. See Huggins, *Harlem Renaissance;* Michael North, *The Dialect of Modernism: Race, Language, and Twentieth-Century Literature* (New York: Oxford UP, 1994); Houston Baker, *Modernism and the Harlem Renaissance* (Chicago: U Chicago P, 1987); Ann Douglas, *Terrible Honesty: Mongrel Manhattan in the 1920s* (New York: Farrar, Straus, and Giroux, 1995); Amritjit Singh, William S. Shiver, and Stanley Brodwin, eds., *The Harlem Renaissance: Revaluations* (New York: Garland, 1989).

5. Van Vechten is best known as the author of *Nigger Heaven* (1926) and the close associate of Alfred A. Knopf and James Weldon Johnson. Mason, universally referred to as "Godmother," is best known as the patron of Langston Hughes, Hurst as Zora Neale Hurston's patron, and Cunard as the promiscuous patron of many African American writers and artists and the editor of *Negro: An Anthology* (1934). Notable exceptions to the scholarly tendency to focus on individual patronage relationships at the expense of a broader critique of consumer capitalism include Hutchinson's *Harlem Renaissance,* Wintz's *Black Culture,* Rhodes's "Writing Up the 'New Negro,'"

and Harold Cruse's *Rebellion or Revolution,* the last of which blames the white bourgeoisie for distorting the New Negro movement and diverting its political energies.

6. See Kevin Dettmar and Stephen Watt, eds., *Marketing Modernism: Self-Promotion, Canonization, Rereading* (Ann Arbor: U Michigan P, 1996); Joyce P. Wexler, *Who Paid for Modernism? Art, Money, and the Fiction of Conrad, Joyce, and Lawrence* (Fayetteville: U Arkansas P, 1997); Lawrence Rainey, *The Institution of Modernism: Literary Elites and Public Culture* (New Haven: Yale UP, 1998).

7. Both Hutchinson and North address this point.

8. See *Publishers Weekly* June 30, 1923: 1934.

9. Book printing and publishing followed women's and men's clothing, newspapers and periodicals, bread and bakery products, millinery and lace, and cigars and cigarettes (*Publishers Weekly* March 3, 1923: 628).

10. The number rose from 788 to 2,142 between 1918 and 1929. See John Tebbel, *A History of Book Publishing in the United States* (New York and London: R. R. Bowker, 1978), 683.

11. "Many industries try to market their goods without appearing to be interested in the bottom line," writes Lori Ween, "but such concerns are even more urgent when it comes to ethnic American literature, which relied on prescribed authenticity and the importance of telling the 'real story' apart from merely selling the commodity of the book" ("This is Your Book: Marketing America to Itself," *PMLA* 118.1 [Jan. 2003]: 92).

12. I am borrowing the term "paratextual" from Gerard Genette, who contends in *Paratexts: Thresholds of Interpretation* (New York: Cambridge UP, 1997) that the meaning of a text is inseparable from the conditions of its circulation as a commodity, including the "peritextual" elements physically attached to the texts and the "epitextual" elements, such as interviews, reviews, and conversations, that lie outside the physical text itself but exert a shaping force on reading communities and reading practices.

13. Pierre Bourdieu writes: "The art trader is not just the agent who gives the work a commercial value by bringing it into a market; he is not just the representative, the impresario, who 'defends the authors he loves.' He is the person who can proclaim the value of the author he defends (cf. the fiction of the catalogue or blurb) and above all 'invests his prestige' in the author's cause, acting as a 'symbolic banker' who offers as security all the symbolic capital he has accumulated (which he is liable to forfeit if he backs a 'loser'). This investment, of which the accompanying 'economic' investments are themselves only a guarantee, is what brings the producer into the cycle of consecration. Entering the field of literature is not so much like going into religion as getting into a select club: the publisher is one of those prestigious sponsors (together with preface-writers and critics) who effusively recommend their candidate" (*The Field of Cultural Production* [New York: Columbia UP, 1993], 77).

14. See Marchand, "Advertising as Social Tableau," in *Advertising the American Dream* 164–205.

15. See Patrick Gilpin, "Charles S. Johnson: Entrepreneur of the Harlem Renaissance," *The Harlem Renaissance Remembered* (New York: Dodd, Meade, 1972), 215–46.

16. See Edward Bernays, *Biography of an Idea: Memoirs of Public Relations Counsel Edward L. Bernays* (New York: Simon and Schuster, 1965). See also "Testimony before the Subcommittee on Overseas Information Programs of the Senate Committee on Foreign Affairs, March 31, 1953," *Congressional Record,* appendix, A1949–A1950.

17. In fact, though Bernays was probably not personally involved in the Urban League's staging of the Civic Club event, he had directed publicity and promotion for the NAACP. In *The Walls Came Tumbling Down,* Mary White Ovington writes: "When the NAACP convened their annual national conference in Atlanta in 1921, Edward Bernays handled the publicity "and the press did well for us. I cannot forget how fully and correctly the Atlanta *Constitution* reported our meetings. Bernays's technique was to make friends of the reporters and do all their work" (178). See also Bernays, *Biography,* chapter 19.

18. *Publishers Weekly* January 27, 1923: 147.

19. If Pound had had things his way, B&L would have been the principal U.S. publisher of modernism tout court. Among those whom Liveright pursued overseas with Pound's help in the early twenties were James Joyce, W. B. Yeats, Wyndham Lewis, H. G. Wells, and George Bernard Shaw, none of whom were ultimately won over. See Rainey 125–26; Dardis 109.

20. Interestingly, this 1926 prize went unawarded. The judges—among whom were DuBois, James Weldon Johnson, Henry Seidel Canby, Charles Johnson, and Irita Van Doren—ultimately found no novel worthy of the award. See Wintz, *Black Culture* 137; Lewis 179.

21. Both entries appear in the Boni and Liveright book catalogs collected in the W. W. Norton papers, series III, box 8, Butler Rare Books and Manuscripts Collection, Columbia University. See page 11 in the spring 1924 catalog and page 9 in the fall 1926 catalog.

22. David Levering Lewis's "dollars and cents salon Negrotarians" are those who only maintained contact with black culture as long as their account books also stayed in the black (99).

23. An excellent example of the deliberate and differentiated program pursued by the new, largely Jewish publishers is Alfred Knopf's formation, in 1927, of the Publishers' Book Table. Because the existing group, the Publishers' Lunch Club, was "not notable in those days for the number of its Jewish members," as John Tebbel understates it, Knopf's group convened "a shifting assortment of authors, publishers, distributors, advertisers, and designers all gathered to discuss how 'to give books the widest attention,' and did so in ways that transformed the marketing practices of the industry." See Jonathan Freedman, *The Temple of Culture: Assimilation and Anti-Semitism in Literary Anglo-America* (New York: Oxford UP, 2002), 169.

24. In addition to the publishers already mentioned, Richard Simon and

Max Schuster were Jewish, as were the founders of Viking, Harold Guinzberg and George Oppenheimer. Together, these largely Jewish companies revolutionized the industry by bringing "modern business methods to a dangerously hide-bound business," writes Freedman (*Temple* 170). He goes on to compare their impact on publishing and on the culture more generally to the effect of the Jewish moguls in Hollywood on what had been an industry dominated by the Edison Trust.

25. See Heinze, chapter 12.

26. See Rainey 106. The balance that a firm like B&L pursued between the symbolic capital and the actual capital generated by its book list was a variation on what Rainey (112–15) explains was the typical tripartite approach to marketing avant-garde work that consolidated modernism as a hegemonic literary movement: a journal publication, publication of a limited edition, and finally publication of a public or commercial edition. The point is that, far from conflicting as outlets for modernist writing, these various modes of publication worked reciprocally to generate commercial success without sacrificing the appeal the work could make to exclusivity and innovation.

27. On Locke's preference for men, specifically on the homosexual dynamics he pursued with Cullen, Hughes, Bruce Nugent, and Claude McKay, see Gloria Hull, *Color, Sex, and Poetry* (Bloomington: Indiana UP, 1987), 8–10.

28. Perhaps for this reason, Ann Douglas's *Terrible Honesty* (81) mistakenly attributes the publication of Nella Larsen's *Quicksand* (1928) to Boni and Liveright (in fact, it was published by Knopf). Larsen's work exhibits the naturalism and frankness toward sexuality that Hull describes as having appealed to such firms as B&L.

29. See Michael Soto, "Jean Toomer and Horace Liveright; or, A New Negro Gets 'into the Swing of It,'" *Jean Toomer and the Harlem Renaissance* (New Brunswick: Rutgers UP, 2001), 166.

30. See Adam McKible, *The Space and Place of Modernism: The Russian Revolution, Little Magazines, and New York* (New York: Routledge, 2000), for an excellent treatment of the role that the little magazines played in the emergence of American modernism, especially as it related to radical politics.

31. Morrison defines American Africanism as "the ways in which a non-white Africanlike (or Africanist) presence or persona was constructed in the United States, and the imaginative uses this fabricated presence served" (6). The virtue of Morrison's account is that it attributes a complexity to primitivism that is absent from analyses that are too eager to simply indict white writers' "racial ventriloquism" as a form of privileged literary slumming (see, e.g., North, *Dialect of Modernism;* Baker, *Modernism and the Harlem Renaissance*) or, conversely, to simply endorse their experimentation with alternate personae as a challenge to normative discourse (see, e.g., Robert Coles and Diane Isaacs, "Primitivism as a Therapeutic Pursuit: Notes Toward a

Reassessment of Harlem Renaissance Literature," *The Harlem Renaissance: Revaluations* [New York: Garland, 1989], 3–71).

32. "Their griefs are transient," Jefferson asserts, adding: "Those numberless afflictions, which render it doubtful whether heaven has given life to us in mercy or in wrath, are less felt, and sooner forgotten with them. In general, their existence appears to participate more in sensation than reflection" (*Notes on the State of Virginia, Jefferson: Writings* [New York: Library of America], 265).

33. Liveright was hopeful that positioning Toomer as an avant-garde modernist would bring an African American audience intuitively interested in *Cane* to Frank's *Holiday* as well. See Soto 185 n. 37.

34. "Fond of vaudeville?" asked one reviewer, "Vaudeville is what Jean Toomer's 'Cane' is called by its publishers . . . The entertainment before the intermission is concerned with the folk-life of the Southern Negro; that after the intermission, with the 'brown life' of Washington. The drama is an 'added attraction'" (quoted in Soto 171). Readers familiar with *Cane* will readily see, as Soto puts it, "B&L's references to [vaudeville] were little more than Madison Avenue shorthand for simple, pliant 'darkies' already familiar to the average consumer thanks to icons like Cream of Wheat's Rastus or Quaker Oats' Aunt Jemima" (Soto 171; see also North 149).

35. Quotations from McKay's correspondence are from letters in the Arthur A. Schomburg Papers in the Schomburg Center for Research in Black Culture at the New York Public Library. McKay also suggested pursuing Knopf and Harcourt Brace (who had published *Harlem Shadows*), assuring Schomburg, "I am certain to suit one of the three." He wrote to Schomburg that Boni was a friend—"I knew him in New York and met him again in Berlin" (correspondence, May 20, 1920)—and, later, that Louise Bryant (John Reed's widow) "knows Boni & Liveright and would help all she can if you can find her address" (correspondence, September 9, 1925).

36. McKay, correspondence, April 28, 1925; June or July 1925; and Sept. 8, 1925. See also Wayne Cooper, *Claude McKay: Rebel Sojourner in the Harlem Renaissance* (Baton Rouge: Louisiana State UP, 1987), chapter 7.

37. Lewis, Wintz, and Hutchinson each discuss this incident. McKay suspected a kind of residual Victorianism, an aversion to representations of "vulgar negroes."

38. I am thinking here of such photographs as Bourke-White's "Louisville Flood Victims" (1937), in which a long queue of desultory African Americans is set off by a giant billboard featuring a gleaming-white family of smiling motorists and the headline "World's Highest Standard of Living . . . There's No Way Like the American Way."

Chapter 6

1. The Schuyler and Hughes essays appeared in the June 16 and June 28, 1926, issues of *The Nation*, respectively.

2. On Schuyler's impact at *The Messenger,* see Hutchinson, chapter 10.

3. Jonathan Veitch reproduces the tables of contents of each issue of the West-Williams incarnation of *Contact* in *American Superrealism: Nathanael West and the Politics of Representation in the 1930s* (Madison: U Wisconsin P, 1997), 156–57.

4. See Veitch, *American Superrealism;* Barnard, chapters 6–8; Philip Brian Harper, *Framing the Margins: The Social Logic of Postmodern Culture* (New York: Oxford UP, 1994), chapter 2; Nathanael West, *Novels and Other Writings* (New York: Library of America, 1997).

5. It would also be reasonable to hear a sexual connotation, since, in keeping with the story's continual references to impotence, "breaking stones" is another way to say "busting balls."

6. Act of March 26, 1790, Ch. 3, 1 Stat. 103.

7. An excellent analysis of Grant, Stoddard, and the cultural context from which Johnson-Reed emerged is Matthew P. Guterl's "Salvaging a Shipwrecked World," the first chapter of his *The Color of Race in America, 1900–1940* (Cambridge: Harvard UP, 2001).

8. The quota system of Johnson-Reed keyed the number of immigrants permitted to enter the United States from a given country to the 1910 population of Americans from that country. Thus, the "Alpine" and "Mediterranean" races of Europeans were disproportionately prevented from immigrating in favor of the "Nordics," as were many other hopefuls whose fellow compatriots had only recently begun to arrive in great numbers and thus represented a small population in 1910. The *Los Angeles Times* headline is quoted in Higham 300. The figures on immigration from Europe are cited in Douglas 305.

9. *Williams v. State of Mississippi* 170 U.S. 213 (1898).

10. The classic treatment of the prominence of "civilization" in the public discourse of this period is Warren Susman's essay "Culture and Civilization: the Nineteen-Twenties," in which he writes: "So much that was produced during the twenties can be seen and read in terms of a thinking that self-consciously considered itself as part of the issue of civilization and even as a technique or instrument involved somehow in sustaining, modifying, destroying, or creating 'civilization.' And this view is a possible and meaningful way toward the establishment of an overview of the period" (*Culture as History: The Transformation of American Society in the Twentieth Century* [New York: Pantheon, 1984], 115).

11. It was actually the "Negroes" and "Indians" that Congress had in mind when it crafted the racially exclusive naturalization law, not "Oriental despots," as Judge Cushman supposed. His presentism notwithstanding, the ruling is instructive in its version of historical determinism: the subjects of a despotic form of government have that form of government "fixed and ingrained" in them. Thus, the form of government toward which the "Orientals" are predisposed is understood to be no less a permanent feature of their constitution than is the "yellow" skin by which whites recognized and racially classified them. As with other racist accounts of the "yellow peril" to

American jobs and social structure in the late nineteenth and early twentieth centuries, here race prejudice is disguised as the preservation of American democratic ideals. Ronald Takaki and Lisa Lowe have written incisively on both the persistence of the "yellow peril" shibboleth in United States history and the variety of forms it has assumed. See Takaki, *Strangers from a Different Shore* (Boston: Little, Brown, 1989); Lowe, *Immigrant Acts* (Durham: Duke UP, 1996).

12. See Higham, chapters 10–11.

13. See Lopez, chapter 4.

14. Schuyler writes in his preface of "America's constant reiteration of the superiority of whiteness," and his novel seems to anticipate the view held by some critical race theorists today that it is only through "constant reiteration" and performance that race is maintained as a coherent, useful concept and category of identity in the face of the contradictions that threaten to undo it. I am thinking specifically of claims advanced by Diana Fuss in *Essentially Speaking* and by Kwame Anthony Appiah in "The Uncompleted Argument: DuBois and the Illusion of Race," *"Race," Writing, and Difference* (Chicago: U Chicago P, 1985), 21–37. To be sure, Schuyler is not the first African American writer to have attributed ideological significance to modern consumer culture, as the present book's first chapter demonstrates. But perhaps because he is a parodist (rather than a realist) and because his gestures are therefore exaggerated, Schuyler's account of the manipulation of public opinion and manufacturing of desire distinguishes him from this tradition and places him, to my mind, closer to such contemporaries as Walter Lippman and Robert Lynd in this country and the Frankfurt theorists who were just then fleeing Nazi Germany.

15. Several of Schuyler's characters are caricatures of prominent Harlem figures, including W. E. B. DuBois. In the case of Crookman's business partners, I think Schuyler used as his model the ubiquitous Caspar Holstein, a West Indian émigré who was both a numbers racketeer and an unscrupulous realtor.

16. Perhaps the best illustration is the radio address delivered late in *Black No More* by Reverend Givens of the Knights of Nordica. Schuyler begins: "[M]illions of people sat before their loud speakers, expectantly awaiting the heralded address to the nation by the Imperial Grand Wizard of the Knights of Nordica. The program started promptly: "Good evening, ladies and gentlemen of the radio audience. This is station WHAT, Atlanta, Ga., Mortimer K. Shanker announcing. This evening we are offering a program of tremendous interest to every American citizen. The countrywide hookup over the chain of the Moronia Broadcasting Company is enabling one hundred million citizens to hear one of the most significant messages ever delivered to the American public" (114). The host goes on to announce the topic of Reverend Givens's talk, "The Menace of Negro Blood": "Rev. Givens, fortified with a slug of corn [liquor], advanced nervously to the microphone, fingering his prepared address. He cleared his throat and talked for upwards of an hour during which time he successfully avoided say-

ing anything that was true, the result being that thousands of telegrams and long distance telephone calls of congratulation came in to the studio. In his long address he discussed the foundations of the Republic, anthropology, psychology, miscegenation, cooperation with Christ, getting right with God, curbing Bolshevism, the bane of birth control, the menace of the Modernists, science versus religion, and many other subjects of which he was totally ignorant. The greater part of his time was taken up in a denunciation of Black-No-More, Incorporated, and calling upon the Republican administration of President Harold Goosie to deport the vicious Negroes at the head of it or imprison them in the federal penitentiary. When he had concluded 'In the name of our Savior and Redeemer, Jesus Christ, Amen,' he retired hastily to the washroom to finish his half-pint of corn [liquor]" (116).

17. Although *Black No More* works with the Marxist categories I have been invoking, Schuyler eventually repudiated his early socialism and made anticommunism a cornerstone of his work. He became a devoted McCarthyite in the 1950s and was reputedly a member sub rosa of the John Birch Society, which stridently opposed immigration. This was indeed an ironic end to a career that began, in Schuyler's essay "The Negro-Art Hokum," with an explicit denunciation of the nativists Madison Grant and Lothrop Stoddard as racist pseudoscientists.

18. On the genesis of the consumer advocacy movement in the early years of the Great Depression, see Marchand, chapter 9.

19. See Christopher Wilson, "The Rhetoric of Consumption: Mass-Market Magazines and the Demise of the Gentle Reader, 1880–1920," *The Culture of Consumption: Critical Essays in American History, 1880–1980* (New York: Pantheon, 1983), 39–64.

20. Walter Lippman's *Public Opinion* (1922) was among the earliest and most cogent articulations of this transformation in twentieth-century American journalism. In particular, see chapter 21, "The Buying Public." For an excellent account of the process by which advertising not only grew more prominent in the official U.S. public sphere of the early twentieth century but in fact conditioned its possibility, see Ohmann 62–117.

21. See Adorno and Horkheimer, "The Culture Industry: Enlightenment as Mass Deception," *Dialectic of Enlightenment* (New York: Continuum, 1994), 120–67. Adorno and Horkheimer's essay must be read as a historically specific response to the rise of European fascism, particularly to fascism's ability to exert control over individual consciousness. But its indictment is directed less at officially fascist configurations of state authority than at corporate authority whose effect, even in "enlightened" states, is to impoverish people's capacity for dissent. In *The Great Depression and the Culture of Abundance,* Rita Barnard also sees West as anticipating the Frankfurt school's ideology critique, reading Miss Lonelyhearts as a Benjaminian "storyteller." Although I look to Adorno and Horkheimer's essay instead, her analysis is instructive. Emphasizing West's concern with "the social, interpersonal, and even material aspects of narrative and counsel," Barnard sees in Miss Lonelyhearts "almost the photographic negative of Benjamin's exemplary and

nostalgic figure" of the storyteller (200, 196). The storyteller's "ability to articulate the unity of his own life imbues experience with unique meaning and authenticity and gives it a public usefulness and relevance," writes Barnard, who concludes, "In short, the storyteller is everything that West's confused advice columnist strives, and fails, to be." For West, the issue in *Miss Lonelyhearts* is not the disappearance of face-to-face, heart-to-heart community (or what the Frankfurt theorists called *gemeinschaft*) but its reinstitution in a community of sob columnists who become the "priests of twentieth-century America" (4). West's story both exposes and satirizes the culture industry's tendency, in Barnard's terms, "to recirculate traditional forms of meaning—often the very meanings it has undermined and replaced" (205).

22. The social pathologies that Adorno and Horkheimer's "The Culture Industry" attributes to mass culture are anticipated closely in *Miss Lonelyhearts*. The price of a long-standing and uncritical adherence to progressive, liberal-capitalist modernization has been enormous. Among its consequences are the triumph of instrumental reason; an ethic of enforced, fraudulent "pleasure"; the prevalence of repetition and its attending pressure to produce new effects; the denaturing of nature; the obliteration of any possibility for popular dissent; the replacement of the media's content by the fact of its total penetration by the profit motive; the sacrifice of art's use value (its anti-utility) to its exchange value; the proliferation of the idiom of advertising, which in turn undermines the possibility for language to signify; the silencing of audiences; and the stunting of creativity by a business ethic of well-planned originality.

23. A more precise term than *resentment* here may be *ressentiment*, as Nietzsche uses it to indicate an act of creative revolt against enslavement, performed by "those who are denied the real reaction, that of the deed, and who compensate with an imaginary revenge" ("Toward a Genealogy of Morals," *The Portable Nietzsche* [New York: Penguin, 1982], 451). Nietzsche's writing on mass culture as a form of enslavement—which was indebted to Kierkegaard, Marx and Engels, and Hegel—was in turn an important precursor to both Weber's work on capitalism's "iron cage" and the work of the Frankfurt philosophers. Both Phillip Brian Harper and Jonathan Veitch use the term *ressentiment* in their analyses of *Miss Lonelyhearts*.

24. In this effort, Michaels contends, in *Our America*, fiction is complicit in a broader white-supremacist cultural project to "make race invisible" and thereby preserve the equation between Americanness and whiteness that was threatened by Reconstruction and immigration.

25. Michaels traces the legacy of this redefinition of race in the works of such American modernists as Cather, Fitzgerald, Hemingway, and Faulkner, arguing that the question "Are you white?" is replaced by the question "Are you American?" but with the latter category still retaining "an ontology of race."

26. The "partially destroyed insect" to which West compares Peter Doyle is one of the many incompletely destroyed bodies that populate his fiction, constant reminders that the height of inhumanity is to fail to extinguish a

suffering life. They always signal too earnest an adherence to the popular myths America tells about itself, and Doyle is no exception. A year later, in *A Cool Million* (subtitled *The Dismantling of Lemuel Pitkin*), West would enumerate the piecemeal dismemberment of the protagonist's body, a result of his naive faith in the Horatio Alger myth. With each successive episode in West's countermyth, Pitkin literally loses a part of himself. Ultimately relieved of his teeth, an eye, a thumb, his scalp, and one leg, he is put out of his misery and shot through the heart. In *Miss Lonelyhearts,* it is the partially destroyed Doyle who does the shooting.

27. Letter from West to Edmund Wilson, cited in Jay Martin, *Nathanael West: The Art of His Life* (New York: Carrol and Graf, 1970), 329.

28. Jonathan Veitch offers the most compelling account of West's unusual stance toward "the masses." At a time when "there was an unparalleled attempt to record, transcribe, or otherwise gain access to the voice and image of the people," Veitch writes, West's attention to the modes through which their voice and image were mediated allowed him to avoid the pitfalls of romanticizing or sentimentalizing "the masses," as many of his populist, Communist, and modernist peers tended to do, or demonizing them, as was the tendency among the Frankfurt academics and the mainstream detractors of "mass culture as social decay," as Patrick Brantlinger has put it. See Veitch 67–69; Brantlinger, *Bread and Circuses: Theories of Mass Culture as Social Decay* (Ithaca: Cornell UP, 1983).

29. The quoted assessment of *Black No More* is George Hutchinson's in *Harlem Renaissance* (286). As an illustration of *Black No More*'s oversight among scholars of whiteness and "passing" literature, note the absence of any reference to Schuyler in the essays comprising the otherwise commendable volumes *Displacing Whiteness: Essays in Social and Cultural Criticism* (Durham: Duke UP, 1997), edited by Ruth Frankenberg, and *Passing and the Fictions of Identity* (Durham: Duke UP, 1996), edited by Elaine Ginsberg.

30. I have relied on Jay Martin's *Nathanael West* for biographical information about West's family. On the eastern European Jewish immigrants' embrace of the American consumer ethos, see Heinze, *Adapting to Abundance.*

Conclusion

1. James Sterngold, "A Racial Divide Widens on Network TV," *New York Times* December 29, 1998: A1, A12.

2. See Lipsitz, *Possessive Investment*, 6–9.

3. In addition to Susan Willis, whose work I discuss in chapter 1, two authors whose work skillfully debunks the willful optimism and Keynesian approach of a book like Wynter's *American Skin* are Elizabeth Chin, an anthropologist, and Ann duCille, a scholar of African American studies. See Chin, *Purchasing Power: Black Kids and Consumer Culture* (Minneapolis: U Minnesota P, 2001); duCille, *Skin Trade* (Cambridge: Harvard UP, 1996).

Bibliography

Adorno, Theodor, and Max Horkheimer. "The Culture Industry: Enlightenment as Mass Deception." *Dialectic of Enlightenment.* Trans. John Cum-
ming. New York: Continuum, 1994. 120–67.
"The Adventures of a Near-White." *The Independent* 75 (Aug. 14, 1913):
373–76.
Agnew, Jean-Christophe. "The Consuming Vision of Henry James." *The Cul-
ture of Consumption: Critical Essays in American History, 1880–1980.* Ed.
Richard Wightman Fox and T. J. Jackson Lears. New York: Pantheon,
1983.
Allen, Theodore. *The Invention of the White Race.* London: Verso, 1997.
Anderson, Sherwood. *Dark Laughter.* New York: Pocket Books, 1952.
Appelbaum, Stanley. *The Chicago World's Fair of 1893: A Photographic Record.*
New York: Dover, 1980.
Appiah, Kwame Anthony. "The Uncompleted Argument: DuBois and the
Illusion of Race." *"Race," Writing, and Difference.* Ed. Henry Louis Gates, Jr.
Chicago: U Chicago P, 1985. 21–37.
Baker, Houston. "Critical Memory and the Black Public Sphere." *The Black
Public Sphere.* Ed. Black Public Sphere Collective. Chicago: U Chicago P,
1995. 5–37.
———. *Modernism and the Harlem Renaissance.* Chicago: U Chicago P, 1987.
Baldwin, Davarian. "Chicago's New Negroes: Consumer Culture and Intel-
lectual Life Reconsidered." *American Studies* 44.1,2 (2003): 121–52.
Baldwin, James. "On Being 'White' . . . and Other Lies." *Essence* 14 (Apr.
1984): 90–92.
Bambara, Toni Cade. "The Lesson." *Gorilla, My Love.* New York: Vintage
Books, 1992.
Barkley Brown, Elsa. "Negotiating and Transforming the Public Sphere:
African American Political Life in the Transition from Slavery to Free-
dom." *The Black Public Sphere.* Ed. Black Public Sphere Collective.
Chicago: U Chicago P, 1995. 111–50.

Barnard, Rita. *The Great Depression and the Culture of Abundance: Kenneth Fear-ing, Nathanael West, and Mass Culture in the 1930s.* Cambridge: Cambridge UP, 1995.

Barthes, Roland. *Mythologies.* Trans. Annette Lavers. New York: Noonday, 1972.

Baudrillard, Jean. *The Mirror of Production.* Trans. Mark Poster. St. Louis: Telos, 1975.

Bennett, Tony. "The Exhibitionary Complex." *New Formations* 4 (1988): 73–102.

Beresford, Charles. "The Future of the American Race." *North American Review* 171 (Dec. 1900): 802–10.

Berlant, Lauren. "National Brands/National Body: *Imitation of Life.*" *The Phantom Public Sphere.* Ed. Bruce Robbins. Minneapolis: U Minnesota P, 1993. 173–208.

———. *The Queen of America Goes to Washington City: Essays on Sex and Citizen-ship.* Durham: Duke UP, 1997.

Bernays, Edward. *Biography of an Idea: Memoirs of Public Relations Counsel Edward L. Bernays.* New York: Simon and Schuster, 1965.

———. "Promotion Expert Urges New Sales Methods for Books." *Publishers Weekly* 97 (Mar. 20, 1926): 933–36.

Besant, Walter. "The Future of the Anglo-Saxon." *North American Review* 163 (Aug. 1896): 129–43.

Black Public Sphere Collective, ed. *The Black Public Sphere.* Chicago: U Chicago P, 1995.

Blair, Sara. *Henry James and the Writing of Race and Nation.* Cambridge: Cam-bridge UP, 1996.

Boas, Franz. "Race and Progress." *Science* 74 (July 3, 1931): 1–8.

Bone, Robert. *The Negro Novel in America.* New Haven: Yale UP, 1958.

Boorstin, Daniel. *The Image; or, What Happened to the American Dream.* New York: Atheneum, 1962.

Borus, Daniel. *Writing Realism: Howells, James, and Norris in the Mass Market.* Chapel Hill: U North Carolina P, 1989.

Bourdieu, Pierre. *Distinction: A Social Critique of the Judgment of Taste.* Trans. Richard Nice. Cambridge: Harvard UP, 1984.

Brantlinger, Patrick. *Bread and Circuses: Theories of Mass Culture as Social Decay.* Ithaca: Cornell UP, 1983.

Brody, Jennifer Devere. *Impossible Purities: Blackness, Femininity, and Victorian Culture.* Durham: Duke UP, 1998.

Brown, Bill. "The Prosthetics of Empire." *Cultures of U.S. Imperialism.* Ed. Amy Kaplan and Donald Pease. Durham: Duke UP, 1993. 129–63.

Brown, Sterling A. "A Century of Negro Portaiture in American Literature." *Massachusetts Review* 7 (Winter 1966).

"Burden of the White Taxpayer." *The Independent* 68 (Mar. 10, 1910): 538–39.

Butler, Judith. *Bodies That Matter: On the Discursive Limits of Sex.* New York: Routledge, 1993.

Calhoun, Craig, ed. *Habermas and the Public Sphere.* Cambridge: MIT Press, 1992.

Calvin, Floyd. "The Digest." *Pittsburgh Courier* Apr. 19, 1924: 20.

Carby, Hazel. "The Multicultural Wars." *Black Popular Culture.* Ed. Michele Wallace and Gina Dent. Seattle: Bay Press, 1992. 187–99.

———. *Reconstructing Womanhood: The Emergence of the Afro-American Woman Novelist.* New York: Oxford UP, 1987.

Castle, W. E. "Race Mixture and Physical Disharmonies." *Science* 71 (June 13, 1930): 603–6.

Cayton, Horace, and St. Clair Drake. *Black Metropolis: A Study of Negro Life in a Northern City.* Chicago: U Chicago P, 1993.

Chin, Elizabeth. *Purchasing Power: Black Kids and Consumer Culture.* Minneapolis: U Minnesota P, 2001.

"The Class Experience of Mass Consumption: Workers as Consumers in Interwar America." *The Power of Culture.* Ed. Richard Wightman Fox and T. J. Jackson Lears. Chicago: U Chicago P, 1993. 135–60.

Cohen, Lizabeth. *Making a New Deal: Industrial Workers in Chicago, 1919–1939.* Cambridge: Cambridge UP, 1990.

Coles, Robert, and Diane Isaacs. "Primitivism as a Therapeutic Pursuit: Notes Toward a Reassessment of Harlem Renaissance Literature." *The Harlem Renaissance: Revaluations.* Ed. Amritjit Singh, William S. Shiver, and Stanley Brodwin. New York: Garland, 1989. 3–71.

Cooper, Wayne. *Claude McKay: Rebel Sojourner in the Harlem Renaissance.* Baton Rouge: Louisiana State UP, 1987.

Cross, Gary. *An All-Consuming Century: Why Commercialism Won in Modern America.* New York: Columbia UP, 2000.

Cruse, Harold. *The Crisis of the Negro Intellectual.* New York: Morrow, 1967.

Cummings, E. E. *The Enormous Room.* New York: Liveright, 1970.

Dardis, Tom. *Firebrand: The Life of Horace Liveright.* New York: Random House, 1995.

Davis, F. James. *Who Is Black: One Nation's Definition.* University Park: Pennsylvania State UP, 1991.

"The Debut of the Younger School of Negro Writers." *Opportunity* May 1924: 143–44.

Denning, Michael. *The Cultural Front.* London: Verso, 1997.

———. "'The Special American Conditions': Marxism and American Studies." *American Quarterly* 38.3 (1986): 356–80.

Douglas, Ann. *Terrible Honesty: Mongrel Manhattan in the 1920s.* New York: Farrar, Straus and Giroux, 1995.

Douglas, Mary, and Baron Isherwood. *World of Goods.* New York: Basic Books, 1979.

DuBois, W. E. B. *Black Reconstruction in America.* New York: Russell and Russell, 1962.

————. *The Emerging Thought of W. E. B. DuBois: Essays and Editorials from "The Crisis."* New York: Simon and Schuster, 1992.

————. *The Souls of Black Folk.* New York: Bantam Books, 1989.

————. "The Souls of White Folk." *W. E. B. DuBois: A Reader.* Ed. David Levering Lewis. New York: Henry Holt, 1995. 453–65.

————. "The Superior Race." *Smart Set* 70 (Apr. 1923): 55–60. Reprinted in *W. E. B. DuBois: A Reader.* Ed. Levering Lewis. New York: Henry Holt, 1995. 470–77.

duCille, Ann. *Skin Trade.* Cambridge: Harvard UP, 1996.

Dyer, Richard. "White." *Screen* 29 (1988): 44–49.

————. *White.* London and New York: Routledge, 1997.

Eagle, Mary Oldham. *The Congress of Women, Held in the Women's Building.* New York: Wilson, 1894.

Edwards, Paul K. *The Southern Urban Negro as a Consumer.* New York: Prentice Hall, 1932.

Ewen, Elizabeth. *Immigrant Women in the Land of Dollars: Life and Culture on the Lower East Side, 1890–1925.* New York: Monthly Review Press, 1985.

Ewen, Elizabeth, and Stuart Ewen. *Channels of Desire: Mass Images and the Shaping of American Consciousness.* 2nd ed. Minneapolis: U Minnesota P, 1992.

Ewen, Stuart. *Captains of Consciousness: Advertising and the Social Roots of the Consumer Culture.* New York: McGraw-Hill, 1976.

Ex Parte Shahid. 205 F. 812 (E.D.S.C. 1913). Reprinted in Ian Haney Lopez, *White by Law: The Legal Construction of Race.* New York: New York UP, 1996. 213–17.

Farred, Grant. *What's My Name? Black Vernacular Intellectuals.* Minneapolis: U Minnesota P, 2003.

Fauset, Jessie. *Plum Bun.* New York: Beacon, 1990.

————. *There Is Confusion.* New York: Boni and Liveright, 1924.

Filene, Edward. "The Present Status and Future Prospects of Chains of Department Stores." Address delivered before the American Economic Association, Dec. 27, 1927. Library of Congress American Memory Project. http://memory.loc.gov/cgi-bin/ampage?collId=cool&itemLink= D?coolbib:1:./temp/~ammem_RQmk::&hdl=amrlg:lg24:00 01 (accessed May 24, 2006).

Fisher, Rudolph. "The Caucasian Storms Harlem." *Black on White: Black Writers on What It Means to Be White.* Ed. David Roediger. New York: Schocken Books, 1998. 216–17.

Fiske, John. *Understanding Popular Culture.* London: Unwin Hyman, 1989.

Flinn, John J. *The Best Things to Be Seen at the World's Fair.* Chicago: Columbian Guide, 1893.

Foucault, Michel. *The History of Sexuality.* Vol. 1. Trans. Robert Hurley. New York: Vintage Books, 1990.

————. "Nietzsche, Genealogy, History." 1971. Reprinted in *The Foucault Reader.* Ed. Paul Rabinow. New York: Pantheon, 1984. 76–100.

Fox, Richard Wightman. "Epitaph for Middletown: Robert S. Lynd and the Analysis of Consumer Culture." *The Culture of Consumption: Critical Essays in American History, 1880–1980.* Ed. Richard Wightman Fox and T. J. Jackson Lears. New York: Pantheon, 1983. 103–41.

Fox, Richard Wightman, and T. J. Jackson Lears, eds. *The Culture of Consumption: Critical Essays in American History, 1880–1980.* New York: Pantheon, 1983.

Frank, Waldo. *Time Exposures.* New York: Boni and Liveright, 1926.

Frankenberg, Ruth, ed. *Displacing Whiteness: Essays in Social and Cultural Criticism.* Durham: Duke UP, 1997.

Fraser, Nancy. "Rethinking the Public Sphere: A Contribution to the Critique of Actually Existing Democracy." *Habermas and the Public Sphere.* Ed. Craig Calhoun. Cambridge: MIT Press, 1992. 109–41.

———. *Unruly Practices: Power, Discourse, and Gender in Contemporary Social Theory.* Minneapolis: U Minnesota P, 1989.

Freedman, Jonathan. "The Poetics of Cultural Decline: Degeneracy, Assimilation, and the Jew in James's *The Golden Bowl.*" *American Literary History* 7.3 (Fall 1995): 477–99.

———. *The Temple of Culture: Assimilation and Anti-Semitism in Literary Anglo-America.* New York: Oxford UP, 2002.

Fuss, Diana. *Essentially Speaking: Feminism, Nature, and Difference.* New York: Routledge, 1989.

Galbraith, John Kenneth. *The Affluent Society.* Boston: Houghton Mifflin, 1958.

Gates, Henry Louis. *Figures in Black: Words, Signs, and the "Racial" Self.* New York: Oxford UP, 1987.

———. Introduction. *The Autobiography of an Ex-Coloured Man.* By James Weldon Johnson. New York: Vintage Books, 1989. v–xxiii.

Genette, Gerard. *Paratexts: Thresholds of Interpretation.* Trans. Jane Lewin. New York: Cambridge UP, 1997.

Giddings, Paula. *When and Where I Enter: The Impact of Black Women on Race and Sex in America.* New York: Bantam Books, 1984.

Gilbert, James. *Perfect Cities: Chicago's Utopias of 1893.* Chicago: U Chicago P, 1991.

Gilmore, Paul. *The Genuine Article.* Durham: Duke UP, 2001.

Gilpin, Patrick. "Charles S. Johnson: Entrepreneur of the Harlem Renaissance." *The Harlem Renaissance Remembered.* Ed. Arna Bontemps. New York: Dodd, Meade, 1972. 215–46.

Gilroy, Paul. *Black Atlantic: Modernity and Double Consciousness.* Cambridge: Harvard UP, 1993.

———. *There Ain't No Black in the Union Jack.* London: Unwin Hyman, 1987.

Ginsberg, Elaine, ed. *Passing and the Fictions of Identity.* Durham: Duke UP, 1996.

Gossett, Thomas. *Race: The History of an Idea in America.* 2nd ed. New York: Oxford UP, 1997.

Govoni, Norman, and George Joyce, eds. *The Black Consumer: Dimensions of Behavior and Strategy.* New York: Random House, 1971.

Gramsci, Antonio. *Selections from the Prison Notebooks.* Ed. and trans. Quentin Hoare and Geoffrey Nowell Smith. New York: International Publishers, 1971.

Gubar, Susan. *Racechanges: White Skin, Black Face in American Culture.* New York: Oxford UP, 1997.

Guillamin, Collette. *Racism, Sexism, Power, and Ideology.* New York: Routledge, 1995.

Guterl, Matthew P. *The Color of Race in America, 1900–1940.* Cambridge: Harvard UP, 2001.

Habermas, Jurgen. *The Structural Transformation of the Public Sphere: An Inquiry into a Category of Bourgeois Society.* Trans. Thomas Burger. Cambridge: MIT Press, 1989.

Hale, Grace E. *Making Whiteness: The Culture of Segregation in the South, 1890–1940.* New York: Vintage Books, 1998.

Hall, Charles E. *Negroes in the United States, 1920–1932.* Washington, DC: U.S. Bureau of the Census, 1935.

Hall, Stuart. "Notes on Deconstructing 'the Popular.'" *People's History and Socialist Theory.* Ed. Raphael Samuel. London: Routledge and K. Paul, 1981.

———. "Race, Articulation, and Societies Structured in Dominance." *Sociological Theories: Race and Colonialism.* Paris: UNESCO, 1980.

Hansen, Miriam. Introduction. *Public Sphere and Experience: Toward an Organizational Analysis of Proletarian and Middle-Class Public Opinion.* By Oscar Negt and Alexander Kluge. Trans. Peter Labanyi. Minneapolis: U Minnesota P, 1993.

Harper, Frances E. W. *Iola Leroy; or, Shadows Uplifted.* Boston: Beacon, 1987.

Harper, Philip Brian. *Framing the Margins: The Social Logic of Postmodern Culture.* New York: Oxford UP, 1994.

Harris, Cheryl. "Whiteness as Property." *Black on White.* Ed. David Roediger. New York: Schocken Books, 1998. 103–18.

Haviland, Beverly. "The Return of the Alien: Henry James in New York, 1904." *Henry James Review* 16 (1995): 257–63.

Heinze, Andrew. *Adapting to Abundance: Jewish Immigrants, Mass Consumption, and the Search for American Identity.* New York: Columbia UP, 1990.

Higham, John. *Strangers in the Land: Patterns of American Nativism, 1860–1925.* New Brunswick: Rutgers UP, 1996.

hooks, bell. "Overcoming White Supremacy." *Zeta* 1 (Jan. 1988): 24–37.

Hopkins, Pauline. *Of One Blood. The Magazine Novels of Pauline Hopkins.* New York: Oxford UP, 1990.

Huggins, Nathan. *The Harlem Renaissance.* New York: Oxford UP, 1971.

Hughes, Langston. "The Negro Artist and the Racial Mountain." *The Nation* June 28, 1926.

Hull, Gloria. *Color, Sex, and Poetry.* Bloomington: Indiana UP, 1987.

Hutchinson, George. *The Harlem Renaissance in Black and White*. Cambridge: Harvard UP, 1995.

Huyssen, Andreas. *After the Great Divide: Modernism, Mass Culture, Postmodernism*. Bloomington: Indiana UP, 1986.

Jacobson, Matthew Frye. *Whiteness of a Different Color: European Immigrants and the Alchemy of Race*. Cambridge: Harvard UP, 1998.

James, Henry. *The American Scene*. New York: Penguin Books, 1994.

———. *The Golden Bowl*. New York: Penguin Books, 1984.

Jameson, Frederic. *The Political Unconscious: Narrative as a Socially Symbolic Act*. Ithaca: Cornell UP, 1981.

———. "Reification and Utopia in Mass Culture." *Social Text* 1 (1979): 130–48.

Jefferson, Thomas. *Notes on the State of Virginia. Jefferson: Writings*. New York: Library of America. 123–325.

Johnson, James Weldon. *Along This Way: The Autobiography of James Weldon Johnson*. New York: Viking, 1933.

———. *The Autobiography of an Ex-Coloured Man*. New York: Vintage Books, 1989.

Johnson, Rossiter, ed. *A History of the World's Columbian Exposition*. New York: D. Appleton, 1898.

Kasson, John. *Amusing the Million: Coney Island at the Turn of the Century*. New York: Hill and Wang, 1978.

Kawash, Samira. "*The Autobiography of An Ex-Coloured Man:* (Passing for) Black Passing for White." *Passing and the Fictions of Identity*. Ed. Ginsberg. Durham: Duke UP, 1996. 59–74.

Kern-Foxworth, Marilyn. *Aunt Jemima, Uncle Ben, and Rastus*. Westport: Greenwood, 1994.

Klein, Naomi. *No Logo: Taking Aim at the Brand Bullies*. New York: Picador, 1999.

Knox, George. "Douglass' Wasted Zeal." *Indianapolis Freeman* Aug. 5, 1893: 1.

———. "No 'Nigger Day,' No 'Nigger Pamphlet.'" *Indianapolis Freeman* Aug. 12, 1893: 4.

Lacapra, Dominick. *History, Politics, and the Novel*. Ithaca: Cornell UP, 1987.

Laclau, Ernesto, and Chantal Mouffe. *Hegemony and Socialist Strategy: Towards a Radical Democratic Politics*. London: Verso, 1985.

Landes, Joan. *Women and the Public Sphere in the Age of the French Revolution*. Ithaca: Cornell UP, 1988.

Larsen, Nella. *Quicksand* and *Passing*. New Brunswick: Rutgers UP, 1991.

Leach, William. *Land of Desire: Merchants, Power, and the Rise of a New American Culture*. New York: Vintage Books, 1993.

Lears, T. J. Jackson. "The Concept of Cultural Hegemony: Problems and Possibilities." *American Historical Review* 90.3 (1985): 567–93.

———. *Fables of Abundance: A Cultural History of Advertising in America*. New York: Basic Books, 1994.

————. *No Place of Grace: Antimodernism and the Transformation of American Culture, 1880–1920.* Chicago: U Chicago P, 1981.

Levine, Lawrence. "The Folklore of Industrial Society: Popular Culture and Its Audiences." *American Historical Review* 97 (Dec. 1992): 1369–99.

————. *Highbrow/Lowbrow: The Emergence of Cultural Hierarchy in America.* Cambridge: Harvard UP, 1988.

Lewis, David Levering. *When Harlem Was in Vogue.* New York: Knopf, 1981.

Lippmann, Walter. *The Phantom Public.* New York: Macmillan, 1925.

Lipsitz, George. "Listening to Learn and Learning to Listen: Popular Culture, Cultural Theory, and American Studies." *American Quarterly* 42.4 (1990): 615–36.

————. "The Possessive Investment in Whiteness." *American Quarterly* 47.3 (1995): 369–87.

————. *The Possessive Investment in Whiteness: How White People Profit from Identity Politics.* Philadelphia: Temple UP, 1998.

Locke, Alain, ed. *The New Negro.* New York: Albert and Charles Boni, 1925.

Long, Richard. "The Genesis of Locke's *The New Negro.*" *Black World* 25.4 (Feb. 1976): 14–20.

Lopez, Ian Haney. *White by Law: The Legal Construction of Race.* New York: New York UP, 1996.

Lott, Eric. *Love and Theft: Blackface Minstrelsy and the American Working Class.* New York: Oxford UP, 1993.

Lubiano, Wahneema, ed. *The House That Race Built.* New York: Vintage Books, 1998.

Lury, Celia. *Consumer Culture.* New Brunswick: Rutgers UP, 1996.

Lynd, Robert. "The People as Consumers." *Recent Social Trends in the United States: Report of the President's Research Committee.* Vol. 2. New York: McGraw-Hill, 1933.

Lynd, Robert, and Helen Lynd. *Middletown in Transition.* New York, 1933.

MacDonald, Dwight. *Against the American Grain.* New York: Random House, 1962.

Manring, M. M. *Slave in a Box: The Strange Career of Aunt Jemima.* Charlottesville: U Virginia P, 1998.

Marchand, Roland. *Advertising the American Dream: Making Way for Modernity, 1920–1940.* Berkeley: U California P, 1985.

Marquette, Arthur. *Brands, Trademarks, and Goodwill: The Story of the Quaker Oats Company.* New York: McGraw-Hill, 1967.

Martin, Jay. *Nathanael West: The Art of His Life.* New York: Carroll and Graf, 1970.

Marx, Karl. *Capital.* Vol. 1. *Marx-Engels Reader.* Ed. Robert C. Tucker. New York: W. W. Norton, 1978.

————. *Economic and Philosophical Manuscripts. Karl Marx: Early Writings.* Ed. and trans. T. B. Bottomore. New York: McGraw-Hill, 1964.

Massa, Ann. "Black Women in the 'White City.'" *Journal of American Studies* 8 (Dec. 1974): 319–37.

May, Lary. *Screening Out the Past: The Birth of Mass Culture and the Motion Picture Industry*. New York: Oxford UP, 1980.

McClintock, Anne. *Imperial Leather: Race, Gender, and Sexuality in the Colonial Conquest*. London: Routledge, 1995.

McHenry, Elizabeth. *Forgotten Readers: Recovering the Lost History of African American Literary Societies*. Durham: Duke UP, 2002.

McKay, Claude. Correspondence. Arthur A. Schomburg Papers. Schomburg Center for Research in Black Culture, New York Public Library.

McKee, Patricia. *Producing American Races: James, Faulkner, and Morrison*. Durham: Duke UP, 1999.

McKendrick, Neil, John Brewer, and J. H. Plumb. *The Birth of Consumer Society: The Commercialization of Eighteenth-Century England*. Bloomington: Indiana UP, 1982.

McKible, Adam. *The Space and Place of Modernism: The Russian Revolution, Little Magazines, and New York*. New York: Routledge, 2000.

McNamara, Kevin. "Building Culture: The Two New York's of Henry James's *The American Scene*." *Prospects: An Annual of American Cultural Studies* 18 (1993): 121–51.

Meier, August, and Elliot Rudwick. "Black Man in the 'White City.'" *Phylon* 26 (1965): 354–61.

Mercer, Kobena. "Black Hair/Style Politics." *New Formations* 3 (1987): 33–54.

Michaels, Walter Benn. "Autobiography of An Ex-White Man." *Transition* 73 (1996): 122–43.

———. *Our America: Nativism, Modernism, and Pluralism*. Durham and London: Duke UP, 1995.

Morris, Charles. *The Nation and the Negro*. Washington, DC, 1891.

Morrison, Toni. *Playing in the Dark: Whiteness and the Literary Imagination*. New York: Vintage Books, 1992.

Mullins, Paul R. *Race and Affluence: An Archaeology of African America and Consumer Culture*. New York: Kluwer Academic/Plenum Publishers, 1999.

Myrdal, Gunnar. *An American Dilemma*. New York: Harper, 1944.

Negt, Oscar, and Alexander Kluge. *Public Sphere and Experience: Toward an Organizational Analysis of Proletarian and Middle-Class Public Opinion*. Trans. Peter Labanyi. Minneapolis: U Minnesota P, 1993.

Nelson, Dana. *National Manhood: Capitalist Citizenship and the Imagined Fraternity of White Men*. Durham: Duke UP, 1998.

"The New Generation." *Opportunity* 2 (Mar. 1924): 68.

Nietzsche, Friederich. "Toward a Genealogy of Morals." *The Portable Nietzsche*. Ed. and trans. Walter Kaufmann. New York: Penguin, 1982. 451–54.

North, Michael. *The Dialect of Modernism: Race, Language, and Twentieth-Century Literature*. New York: Oxford UP, 1994.

Ohmann, Richard. *Selling Culture: Magazines, Markets, and Class at the Turn of the Century*. London: Verso, 1996.

Omi, Michael, and Howard Winant. *Racial Formation in the United States from the 1960s to the 1990s.* 2nd ed. London: Routledge, 1994.

O'Neill, Eugene. *The Emperor Jones. Nine Plays by Eugene O'Neill.* New York: Random House, 3–38.

Packard, Vance. *The Hidden Persuaders.* New York: D. McKay, 1957.

Patten, Simon. *The New Basis of Civilization.* London: MacMillan, 1907.

Peiss, Kathy. *Cheap Amusements: Working Women and Leisure in Turn-of-the-Century New York.* Philadelphia: Temple UP, 1986.

Peplow, Michael. *George S. Schuyler.* Boston: Twayne, 1980.

Perkins, Huel D. "Wallace Thurman: Renaissance Renegade?" *Black World* 25.4 (Feb. 1976): 29–35.

Posnock, Ross. "Henry James, Veblen, and Adorno: The Crisis of the Modern Self." *Journal of American Studies* 21 (1987): 31–54.

Potter, David. *People of Plenty: Economic Abundance and the American Character.* Chicago: U Chicago P, 1954.

Radway, Janice. *A Feeling for Books: The Book-of-the-Month Club, Literary Taste, and Middle-Class Desire.* Chapel Hill: U North Carolina P, 1997.

Rainey, Lawrence. "The Price of Modernism: Publishing *The Waste Land.*" *T. S. Eliot: The Modernist in History.* Ed. Ronald Bush. London: Cambridge UP, 1991.

Rampersad, Arnold, ed. *The New Negro: Voices of the Harlem Renaissance.* New York: Simon and Schuster, 1997.

Reed, Christopher. *All the World Is Here! The Black Presence at White City.* Bloomington: Indiana UP, 2000.

Reuter, E. B. "Civilization and the Mixture of Races." *Scientific Monthly* 31 (Nov. 1930): 442–49.

Rhodes, Chip. "Writing Up the New Negro: The Construction of Consumer Desire in the Twenties." *Journal of American Studies* 28.2 (1994): 191–207.

Richards, Thomas. *The Commodity Culture of Victorian Britain: Advertising and Spectacle, 1851–1914.* London: Verso, 1990.

Riesman, David. *Abundance for What?* Garden City: Doubleday, 1964.

Robbins, Bruce, ed. *The Phantom Public Sphere.* Minneapolis: U Minnesota P, 1993.

Roediger, David. *Toward the Abolition of Whiteness.* London: Verso, 1994.

Rogin, Michael P. *Blackface, White Noise: Jewish Immigrants in the Hollywood Melting Pot.* Berkeley: U California P, 1998.

Rosenzweig, Roy. *Eight Hours for What We Will: Workers and Leisure in an Industrial City, 1870–1920.* Cambridge: Cambridge UP, 1983.

Rydell, Robert. *All the World's a Fair: Visions of Empire at American International Expositions, 1876–1916.* Chicago: U Chicago P, 1984.

———. "The World's Columbian Exposition of 1893: Racist Underpinnings of a Utopian Artifact." *Journal of American Culture* 1 (1978): 253–75.

Salmon, Richard. *Henry James and the Culture of Publicity.* Cambridge: Cambridge UP, 1997.

Schomburg, Arthur A. Papers. Schomburg Center for Research in Black Culture, New York Public Library.

Schultz, Alfred. *Race or Mongrel?* New York: Little, Brown, 1908.

Schuyler, George. *Black No More.* New York: Modern Library, 1999.

Seltzer, Mark. *Henry James and the Art of Power.* Ithaca: Cornell UP, 1984.

Sewell, May Wright, ed. *The World's Congress of Representative Women.* 2 vols. Chicago and New York: Rand McNally, 1894.

Singh, Amritjit, William S. Shiver, and Stanley Brodwin, eds. *The Harlem Renaissance: Revaluations.* New York: Garland, 1989.

Soto, Michael. "Jean Toomer and Horace Liveright; or, A New Negro Gets 'into the Swing of It.'" *Jean Toomer and the Harlem Renaissance.* Ed. Geneviève Fabre and Michel Feith. New Brunswick: Rutgers UP, 2001. 162–87.

Starkey, Marion. "Jessie Fauset." *Southern Workman* May 1932: 218–19.

Strasser, Susan. *Satisfaction Guaranteed: The Making of the American Mass Market.* New York: Pantheon, 1989.

Susman, Warren. *Culture as History: The Transformation of American Society in the Twentieth Century.* New York: Pantheon, 1984.

Sylvander, Carolyn Wedin. *Jessie Redmon Fauset: Black American Writer.* Troy, NY: Whitston, 1981.

Tebbel, John. *A History of Book Publishing in the United States.* 4 vols. New York and London: R. R. Bowker, 1978.

Thompson, Mildred. *Ida B. Wells-Barnett: An Exploratory Study of an American Black Woman, 1893–1930.* Brooklyn: Carlson, 1990.

Toomer, Jean. *Cane.* New York: Boni and Liveright, 1923.

———. *A Jean Toomer Reader: Selected Unpublished Writings.* Ed. Frederick L. Rusch. New York: Oxford UP, 1993.

———. *The Wayward and the Seeking: A Collection of Writings by Jean Toomer.* Ed. Darwin Turner. Washington, DC: Howard UP, 1982.

Trachtenberg, Alan. "Conceivable Aliens." *Yale Review* 82.4 (Oct. 1994): 42–64.

———. *The Incorporation of America: Culture and Society in the Gilded Age.* New York: Hill and Wang, 1982.

Turner, Patricia. *Ceramic Uncles and Celluloid Mammies: Black Images and Their Influence on Culture.* New York: Anchor Books, 1994.

Vann Woodward, C. *The Strange Career of Jim Crow.* 3rd ed. New York: Oxford UP, 1974.

Veblen, Thorstein. *Theory of the Leisure Class.* New York: Macmillan, 1899.

Veitch, Jonathan. *American Superrealism: Nathanael West and the Politics of Representation in the 1930s.* Madison: U Wisconsin P, 1997.

Wald, Gayle. "The Satire of Race in James Weldon Johnson's *Autobiography of an Ex-Colored Man.*" *Cross-Addressing: Resistance Literature and Cultural Borders.* Ed. John C. Hawley. Albany: State University of New York Press, 1996. 139–55.

Wall, Cheryl. *Women of the Harlem Renaissance.* Bloomington: Indiana UP, 1995.

Warner, Michael, ed. *Fear of a Queer Planet: Queer Politics and Social Theory.* Minneapolis: U Minnesota P, 1993.

————. "The Mass Public and the Mass Subject." *Habermas and the Public Sphere*. Ed. Craig Calhoun. Cambridge: MIT Press, 1992. 377–401.

Warren, Kenneth. *Black and White Strangers: Race and American Literary Realism*. Chicago: U Chicago P, 1993.

Weems, Robert E. *Desegregating the Dollar: African American Consumerism in the Twentieth Century*. New York: New York UP, 1998.

Ween, Lori. "This Is Your Book: Marketing America to Itself." *PMLA* 118.1 (Jan. 2003): 90–102.

Wells, Ida B. *Crusade for Justice: The Autobiography of Ida B. Wells*. Ed. Alfreda Duster. Chicago: U Chicago P, 1970.

————. Letter. *Cleveland Gazette* July 22, 1893: 1.

————, ed. *The Reason Why the Colored American Is Not in the World's Columbian Exposition: The Afro-American's Contribution to Columbian Literature. Selected Works of Ida B. Wells-Barnett*. New York: Oxford UP, 1991. 46–137.

West, Nathanael. *Miss Lonelyhearts* and *The Day of the Locust*. New York: New Directions, 1962.

————. *Novels and Other Writings*. New York: Library of America, 1997.

White, Walter. "Why I Remain a Negro." *Saturday Review of Literature* 30 (Oct. 11, 1947): 13——14, 49–52.

Wicke, Jennifer. *Advertising Fictions: Literature, Advertisement, and Social Reading*. New York: Columbia UP, 1988.

Wiegman, Robyn. *American Anatomies: Theorizing Race and Gender*. Durham: Duke UP, 1995.

Williams, Raymond. "Advertising: The Magic System." *New Left Review* 1960.

Williamson, Judith. *Decoding Advertisements: Ideology and Meaning in Advertising*. London: Marion Boyars, 1978.

Willis, Susan. *A Primer for Daily Life*. London: Routledge, 1991.

Wilson, Christopher. "The Rhetoric of Consumption: Mass-Market Magazines and the Demise of the Gentle Reader, 1880–1920." *The Culture of Consumption: Critical Essays in American History, 1880–1980*. Ed. Richard Wightman Fox and T. J. Jackson Lears. New York: Pantheon, 1983. 39–64.

Wilson, Dreck Spurlock. "Black Involvement in Chicago's Previous World's Fairs." Unpublished manuscript, Library of the Chicago Historical Society, 1984.

Wintz, Cary. *Black Culture and the Harlem Renaissance*. College Station: Texas A&M UP, 1996.

————, ed. *The Emergence of the Harlem Renaissance*. New York: Garland, 1996.

"The Women and the World's Fair." *New York Age* Oct. 24, 1891.

Wynter, Leon. *American Skin: Pop Culture, Big Business, and the End of White America*. New York: Crown, 2002.

Wynter, Sylvia. "Sambos and Minstrels." *Social Text* 1 (Winter 1979): 149–56.

Index